Contents

Introduction

Over the centuries, Western man has been positively obsessed by the ancient Greeks and Romans. The obsession goes beyond anything that can be explained in terms of their achievements or even their failings. The achievements were real enough: in art, literature, philosophy, engineering, science, mathematics, law, politics, war. The failings – the Greeks' suicidal infighting, the Romans' cruelty and destructive ambition – are just as familiar and at least as widely imitated. One source of their special interest for us is obvious: the Mediterranean civilisation of Greece and Rome was the direct ancestor of our own 'Western' civilisation. Though the Goths, Franks and other barbarian peoples were largely responsible for destroying the Roman Empire in the West, they then settled amongst its ruins and took over as much as they could understand of its culture, titles, customs and skills. Even when the Christian West had emerged as a distinctive society, its rulers, artists and thinkers returned again and again to Greece and Rome – to create a 'Holy' Roman Empire in the Middle Ages, to effect a rebirth of art and letters in the fourteenth-century Italian Renaissance, to reawaken republican virtue of the Roman type in the French Revolution. As a result of this constant backwards-looking, our culture has become saturated with Greco-Roman words, ideas and images. 'Politics' and 'democracy', the English public school system, the British Museum and the Washington Capitol, the key pattern, the Fascist salute, the United States eagle, church dioceses, the Olympic Games: all are either inherited or imitated from the Greeks and Romans. No civilisation has admired and sought to copy one of its predecessors to anything like the same extent; and if knowledge of the 'classics' is no longer thought essential to a sound education, the influence persists in smaller, subtler ways.

The parent-child relationship of Greco-Roman to Westerner would not have been so prolonged if it were not for the quite distinctive human qualities of the 'parents'. The Greeks and Romans are the first peoples in history who speak to us fully and freely, expressing the whole range of their experiences and attitudes. Other ancient cultures have left behind buildings, monuments and artifacts, laws and commandments, mythologies and handbooks of ritual; but only occasionally does a diplomatic letter or school exercise enable us to visualise a Sumerian or Egyptian or Hittite in a less-than-fixed attitude, acting and reacting outside a conventional and general order of things. By contrast, thousands of Greeks and Romans are alive to us, whether gleefully scratching 'Gaius slept here with Julia' on the wall of a bedroom, or debating Socrates' proposition that the unexamined life is not worth living. Archaeologists work wonders in reconstructing the *how*, and even the *why,* of life in the past; but nothing can supply the extra dimension of full humanity except the jokes, sayings, comments and sheer argumentative variety of literate and self-aware peoples with a taste for self-expression. Few peoples have had both the opportunity and the taste; the great surviving literature of Greece and Rome – ranging from careless *grafitti* and jotted-down witticisms to highly-wrought lyrics – provides us with the first, and arguably the finest, broad view of human life as understood by the human beings who experienced it. Though political history and high achievement must claim a large share in any account of the Greeks and Romans, this book also tries to capture the flavour of Greek and Roman life – of ordinary as well as extraordinary experience, and of the attitudes that shaped or were shaped by that experience.

Early Civilisations and the Heroic Age

THE HUMAN ACHIEVEMENT

Even before the Greeks and Romans appeared on the scene, important human advances had been made. Over wide areas of Europe and Asia, men had discovered how to grow crops and domesticate animals, and had given up hunting and settled down as farmers. Spinning, weaving and the art of pottery had been invented. Tools and weapons of stone had been supplemented by harder ones of copper and bronze. Trade was carried on by land and sea. And before the emergence of the earliest civilisations men had begun to live and work in cities.

The early civilisations developed in the great river valleys of the Tigris–Euphrates and the Nile, which were capable of yielding rich harvests if they were properly irrigated. This was made possible by the employment of a large organised labour force, which in turn required for its effective use a strong state apparatus, specialised administrators and reliable records; hence the earliest of all civilisations, Sumer in Mesopotamia, also gave birth to the earliest known form of writing. The surpluses produced by successful farming of the rich alluvial soils of Sumer and Egypt went to further strengthen the state, priesthood and army, and also to finance monumental art and great building projects such as the pyramids. (However, less advanced societies along the shores of the Mediterranean and Atlantic also showed themselves capable of monumental building, notably the megaliths of Stonehenge in England,

Carnac in Brittany, and other sites.)

In the third millennium BC civilisation began to spread from the older centres. The Indus Valley in India became the site of a vast and enigmatic society that may have evolved independently or through some degree of contact with Sumer. Asia Minor (roughly the area of modern Turkey-in-Asia) had become civilised through such contacts, and trade brought the eastern Mediterranean in touch with both Sumer and Egypt.

Above
Greek coin with representation of the Minotaur.

Opposite
Bull rhyton (drinking vessel) from the palace at Knossos. Archaeological Museum, Heraklion.

CRETE: EUROPE'S FIRST CIVILISATION

By about 1900 BC, when the first Greek-speaking peoples appeared on what is now the Greek mainland, the island of Crete was beginning to develop a flourishing and distinctive culture. For all we know, something of the sort may also have been about to happen on the mainland, whose inhabitants were probably related to the Cretans; but if so, the Greek incursions must have aborted the process, though we do not know whether the invaders massacred, drove away or simply absorbed the earlier inhabitants. It was Crete that went on to achieve greatness, and it was from the Cretans that the Greeks were to learn their first lessons in the arts of civilisation.

Crete figures most prominently in Greek legend as the domain of King Minos, who is said to have exacted a tribute of seven youths and seven girls from Athens every year; these were sacrificed to the Minotaur, a monstrous man-bull who was housed in the centre of a labyrinth. Eventually the Athenian hero Theseus managed to slay the Minotaur with the help of the king's daughter, Ariadne, who provided him with a magic sword and the length of thread he needed to find his way out of the labyrinth.

Like many ancient legends, this one probably has some kind of basis in fact. The *labrys*, a double-headed axe, was a widely used symbol in Crete, evidently with a cultic significance; and *labyrinth* is now taken to mean the palace or hall of the double axe.

The bull too was the object of a cult, though it seems to have been the animal itself, not human beings, that suffered at sacrificial ceremonies. The surviving evidence shows only one kind of young man or woman faced with an enraged bull: the bull-leaper, a trained acrobat who apparently seized the bull by its horns and somersaulted right over it. It seems possible that the story of Minos includes confused recollections of palace complexes that seemed like labyrinths to rustic Greek visitors, and perhaps also of Greek casualties among the less skilful acrobats employed at Crete.

After its fall, Cretan civilisation was forgotten until about 1895, when the island's great palaces began to be uncovered by the British archaeologist Sir Arthur Evans. He called the entire culture 'Minoan', after the legendary Minos; and in spite of objections, the adjective has been generally accepted. But if the name of Minos suggests cruelty and gloom, everything else we know about Minoan culture suggests the opposite. The palaces at Knossos, Phaestos, Mallia, Hagia Triada and elsewhere have an atmosphere of peace, gaiety and civilised leisure. They are complexes of rooms (guest-, store-, administrative, cult, work-, and public rooms) built round an open courtyard with an eye to comfort rather than grandeur. The buildings were sophisticated constructions of stone and wood, yet there are no traces of fortifications; and the impression of peace and security is reinforced by the fact that Minoan soldiers do not appear to have worn body armour until the culture was controlled from outside and unmistakably in decline. The rest of our picture of Minoan society comes from surviving fragments of the bright, cheerful frescos that covered the walls, executed in a vividly expressive cartoon-like style; and from statuettes, plaster reliefs, painted pottery and sarcophagi, and stones carved for use as seals; the Minoans did develop a system of writing, but it has not so far been deciphered. In paintings the people of Minoan Crete seem relaxed, attractively dandified creatures – the men striding about in neat loincloths and boots, the groups of gossiping women well-made-up, with puff-sleeved tunics

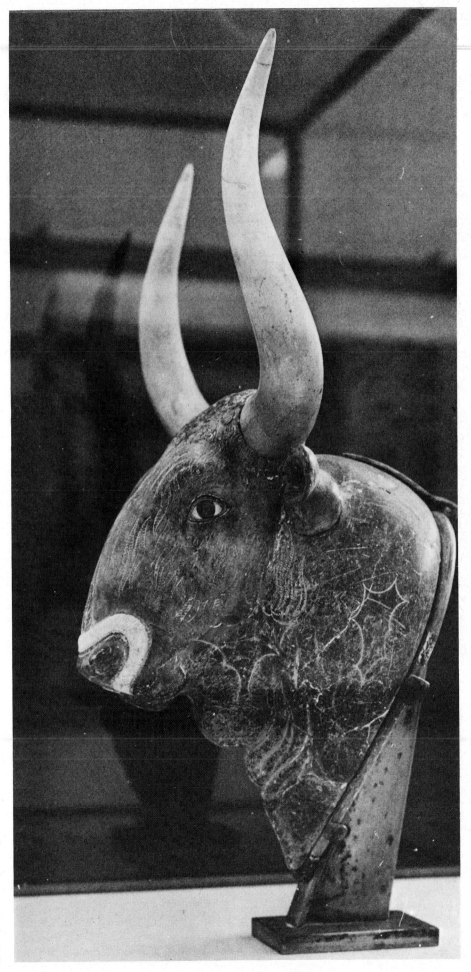

Above
'La Parisienne': fresco from Knossos,
sixteenth to fifteenth century BC.
Archaeological Museum, Heraklion.

Above centre
Storage rooms and jars at the palace at
Knossos.

Opposite top
Throne and fresco of lions at the 'Palace
of King Minos', Knossos.

Opposite bottom
Bronze statuette of Minoan bull-leaping
rite. British Museum, London.

open at the front to show their breasts,
and flounced skirts.

The palaces are the most striking
feature of Minoan society, apparently
forming self-contained communities
of impressive complexity. But town
life also flourished, and there is evidence of considerable luxury in the
larger houses. Much of the wealth
must have been generated by trade,
and it seems likely that Crete possessed
a large merchant navy; the Minoans
certainly had a marked taste for
marine subjects on their frescos and

pottery, accommodating octopi and
other sea creatures to the spiral and
tendril-like patterns they favoured.

Minoan prosperity survived the
unidentified disaster – earthquake or
invasion – that struck the island
around 1700 BC. The destroyed
palaces were rebuilt on an even larger
scale than before, and Minoan
colonists began to settle in some of the
Greek islands and (perhaps more
tentatively) at Miletus on the coast of
Asia Minor. In fact Minoan civilisation reached its apogee in the seven-

teenth and sixteenth centuries; as we shall see, it exercised an unmistakable and strong influence on the more backward culture of the mainland Greeks. The decline of Minoan Crete may have causes we know nothing about, but it manifested itself in another catastrophe, or series of catastrophes, which occured around 1500-1450 BC. At least some of the damage must have been done by the eruption of the volcano-island of Thera (modern Santorini), which virtually exploded. One view – hotly disputed – is

Above
Glazed earthenware figure of a goddess
with snakes. Archaeological Museum,
Heraklion.

Opposite top
The 'Harvesters' Vase', showing a
procession; from the palace at Hagia
Triada. About 1550-1500 BC.
Archaeological Museum, Heraklion.

Opposite bottom
Gold pendant from Mallia, showing
two bees holding a cake of honey
between their feet. Middle Minoan
period, 2000-1500 BC. Archaeological
Museum, Heraklion.

Above
Cretan storage jar with double-axe decoration. Late Minoan period, 1500-1400 BC. Archaeological Museum, Heraklion.

Opposite
A fine example of the Cretan taste for marine subjects. Jar from the Middle Minoan period, 2000-1500 BC. Archaeological Museum, Heraklion.

that this created an immense tidal wave, the effects of which must have been felt all over the eastern Mediterranean; and it has been suggested that the destruction of Thera was the origin of the Atlantis legend of a vast drowned continental civilisation. Whatever the effects of the volcanic eruption, it seems to have been followed within a generation or so by a still more serious man-made disaster – perhaps the devastation of a Thera-enfeebled or merely decadent Crete by Greek or other barbarian marauders. By about 1450 BC Knossos was evidently under the control of Greeks who imported a militaristic element into the Minoan culture;

elsewhere on the island the shattered palaces were not rebuilt and the communities were probably tributary to Greek-held Knossos. The alien occupation was short-lived; around 1400 BC another catastrophe ended the Greek presence, though it seems not to have affected the by-now-flourishing mainland culture. The distinctive Cretan civilisation never recovered; the future lay with the Greeks.

MYCENAE, RICH IN GOLD
The people who entered mainland Greece around 1900 BC soon spread out and settled its lowland and coastal areas. The most abundant evidence of their culture has been found in the Peloponnese, the large peninsula comprising the whole of southern Greece. Here, at Mycenae, Tiryns and Pylos, chiefs or kings lived in forbidding, strongly fortified palaces sited on strategically placed hills. Mycenae, controlling the land route to central Greece through the Isthmus of Corinth, was in legend the stronghold of the High King of all the Greeks, and has in fact yielded the richest finds to the archaeologist; the result is that the entire early Greek culture has been labelled 'Mycenaean', and its members are often indiscriminately described as Mycenaeans. The most important centre outside the Peloponnese was probably Thebes, which according to legend was ruled by King Oedipus, who was doomed to unwittingly murder his father and marry his mother (hence 'Oedipus complex', the modern psychoanalytical term for the child's jealous hostility towards his father).

Somewhere around 1600 BC Mycenae became really wealthy, as the contents of its graves have shown. The poet Homer called Mycenae 'rich in gold'; and so it proved when, two-and-a-half thousand years later, the settlement was excavated. Mycenae's rulers were buried with quantities of swords, daggers and ornaments, made of gold, bronze or rock crystal, hammered, engraved, inlaid or carved with impressive skill. The influence of Minoan art is very strong at this stage, and some kind of contact between the two cultures – whether political or economic – may account for the sudden appearance of so much wealth

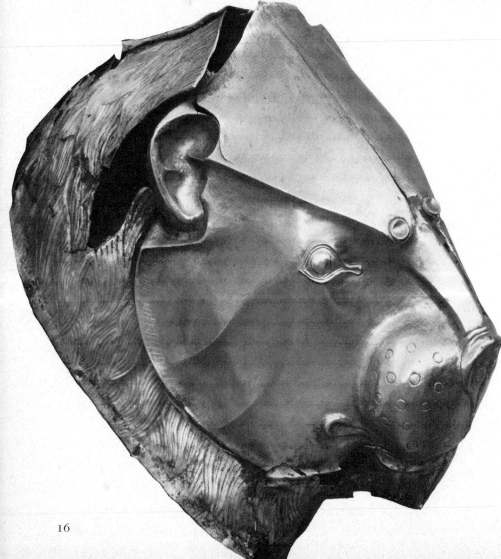

Above
Grave circle A at Mycenae, where the richest discoveries were made.

Left
Lion-headed gold rhyton (drinking vessel) from a grave in the citadel at Mycenae. About 1550 BC. National Archaeological Museum, Athens.

Opposite
The 'Lion Gate' leading to the citadel at Mycenae.

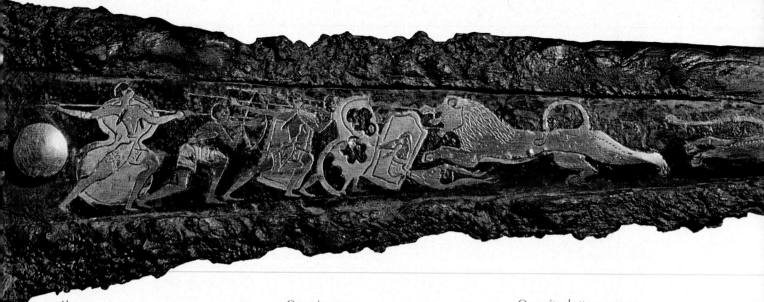

at Mycenae. But there is evidently no question of a Cretan occupation or colonisation. Among the most splendid archaeological discoveries at Mycenae were masks of beaten gold, placed over the faces of dead kings; and these show the kings with beards and moustaches, unlike the clean-shaven Cretans. Their skeletons indicate that they were also taller than the islanders. Unlike the Minoans they valued amber goods, which had to be imported from the Baltic, and their carvings on stone grave markers show they were familiar with the horse-drawn chariot, which was still unknown on Crete. (The horse had been domesticated on the Eurasian steppe a century or so earlier.) The emphasis on weaponry, the massiveness of the citadels, the organisation of the palace, centred on a great hall of the type that inevitably suggests the roistering feasts of Homeric heroes: altogether Mycenaean civilisation in the sixteenth and fifteenth centuries gives the impression of an aggressive vigour that has not yet been tamed or sapped by wealth.

Not surprisingly, it has been suggested that this aggressive people owed their wealth to piracy as well as trade or home production; in either case they must have been experienced seafarers. As we have seen, they succeeded in establishing themselves on Crete in about 1450 BC. It may well have been the Mycenaeans who devastated the Minoan palaces, perhaps from their base at Knossos, whose late culture shows it to have been a Mycenaean enclave.

Presumably Mycenaean writing dates from the short-lived Greek occupation of Crete; the script of the Mycenaeans employed ('Linear B') was an adaptation of the script used by the Minoans ('Linear A') to write their own non-Greek language. Minoan Linear A remains undeciphered, but as recently as 1952 the brilliant scholar Michael Ventris identified Linear B as an early form of Greek. It survives mainly in the form of records scratched on to tablets of damp clay, which have been preserved by accident – baked hard in the disastrous fires in which earthquakes and invasions culminate while societies perish. Linear B tablets have been found not only at Knossos, but also on the mainland at Pylos, Mycenae and Thebes; apart from a few inscriptions painted on pottery, there are no other relics of Mycenaean writing, though it is quite possible that more significant communications have been lost through being entrusted to parchment or other perishable materials. The contents of the tablets are essentially civil service memoranda – lists of stores, allocations, jobs scheduled to be done for the authorities, and so on. They reveal that Mycenaean society was complex and highly specialised (from a separately functioning king and commander-in-chief down to craft-distinctions whose meaning we can now only guess at); and also that it was strictly controlled from the top. It was, in fact, a small-scale version of the great empires of Mesopotamia and Egypt.

Although they left or were driven out of Crete around 1400, the Mycenaeans were more prosperous than ever in the fourteenth century. They had contacts with the Lipari Islands and the Italian mainland, and established trading posts in Syria. In Egypt, Mycenaean pottery has been found in the ruins of Pharoah Akhenaton's capital, Tel-el-Amarna, some two hundred miles up the Nile. And around 1300 the ruler of the Hittite empire in Asia Minor wrote to a fellow-ruler who is generally believed to have been the king of Mycenae, explaining his violation of Mycenaean(?) territory on the west coast of Asia Minor. The injured party was 'king of the Ayyiwah'; and 'Ayyiwah' has been plausibly interpreted as a Hittite's attempt to get his tongue round 'Achaeans', Homer's name for

the Greeks of Mycenaean times. Rulers of empires sometimes have good reason to cultivate their lesser brethren, but if the 'king of the Ayyiwah' *was* the king of Mycenae, with an outpost in Asia Minor, he must have carried a fair amount of political weight. The assumption that the Greek king in question was the ruler of Mycenae, is not, of course, unchallengeable; but both later tradition and the wealth of Mycenae – far exceeding that of any other fourteenth-century site – make it probable.

The Trojan War

The thirteenth century was, at the least, a time of strain for the Mycenaeans. At Mycenae itself there is evidence of declining trade and less competent home production. The massive cyclopean walls of the citadel were extended, and an underground passage was constructed that leads to a spring outside the walls – surely a clear indication of a keener sense of insecurity. Similar measures were taken at Tiryns, and an underground stairway has also been discovered at Athens, which has otherwise left few traces in the Mycenaean record.

If the legendary Trojan War ever took place, it must have been in this troubled century. The war is supposed to have been caused by the

Opposite, top left
Vault of the 'Tomb of Clytemnestra' at Mycenae, showing the skill of Mycenaean building techniques.

Opposite, top right
Cyclopean masonry; part of the citadel at Tiryns.

Opposite bottom
Minoan and Mycenaean writing on clay tablets: Linear A (right) and Linear B (left).

Above
Greek bas-relief of Paris carrying off Helen of Troy. Musei Vaticani.

as if despairing of victory, leaving a gigantic wooden horse on the shore; the rejoicing Trojans hauled the horse into the city; and in the dead of night Greek warriors emerged from their hiding-place in the horse's belly, opened the gates to their comrades, sacked and burned Troy, and led the survivors away into slavery.

The story would need to be outlined here even if it had been proved wholly fictional, since it has a vital place in Greek culture simply as a story. For the Greeks, the war was at once heroic history and a kind of archetype of human experience – particuarly those parts of the action described in Homer's great epic poem the *Iliad*, dating from several centuries later. The works of Homer acquired a unique authority: they were not only great literature but also ancestral history, repositories of wisdom, and an inexhaustible quarry for later writers, who might bring radically diverse attitudes to bear on the same materials. The only rough equivalent in our culture is the Bible, whose sayings are also quoted in all sorts of contexts, and whose stories are also believed by some while being continually reinterpreted or reworked in polemic or fiction. The Trojan War and its aftermath, like the story of Oedipus and his children, permeated the Greek imagination for well over a

Above right
Heinrich Schliemann, who excavated Troy and Mycenae, and his wife Sophia (*above*) wearing gold jewellery discovered at Troy.

Opposite
Mycenaean gold work: one of the Vaphio cups found at Sparta. National Archaeological Museum, Athens.

elopement of Helen, Queen of Sparta, and Paris, one of the sons of King Priam of Troy. The deserted husband was Menelaus, King of Sparta and brother of Agamemnon, who was King of Mycenae – and, as we should expect, High King or overlord of all the Greeks. Under Agamemnon's leadership a Greek armada sailed for Troy to avenge Menelaus and bring back Helen; and in the course of a ten-year siege heroes on both sides such as Achilles and Hector found glory and death. Finally the city was taken by a ruse: the Greeks sailed away

thousand years after the occurrences that gave rise to them.

The site of Troy remained unknown until 1870, when it was discovered by the German businessman-turned-archaeologist Heinrich Schliemann. He succeeded where others had failed because of his passionate belief in the accuracy of the *Iliad*. The clues provided by the epic encouraged Schliemann to excavate a mound on the north-west coast of Asia; and the city beneath it must indeed be ancient Troy. This was by no means Schliemann's last contribution to ar-chaeology. He went on to make the first serious excavations at Mycenae and Tiryns, and his fabulous finds included the gold death masks in the Mycenaean graves – masks that he wrongly but understandably took to be those of the Trojan War heroes. After examining the seemingly noblest of the masks, he wrote with touching enthusiasm 'I have looked upon the face of Agamemnon!'

Later investigation revealed not one but nine Troys: the site was a good one, controlling the entrance to the Black Sea, and it had been settled, razed and repeopled again and again from the Early Bronze Age to Roman times. Homer's Troy is now thought to be 'Troy VIIa', which was destroyed by fire in about 1250 BC. Large storage jars have been found buried in the floors of the houses, suggesting careful preparations to withstand a siege; and there are various indications that the end was accompanied by human violence. So it looks as though here, too, Greek legend has a basis in fact.

DECLINE AND FALL

Whether the Trojan War represented a triumph for the Greeks or a fatal distraction, in the years that followed Mycenaean society went into rapid decline. The continuations of Trojan War legend hint at internal troubles in several states. Agamemnon returned to Mycenae only to be murdered by his wife Clytemnestra and her lover; he was avenged a generation later by his children Orestes and Electra. In Homer's other great epic, the *Odyssey*, the hero is Odysseus, shrewdest of the Greek leaders at Troy; after years of war and wandering he returns to his palace at Ithaca to find it occupied by a gang of outsiders, each hoping to take over Odysseus' wife and kingdom; Odysseus, more fortunate than Agamemnon, kills them all.

The archaeological record is less eloquent but still more sombre. Within fifty years of the supposed date of the Trojan War, the great Mycenaean centres had been devastated; Mycenae seems to have made a temporary recovery, but a second catastrophe around 1150 BC ended its greatness for ever. The population of many areas fell sharply as refugees fled *en masse* to safer places such as the north-west corner of the Peloponnese and the Aegean islands. Greece was in fact only one sector of a general upheaval that set peoples wandering over the whole eastern Mediterranean. Egyptian records give a fairly clear picture of 'Peoples of the Sea' who twice descended on the Nile delta; they were beaten off by the Egyptians, but did bring down the mighty Hittite empire. Mycenaean Greeks were among the Peoples of the Sea – and, interestingly enough, there are references in the *Odyssey* to raids on Egypt, and Helen's husband Menelaus is supposed to have been in Egypt before returning home from the war.

Like many other past aggressors, the Mycenaeans among the Peoples of the Sea may well have been refugees themselves, set in motion by the invaders of their own land. We do not know who these invaders were – only that the ultimate occupants of much of central and southern Greece were a new Greek-speaking people, the Dorians. Even this fact is known only through studies of the distri-

bution of Greek dialects, which show a large bloc of Doric speakers bordered or interspersed with others, including Greeks speaking a dialect far closer to the language of the Linear B tablets. The Dorians may have destroyed Mycenaean culture, or they may merely have been the beneficiaries of its destruction. This was so complete that the art of writing was itself lost – the only known example of such a cultural regression. For roughly 450 years (1200-750 BC) the Greeks were illiterate and unable or unwilling to build anything of substance, though they preserved their farming and craft skills. Understandably, the period has been called the Dark Age of Greece.

THE SHAPING OF THE FUTURE

During the darkness, certain develop-

ments can be identified that helped to make possible the future glory of Greece. The invasions and migrations extended the area of Greek settlement, effectively making the Aegean a Greek lake. Fleeing Mycenaeans established themselves on Cyprus. Others crossed from the eastern mainland to Lesbos, Chios and Samos, and on to the west coast of Asia Minor; the central section of the coast, Ionia, played a distinguished part in later Greek history, and the population was to remain predominantly Greek for almost three thousand years. The Dorians also broke out of the mainland; they reached Crete and Rhodes, and may even have taken some part in the settlement of Ionia.

There was clearly no racial-linguistic hostility between the older Greek-

Opposite
Excavation of the walls of Troy.

Above
Bowl from Paestum with a painting of the mythical hero Odysseus tied to the mast of his ship in order to hear the song of the Sirens without being lured to disaster by them; Odysseus' men have their ears plugged with wax. About 330 BC. Antikenmuseum, Berlin.

speaking inhabitants and the new-comers. Greek legend even pictures the Dorians as *Heracleidae* (children of Hercules) righteously returning from exile rather than invading the alien territory of Mycenaean Greece: a neat bit of ethnic embroidery in the interests of cultural integration.

In the eleventh century, iron tools and weapons began to be widely used by the Greeks. The social consequences were important, since – as it has been well said – iron was a more democratic metal than bronze. Bronze is an alloy of copper and tin, neither of which was widely available; so its technological supremacy favoured kings and warrior castes who could monopolise its use. This fact alone explains much of the fearsome militarism that characterised the Bronze Age. By contrast, iron ore could be mined with reasonable ease in many places, which meant that tools and weapons were more widely distributed in a community.

This made possible the emergence of the Greek city-state form that was to spread all over the Mediterranean world. The Mycenaean state accurately reflected the Bronze Age situation: it was run by an authoritarian, militaristic minority, served by a bureaucratic apparatus intended to control much of everyday life. The city-states that emerged from the Dark Age were much simpler institutions: small, virtually self-sufficient agricultural communities, well able to support the city that served each as a meeting-place, market town and wartime refuge rather than a 'capital' in the modern sense. Such communities had little need for centralised organisation, and provided at least a basis for wide participation in public affairs. Their unstructured nature made possible the glorious if incorrigibly erratic doings of the Greeks in the age to come.

25

The Great Age
of the City-State

LITERACY AND LITERATURE

If the Greeks and Romans are the first peoples in history who speak to us fully and freely, part of the reason lies in the new tool now placed at their disposal – the alphabet. The older forms of writing involved using hundreds of pictures or signs to stand for objects or syllables; knowledge of them must have been the monopoly of a narrow caste of professional scribes. But the alphabet, with only twenty-odd letters which could be permutated to convey every known word, was easy to learn as well as quicker and more convenient to use. Writing, widely (relatively widely) practised and understood, became the potential medium for recording all kinds of facts, experiences and feelings. The Greeks were the first people to exploit this possibility, although they were not the inventors of the alphabet: they learned it from the Phoenicians somewhere around 750 BC, almost certainly through trading contacts with this vigorous mercantile people. Significantly, Greek trade and colonisation had begun to boom at this very time.

The earliest tangible result of adopting the alphabet was the writing-down of the *Iliad* and the *Odyssey*. Scholars have debated endlessly about the identity of the author and the subject matter of the poems. Did Homer write one, both or neither of them? Was he, as tradition insisted, a blind bard from one of the Ionian cities? Or is 'Homer' just a tag for the collective efforts of many generations? The nineteenth-century Eng-

lish writer Samuel Butler argued that Homer was a woman; Lawrence of Arabia, who translated the *Odyssey*, regarded the author as a landlubber, ignorant of the seafaring he (or she) described. Modern opinion holds that the epics are unmistakably products of a long oral tradition; Homer, if he existed, was perhaps an Ionian genius who linked, shaped and polished the mass of traditional material. Clearly the Homeric and Mycenaean worlds resemble each other in many ways – in the forms of the names mentioned and the places listed, for example; as we have seen, Schliemann discovered the site of Troy through accepting the documentary value of the *Iliad*. Equally clearly, the bards of the Dark Age adapted traditional matter so that it squared with the world they knew: the Bronze Age heroes are familiar with iron; they cremate their dead instead of burying them as the Mycenaeans did; and their kings are simple war-leaders, not the supreme bureaucrats we glimpse in the Linear B tablets.

Once written down, the Homeric poems were fixed, so that they seemed to later Greeks to represent an increasingly remote past; their all-pervading influence has already been indicated. Though the withering of the oral tradition has often been regretted, the literature that replaced it was of unexampled variety and expressiveness. Language and literature, together with religion and ritual, were significantly unifying elements among a people much-divided and increasingly scattered.

TRADE AND COLONISATION

The later centuries of the Dark Age seem to have been fairly peaceful. At any rate the Greek population increased, and carried on increasing, over a long period. This put an intolerable strain on the simple Greek economy, which was based on exploiting strictly limited expanses of soil – and relatively poor soil at that, occurring in the lowland areas hemmed in by the mountain ranges that dominate the Greek landscape.

The Greeks tried several responses. One was to increase trade, for example exporting pottery and olive oil in return for the cereals produced in Egypt and the lands beyond the Black Sea. Another was to export men, relieving the pressure on resources at home. Many Greeks served as mercenary soldiers in Asia and Egypt; some of them scratched their names on one of the famous colossal statues of Abu Simbel. A third response, combining the advantages of the first two, was to send out colonies from a mother-city to set up a new city-state on unoccupied or unconquered territory. With little room for further expansion in the Aegean, the Greeks looked further afield, beginning with a humble trading post in northern Syria around 800 BC and bursting out to the west by the mid-eighth

Opposite
The flourishing art of the Greek colonies in Italy: the sack of Troy by 'the Nazzano painter', on a mixing bowl. About 400-350 BC. Museo Nazionale di Villa Giulia, Rome.

century. The Egyptians, Phoenicians and Etruscans effectively barred the way in many places, but Southern Italy and Sicily were so densely settled, and proved so rich, that the area became known as 'Greater Greece'. Few mainland or Aegean Greek cities could match the wealth and power of ancient Syracuse; and the inhabitants of Sybaris were so renowned for luxury-loving that 'sybarite' is still used in English as a term of politely puritanical abuse. Ionian Greeks established a colony at Massilia, now Marseilles in France, which in turn gave birth to colonies on the Riviera (Nice, Antibes, Monaco) and the Spanish coast. Attracted by the trading possibilities offered by Scythian wheat, fish and timber, Greek cities also established colonies and trading posts along the north (Thracian) coast of the Aegean, on the Hellespont (modern Dardanelles), the Sea of Marmara and the Bosporus, and finally right round the shores of the Black Sea. Virtually all the Greek city-states played some part in the colonising movement – even the little island of Thera, which was responsible for founding Cyrene, easily the most important Greek settlement on the North African coast. The colonising impulse lasted for about two and a half centuries, petering out only after 500 BC.

A colony was not a possession of the mother-city, and was not expected to look to it for help after the first few years of settlement. There was no shared citizenship; apart from a few short-lived exceptions the colony was completely independent; and although there was generally some kind of sentimental tie, war between mother-city and colony was not unthinkable. For this reason, no individual state gained in political power from this mass-movement of the Greek people: the Greeks remained curiously small-scale, if not parochial, in their political thinking and political passions. But trade and colonisation did enormously enrich the Greek world and make Greek society more complex, contributing to the political turmoil of the following centuries.

TURMOIL AND TYRANNY

The growth of wealth and trade upset the social and political order. By the end of the eighth century kingship had long disappeared from most states, or had been reduced to a near-ceremonial role. Political power lay with the aristocracy (aristoi, 'best people'), and was based on its large landholdings, military prowess and traditional prestige. The aristoi had encouraged the colonising movement, since population growth threatened their power by increasing the numbers of the poor and discontented; but the long-term effects of colonisation and trade proved to be at least as disruptive. As part of their far-flung trade the Greeks exported items such as oil and wine, pottery and metalwork;

Opposite
Bronze figure of a Scythian archer.
About 500 BC. From Santa Maria di
Capua. The Greeks had a good deal of
contact with this south Russian people,
and the barbarian 'constabulary' at
Athens were known as 'Scythian
archers'. British Museum, London.

Above
Colonial Greek architecture: the temple
at Agrigento in Sicily.

Left
Colonial Greek art: Acteon being torn
to pieces by hounds at the command of
the goddess Artemis. Carving from a
temple at Selinus in Sicily. Museo
Nazionale, Palermo.

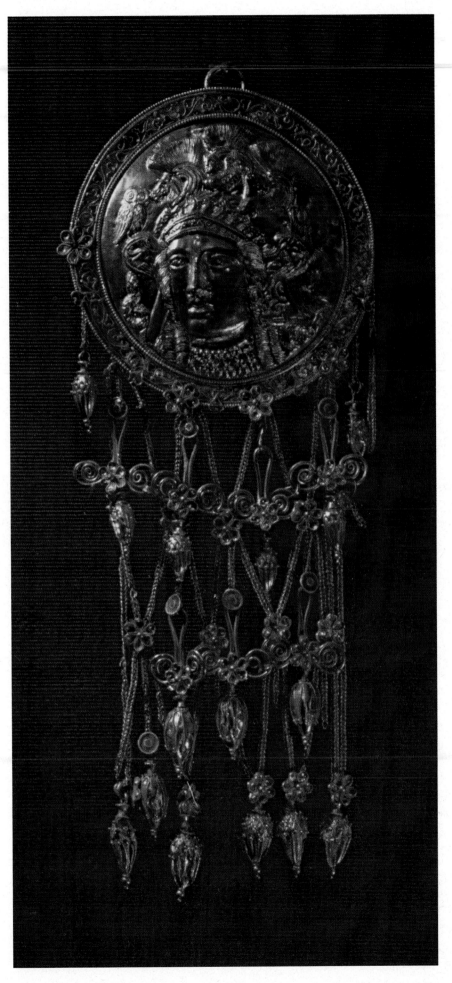

Opposite
Mounted Greek warrior with attendant.
Amphora by Lydos. About 540 BC.
Museo Archeologico Nazionale, Naples.

Above
Greek art for export: sculptured
lekythos (vase) in the form of a dancing
barbarian, found in a Scythian barrow
grave in southern Russia. Sixth to fourth
centuries BC.

Right
Gold and enamel pendant medallion
with relief head inspired by a famous
statue: the colossal Athena Parthenos of
Phidias, destroyed in antiquity. Found in
Scythia (southern Russia). Sixth to
fourth century BC. Hermitage Museum,
Leningrad.

and this produced not only wealthy merchants but a whole class of non-aristocratic landowners and other men of substance. Later, coinage was introduced: that is, precious metal whose purity could be relied on because it was guaranteed by the state which minted it. This, the first true money, was introduced into Greece at about the end of the seventh century from Lydia, a powerful non-Greek kingdom which had grown up to the south of Ionia. As well as facilitating trade, money made transfers of property easier, breaking up the older patterns of land-holding and the loyalties that went with them.

In this situation the aristocrats struggled to maintain their privileges and powers, but their position was fatally weakened by a change in military tactics and technology. Until about 700 BC the mounted man (and that meant the aristocrat, who could afford the heavy cost of a horse and equipment) was supreme. Then new tactics were devised, and the cavalryman went down before a moving wall of shields, borne by armed and armoured infantrymen – the hoplites. The aristocracy had lost its military justification, and any man who could afford the new, far less expensive equipment, was of value to the state and a potential aspirant to political rights; in fact, the hoplites virtually constituted a separate social class.

In the complicated struggles that ensued, the most frequent victor was a general or maverick aristocrat who seized power, with a greater or lesser degree of popular support, and became a tyrant. 'Tyrant' was the term used by the Greeks for a ruler whose authority had no legal or constitutional basis; initially it did not necessarily imply moral disapproval, let alone blood-thirstiness on the part of the tyrant himself.

Most tyrants tried to destroy the

Opposite top
The Greek foot-soldier: duel between two hoplites. From Locri in southern Italy. About 525 BC. Museo Nazionale, Reggio Calabria.

Opposite bottom
Athenian silver coin with the head of the tyrant Pisistratus on the obverse and the owl of Athena, symbol of Athens, on the reverse. About 566 BC. British Museum, London.

Above
Ostraca: broken pieces of pottery used for voting at Athens. The example at the top carries the name of Athens' great leader, Pericles.

Left
A hero receiving his helmet. Tomb relief. About 480 BC. British Museum, London.

power of the aristocracy, if only because it threatened their own. They also made more or less serious gestures towards the redistribution of land – a measure eagerly hoped for by the poor, to whom the new money economy often meant no more than burdensome debts accumulating on inadequately profitable holdings. Tyrannies were generally short-lived, since they either failed to be useful or quickly outlived their usefulness once they had carried out the 'popular' programme. One of the more important exceptions was Corinth, the leading Greek city-state for much of the seventh century, where the tyrant Cypselus and succeeding members of his family controlled the state for about seventy years.

Even Athens, later the doyen of democracies, underwent a period of turmoil and tyranny. Her crisis occurred later than those of most other states, perhaps because popular energy had been diverted by expansion into Attica, the relatively large area of countryside surrounding the city – where, as luck would have it, no rival settlements had survived the fall of the Mycenaean culture.

When tensions did begin to build up, there was an attempt to avoid faction-fighting and tyranny by appointing a universally respected man to mend the laws and the constitution. In the late 590s Solon, an aristocrat who was also experienced as a merchant, was given full powers. He cancelled all debts, abolished slavery for debt, and rescued as many as possible of those who had already been so enslaved. He also gave the poorer citizens a greater role in public affairs, and took measures to protect their rights, while leaving the old aristocracy the leading position in the state. Then, in a last high-minded gesture, he set out on his travels for ten years, putting to an immediate test the new laws' capacity for survival without the backing of his authority.

Solon's laws survived, but his liberal-conservative reforms failed to prevent party strife or economic discontents. Finally the state was taken over by Pisistratus. He might be described as a career-tyrant, since the successful coup of about 546 BC was his third attempt in fifteen years; and

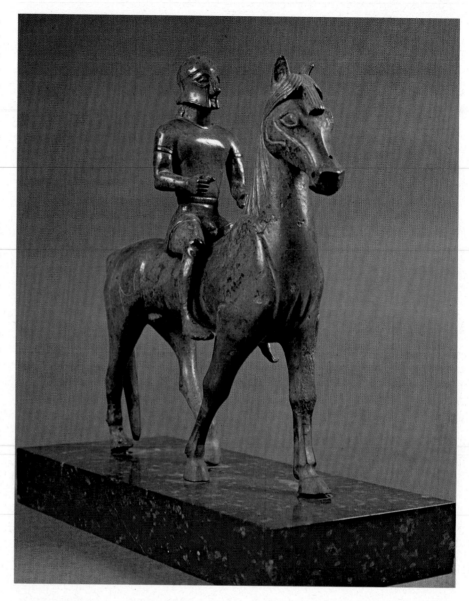

once established he remained in power until his death in 527. Pisistratus was the most successful of all the tyrants, observing legal forms and reconciling most of his opponents while immensely stengthening the state. He must have benefited from Athens' increasing prosperity, which swelled his tax revenues; but he used the revenues sensibly by giving long-term loans to poor farmers, probably to help them change over from cereal to vine and olive cultivation for the export market. Like other populist dictators he also impressed and employed the population by undertaking great public works and encouraging spectacular festivals.

Pisistratus' son Hippias inherited the tyranny but was expelled from Athens in 510 BC as a result of Spartan intervention. Soon afterwards Cleisthenes, one of the party leaders, took up the popular cause, greatly increased the number of Athenian citizens, and put through the reforms that committed Athens to democracy.

OLIGARCHS AND DEMOCRATS
By the end of the sixth century, the age of Greek tyrants was over. But political conflict within the states merely assumed a different form – between the oligarchic party, which aimed to restrict political rights, and the democrats, who favoured giving some voice in public affairs to all citizens. The oligarchs represented a fusion of the old aristocracy and new rich; the democrats were generally drawn from the poorer classes of citizens, though their leadership was often dominated by aristocrats and their followers, who might champion the popular party from ambition, idealism or – probably the most

Opposite
Bronze statuette of a Greek cavalryman.
About 550 BC. British Museum,
London.

Above
The Acropolis, the citadel of Athens,
holds the ruins of the Parthenon and
other temples of Greece's classical age.

Left
Greek warship represented on a seal:
Athens in particular became a
Mediterranean naval power in the fifth-
century BC. British Museum, London.

common – traditional alignment. At Athens, the Alcmaeonid family gave the democratic cause the reformer Cleisthenes; Pericles, the most famous of all Athenian leaders; and a number of others. Democracy, as we shall see later, was never intended to apply to the non-citizen majority of foreign residents, women, children and slaves.

The fifth century BC was, like the twentieth century AD, one in which ideology, patriotism and self-interest produced political confusion. A democratic state might intervene in the affairs of another state to help fellow-democrats, or might support an oligarchy which expediency made an ally; oligarchs might put loyalty before party, or might conspire to betray their city to an alien army; and so on, through all the possible permutations of interest and conviction. By any standards the Greeks were extraordinarily volatile and violent, and the fifth-century record is full of changes

of régime, gross betrayals, broken oaths and harsh reprisals.

In this unstable world there were two fixed points: Athens and Sparta. They were the largest, strongest and most stable of Aegean Greek states, the one committed to democracy and the other to oligarchy. Both had an unusually large territorial base, having concentrated on expansion rather than colonisation. But whereas Athens had integrated Attica into the city-state, making Athenians of its inhabitants, the Spartans remained a kind of master-race holding down far more numerous peoples, many of them reduced to the status of serfs (helots). To maintain their fragile mastery the Spartans turned themselves into a people of full-time professional soldiers, living an austerely dedicated and largely communal life from which luxury, trade and culture were virtually absent. Sparta had the finest sol-

diers in Greece, and also the most conservative and unimaginative leaders. Ultimately hers was a sterile society, politically as well as culturally. By the fifth century she was easily the largest Greek state; but with no more than some 8,000 citizen-soldiers, further expansion by mere conquest would have been intolerably dangerous. In all her later wars, therefore, Sparta found it impossible to exploit her victories other than by setting up friendly oligarchic régimes in defeated cities. Spartan conquests were bound to be temporary, and much of her policy had the negative aim of stemming the growing influence of democratic Athens.

THE PERSIAN WARS

Hostility between Greek and Greek was so ingrained that it took the threat of being enslaved by an alien superpower to produce even a partial and

Opposite
Greek charioteers on an Athenian vase.
National Archaeological Museum,
Athens.

Above
The Greek archer: pediment statue of
the mythical hero Heracles, from the
temple at Aegina. About 490 BC.
Staatliche Antikensammlungen und
Glyptothek, Munich.

temporary unity. The super-power was Persia, the latest and most formidable of the empires of Western Asia. In the 540s, under Cyrus the Great, the Persians swept through Asia Minor, destroyed the Lydian kingdom of Croesus – still a byword for fabulous wealth – and captured the Greek coastal cities in Ionia; only a few years later, Egypt had been subdued, and the Persian empire stretched from India to Libya.

The Persians showed little interest in European Greece, which they could only have reached by land after a march right round the shores of the Black Sea. The situation changed when the Asiatic Greeks revolted in 499. Athens came to their aid, albeit briefly and rather half-heartedly; and when the revolt was crushed after a gruelling six-year struggle, the Persian king Darius turned his resentment against Athens. In 490 a Persian force was landed on the Attic mainland, only to be routed at Marathon by the Athenians led by Miltiades; the Spartans sent an army to help, but it arrived too late.

The battle of Marathon was the greatest feat of Athenian arms; but in Persian terms the whole expedition was no more than a raid that went wrong. After ten years of other distractions, Darius' son and successor, Xerxes, led a major Persian effort to break into Europe. He collected an enormous army, bridged the Hellespont with boats, and invaded Greece by land and sea. Some Greek states were bought off by the Persians, but Sparta, Athens and others had united even before the invasion in a defensive league; the Athenians tactfully yielded overall command on land and sea to the Spartans, though the Athenian leader Themistocles seems to have been the brains behind the subsequent campaign. The Greeks' hopes lay chiefly in the Spartan army and the Athenian navy, which had fortunately been much enlarged by the foresight of Themistocles. However, it seemed unlikely that the Greek forces could hold up against the sheer weight of the Persian onslaught.

Xerxes' army came down from the north through Thessaly, and the Spartan King Leonidas, commanding a hastily assembled mixed force, made a

stand at Thermopylae where a narrow pass controlled the coastal route into central Greece. When the Persians discovered a mountain path that outflanked the Greeks, Leonidas and his personal guard of 300 fought to the last man while the rest of the Greek forces made their escape. The episode is one of the most famous in history, though 'the 300 Spartans' are rather unfairly remembered in legend at the expense of the 1,100 Boeotians who also

formed part of the rearguard – perhaps because Thebes and other Boeotian cities now made peace with the apparently irresistible Persians.

Meanwhile, the Greek navy was forced back at Artemisium, though the Persians and their Phoenician allies suffered considerable losses from battle and weather. The way to central Greece now lay open. Athens was evacuated and the Spartans prepared to make a stand on the narrow

Isthmus of Corinth. But Themistocles persuaded the allies to fight the enemy at sea. The Persian and Phoenician fleets were lured into the straits at Salamis and destroyed in one of the decisive battles of world history. Xerxes returned to Asia; in the following year the army he left behind was destroyed at the battle of Plataea, while the remains of his navy were wiped out at Cape Mycale. European Greece was saved, the Asiatic Greeks again rose in revolt, and the initiative in the war changed hands.

THE ATHENIAN EMPIRE

Over the following decades the Greeks carried the war into Asia and even intervened against the Persians in rebellious Egypt. The Spartans – always careful of their limited manpower and reluctant to commit their forces far from home – soon began to hold back, leaving Athens effectively

Opposite
Bust of Themistocles, the Athenian general largely responsible for the great naval victory over the Persians at Salamis.

Above
The Parthenon, perhaps the most famous building of ancient times.

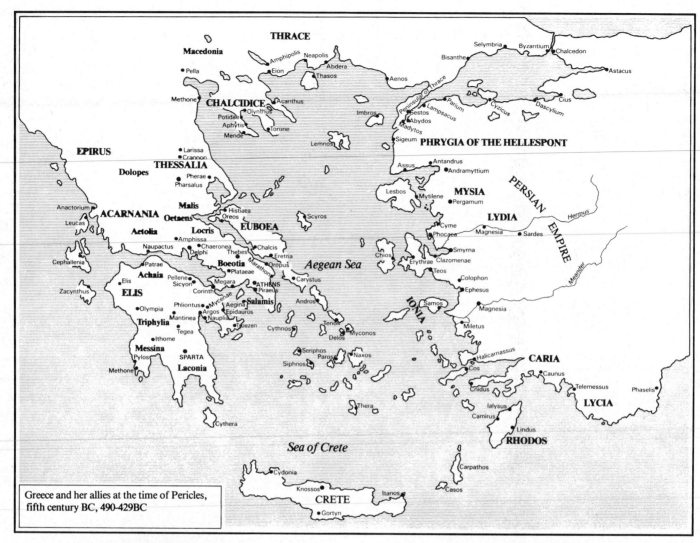

THRACE
Macedonia
Selymbria • Byzantium • Chalcedon
Bisanthe
• Pella
Amphipolis Neapolis
Eion
Astacus
Abdera
Aenos
Parium
Methone
CHALCIDICE
Acanthus
Cyzicus
Dascylium
Cius
Olynthus
Peninsula of Thrace
Lampsacus
Potidae
Imbros
Sestos
Aphytis
Abydos
Mende
Torone
Madytos
Lemnos
Sigeum PHRYGIA OF THE HELLESPONT
EPIRUS
Larissa
Crannon
Assus Antandrus
Andramyttium
Dolopes
THESSALIA
Pherae
Pharsalus
MYSIA
Lesbos
Mytilene
Pergamum
PERSIAN
Anactorium
ACARNANIA
Malis
Histiaea
Oreos
LYDIA
Leucas
Oetaens
Scyros
Cyme
Phocaea
Magnesia
Sardes
EMPIRE
Aetolia
Locris
EUBOEA
Amphissa
Naupactus
Chaeronea
Chalcis
Delphi
Thebes
Eretria
Smyrna
Hermus
Cephallenia
Boeotia
Oropus
Aegean Sea
Chios
Clazomenae
Erythrae
Meander
Plataeae
Marathon
Teos
Patrae
Achaia
Pellene
Sicyon
Corinth
Megara
Carystus
Colophon
Elis
ATHENS
Piraeus
Ephesus
ELIS
Mycenae
Aegina
Salamis
Andros
IONIA
Zacynthus
Phliontus
Argos
Epidauros
Nauplia
Samos
Magnesia
Olympia
Mantinea
Troezen
Tegea
Cythnos
Tenos
Miletus
Triphylia
Ithome
Myconos
Delos
Messina
Pylos
SPARTA
Seriphos
Paros
Naxos
Halicarnassus
CARIA
Methone
Laconia
Siphnos
Cos
Caunus
Cnidus
Telemessus
Phaselis
Ialysus
LYCIA
Camirus
Lindus
RHODOS
Cythera
Thera
Sea of Crete
Carpathos
Cydonia
Casos
Knossos
Itanos
Greece and her allies at the time of Pericles,
fifth century BC, 490-429BC
CRETE
Gortyn

Above
Greek helmets. (left) Ashmolean
Museum, Oxford: (right) Deutsches
Archäeologisches Institut, Athens.

Opposite
Naxian marble lion on the island of
Delos: presented by the people of
Naxos to form an avenue at the
sanctuary of Apollo.

in charge of the war effort. The Greeks were less successful as aggressors, and the conflict eventually petered out in the mid-fifth century. Its chief results were to restore Greek predominance in the Aegean and to greatly increase the power and prestige of Athens.

The political basis of Athenian power was the Delian League, founded in 478 to carry on the war. The members were Athens, her active allies, and the liberated Aegean islands and Asiatic Greek cities. All these essentially naval states contributed ships and money to the League's resources; the common treasury was kept at Delos, a small island sacred to Apollo. With her wealth, trade and dominating fleet, Athens led the League from the start; and it rapidly began to turn into an Athenian empire. First Naxos, and later Thasos, Samos and others, found that resignation from the League was simply not permitted. Revolt was punished lightly but shrewdly – by dismantling the malcontents' navy and making their contribution to the League a purely monetary one, a policy that increased Athens' advantage and gave her funds for yet more ships. Member-states that contributed only money to the League gradually slipped into dependant status; and within fifty years this was the fate of virtually all of them. One by one local mints were closed, and Athenian silver coinage became the standard currency throughout the empire. The imperial reality was openly acknowledged in 454, when the treasury was transferred from Delos to Athens herself; and after peace was made with Persia in 449 it soon became clear that Athens contemplated no change in the situation. The wartime league was now an empire, 'protected' by her navy and paying annual tribute to her for the privilege.

Unlike Sparta, fifth-century Athens was brilliant as well as powerful. The flowering of the Greek genius was not confined to Athens, but in this age it found its most concentrated expression there. The first true dramas developed out of religious ritual under the hands of the Athenians Aeschylus, Sophocles, Euripides and Aristophanes. The first true historian,

Herodotus of Halicarnassus, made Athens his home and inspiration; the next, Thucydides, was an Athenian general. Philosophy was transformed by Socrates and Plato. And sculptors developed the mature Classical style and used it to adorn the Parthenon and other great new buildings whose ruins are still among the wonders of the world; they were put up to replace the temples destroyed by the Persians in 480 – and, it must be said, were largely paid for by the tribute levied on Athens' subject-states.

Athenian democracy functioned remarkably well for most of the fifth century, until the strains of war began to tell on the citizens' nerve and temper. The guiding spirit of Athens for thirty years – from about 460 BC until his death in 429 – was Pericles, an aristocrat entirely convinced of the virtues of democracy. In his speeches he held up the ideal of a free and open

Opposite
Statue of the Athenian dramatist Sophocles. Musei Vaticani.

Above
Early Greek ships: from a fifth-century BC bowl. British Museum, London.

Right
The Greeks at war: the mythical hero Achilles slays Penthesilea, Queen of the Amazons, in this vase painting by Exekias. About 530 BC. British Museum, London.

society, and put forward Athens as the fulfilment of the ideal; but he also supported a proposal to restrict citizenship to those who could show that *both* of their parents had been citizens: perhaps, like later democratic politicians, he sometimes had to bend with the wind rather than direct it. Whether he should be blamed for Athens' ultimately disastrous foreign policy is a matter of opinion; but he was certainly a convinced imperialist, and there is little indication that he tried to restrain Athenian bellicosity during his years of influence.

Despite some reverses, the Athenian empire was strengthened by the war of 460-445 against the Peloponnesians, supported rather unenthusiastically by the Spartans, who were still recovering from the effects of an earthquake and a massive helot revolt. At one moment Athens even succeeded in overrunning central Greece and conquering Boeotia; but long-term control of inland territory was beyond her resources, and the Boeotians liberated themselves without much difficulty. Yet Athens already felt strong enough to conduct this war while still engaged in the unfinished conflict with Persia. Her intervention in Egypt proved disastrous, culminating in the destruction of an entire fleet; but in 449 the Persians nonetheless negotiated a peace that left the Athenians in effective control of the Aegean. The war with the Peloponnesians ended four years later in the signing of a thirty years' peace.

THE PELOPONNESIAN WAR
The Thirty Years' Peace lasted less than half the appointed time. Athens helped Corcyra (Corfu) to fight off an attack by Corinth; Sparta sided with Corinth; and in 431 BC war broke out between the two over-helpful big powers. It may well have been inevitable, since Greece had been increasingly divided between two power blocs: the Spartan-dominated Peloponnesian League and the Athenian empire *alias* the Delian League. In general terms the struggle was also one between oligarchy and democracy, though Athens tolerated oligarchies in her subject-states if they accepted her leadership. On the other hand, even the Athenian historian

Thucydides admitted that Athenian imperialism made all the Greeks uneasy, and that oligarchic Sparta was widely regarded as a potential liberator.

The war was long and exhausting because a decisive engagement was almost impossible to bring about. Athens, supreme at sea, could inflict only limited damage on the land mass of the Peloponnese and central Greece. The famous Spartan army could ravage Attica but could not take Athens, sheltered behind her impregnable 'Long Walls', which surrounded the city and stretched for five miles down to the Piraeus, her port, thus ensuring contact with the fleet and supplies from abroad.

In 430 Athens was weakened by a devastating plague, which carried off Pericles in the following year. Nonetheless, the conflict dragged on until a truce was arranged in 421. When it broke out again in 414, Athens was already committed to an attack on Syracuse in Sicily, which was a major supplier of the Peloponnesian states. This proved to be the turning-point of the war: the Athenians were encircled, and in 413 the entire Sicilian expeditionary force, ships and men, was wiped out. Still Athens fought on, building a new fleet and desperately trying to maintain her crumbling empire; despite everything that has been said about her methods, Athenian imperialism must have had its attractive side, since a surprising number of cities remained loyal to her in adversity. The end came when her grounded fleet was destroyed at Aegospotomi (405); unsupplied by sea, Athens was besieged, starved, and finally surrendered to the Spartans in 404.

THE APPROACH OF A NEW AGE

The outcome of the Peloponnesian War was purely negative: the Athenian empire disappeared, and with it any prospect of a united, stable Greek state. Athens might just have achieved this, though a policy of shared citizenship would have been a more reliable basis for unity than naval power and ideological sympathy. For reasons already noted, there was no prospect of the Spartans maintaining more than a general hegemony in Greece; they even proved incapable of controlling fallen Athens, which soon expelled the Spartan-installed oligarchy, the 'Thirty Tyrants'. At once arrogant and politically incompetent, Sparta was soon at odds with Thebes, Corinth and a revived Athens. Too rigid to adapt to new military tactics, and weakened by a catastrophically declining birth rate, Sparta was smashed by the Thebans under Epaminondas, and never fully recovered; while Theban supremacy proved even more short lived. Fourth-century Greece was as fragmented as ever, though just beginning to formulate ideals of 'Panhellenism' that cut across parochial loyalties when a new power appeared on the fringe of the Greek world. Macedon entered the arena and a new age began.

Opposite
Statuette of the Athenian philosopher Socrates. British Museum, London.

Above left
Bust of the Athenian statesman Pericles. British Museum, London.

Above
Bust of the Athenian historian Thucydides. Museo Capitolino, Rome.

The Greek Experience

THE POLIS AND THE GREEK WAY OF LIFE

Although they fought one another savagely, the Greeks thought of themselves as one people – the Hellenes – inhabiting a fragmented but distinct entity they called Hellas. They shared a common language and religion which brought them together, regardless of their city of origin, at the great Panhellenic festivals and games. Their name for a non-Greek was *barbaros*, a barbarian, though the word was originally no more than a mild expression of contempt for the unintelligible 'bar-bar-bar' of jabbering foreigners. The contempt had intensified as the Greeks came to consider their way of life superior to that of (for example) the Persian, who was dwarfed by the monstrous size of his state, powerless to influence events and an equal citizen only in so far as he shared a universal slavery. In other words, the Greek state and the Greek concept of citizenship were a major part of what it meant to be Greek.

Late in the fourth century, when the glories of Athens and Sparta had vanished, the philosopher Aristotle stated firmly 'Man is a political animal' – by which he meant an animal fitted by nature to live in a *polis*, the Greek word for a city-state and the way of life it embodied. The normal polis consisted of an area of countryside surrounding a single walled city with a dominating citadel, or acropolis ('*the*' Acropolis at Athens is simply the most famous example), and a market place or agora. With the

exception of Sparta, the polis was very small; even at Athens, hardly any part of the countryside was more than twenty kilometres from the city, and most of the population lived outside the walls, travelling in for social or civic purposes. The leading states seem to have had a citizen population of only 10-20,000. (Here Athens was the exception, as her commercial and maritime greatness might lead us to expect: just before the Peloponnesian War she is estimated to have had 40,000 citizens and a total population of about 300,000). In the eyes of the philosophers, even these modest figures were too high: Plato proposed five thousand as the ideal number, while his one-time pupil Aristotle held that every citizen should be able to recognise every other citizen in the city. However, Plato and Aristotle were writing after the disasters of the late fifth century and with more than a touch of nostalgia for the old self-sufficient polis, uncorrupted by trade, luxury and ideas. Still, as far as the normal Greek was concerned, smallness was certainly one of the virtues of the polis: he lived in a society whose workings he could understand, and which he as an individual could hope to influence. The 'failure' of the Greeks to unite, though undoubtedly disastrous in the long run, must be understood with this point of view in mind.

The Greeks despised the Persians because the most powerful of them could be killed at the whim of their king – which made them rather worse off in practice than most Greek slaves.

In the polis, citizens lived under the law. It might be reactionary or excessively severe, like the late seventh-century Athenian code issued by a certain Draco, whose name has passed into adjectival cliché ('draconian'); but it was known to all and applied to all. That, at least, was how things were supposed to be; and although the reality was less than perfect (especially where political passions got the upper hand), reverence for the law was deeply ingrained among the Greeks. Few, however, would have gone as far as Socrates – yet another philosopher – who refused several chances to escape after being sentenced to death on a politically motivated charge of impiety, arguing that the wrongness of the verdict was no excuse for disobeying the law.

The rule of law was common to all the main forms of government, operating in oligarchic Sparta at least as rigorously as in democratic Athens. The main differences between oligarchies and democracies lay in the balance of powers between the political institutions, and in how widely citizenship was extended. In most Greek states the basic political process was the same: a Council prepared and recommended laws and acts of state; an Assembly voted their approval

Opposite bottom
The sports stadium at Delphi.

Opposite top
Athletes in training. Bas-relief from an altar-base, about 510 BC. National Archaeological Museum, Athens.

or disapproval; and magistrates then carried out the decisions that had been arrived at. In oligarchies the Council tended to carry the greatest political weight, since it was necessarily a small body and could be kept a select one by attaching property or age qualifications to membership. By contrast, in full democracies an Assembly consisting of all the citizens was the centre of power. Naturally there were all sorts of shades and variations of practice among the hundreds of Greek city-states, in this as in other aspects of life.

The situation was much the same with regard to citizenship. In oligarchies, those who owned less than a certain amount of land could not be citizens; or if they could, they enjoyed only limited rights (for example the right to vote but not the right to hold office). At best, the Greek concept of citizenship was a narrow one: even the most radical democracy excluded women (they might technically be citizens, but never possessed political rights), children, slaves, and the often large population of resident foreigners created by the growth of trade. If the exclusion of women and slaves was inevitable in terms of the social order, the exclusion of foreigners and various other free men indicates that the Greeks never entirely freed themselves from a conviction that the state was fundamentally a collection of tribes and families, established since remote antiquity, which 'strangers' could not conceivably join; the division of the polis into tribes probably originated with the Dorian settlements, and though they were much modified over the centuries, membership of a tribe remained a condition of citizenship, and most civic activity was organised on a basis of tribal groupings. But citizenship was a matter of place as well as birth: presumably it was unthinkable for the colonist to remain a citizen of his old polis once he was unable to attend public meetings or carry out any of his local religious duties. Only Athens in her high imperial phase experimented with a wider citizenship, sending out some colonies whose members remained Athenians. These were settled at strategic points or used to keep an eye on unreliable allies; they retained

the rights and duties of citizens, and were exempt from the tribute paid by subject-cities. Extending citizenship beyond this, to the subject-cities themselves, was never a political possibility.

In Greek society, then, it was characteristic that a man's ultimate loyalties should be to the immediate and tangible; and for this people, who lived so much out-of-doors, the polis was a larger home and an extended family circle, evoking an intense but close-bounded piety. The obverse of this attractive particularism was the dangerously limited manpower of the state and the impossibility of turning subjects or allies into fellow-citizens in a larger political association. The first factor hastened Sparta's decay, the second restricted the effectiveness of the Athenian empire; and divided Greece, which had only narrowly escaped Persian domination, failed to adapt to a changing world and went down before the single-minded kings of Macedon.

A CONTRAST IN SYSTEMS: ATHENS AND SPARTA

The development of Athenian democracy involved a gradual transformation of the institutions inherited from the Dark Age. Aristocratic Athens was ruled by a council, the Areopagus, and three magistrates or archons. These survived the age of Solon and Pisistratus as prestigious conservative institutions, and subsequent Athenian reformers shrewdly worked to render them innocuous rather than trying to destroy them. For example, Cleisthenes introduced a new, elected council (the Council of Five Hundred) which a later democrat, Ephialtes, made supreme by limiting the powers of the Areopagus to those of a court dealing with crimes of violence. Similarly, the archons were pushed into the background by the strategoi, who were the ten military commanders, elected annually by the Council of Five Hundred. The military function of their office remained a genuine one, but its growing importance can be gauged from the fact that both Themistocles and Pericles were strategoi; indeed Pericles was elected to the office almost continuously for some years before his death, and it was the

basis of such formal executive power as he possessed.

The enhanced importance of the Five Hundred and the strategoi was not achieved for their sakes but to promote the supremacy of the Assembly – the full citizen body, which was as close as Antiquity ever came to the Sovereign People in session. Other institutions had to be maintained in subordination. The Five Hundred were chosen annually by lot, which meant that bribery and influence could not be brought to bear on the selection; and since no member could serve on the council more than twice, there was no possibility of the membership developing an *ésprit de corps* that might convert it into a separate pressure-group. (The rapid rotation also meant that a high percentage of the citizen population would hold public office at some point in their lives – another democratic advantage.) In other words, a sophisticated attempt was made to ensure that the council did its job – prepared legislation – and nothing else; the Athenians had thoroughly grasped the dangers of 'steering' committees which in fact operate to run everything. All real power lay with the Assembly, meeting about once every ten days, which could approve, modify or reject any suggestion, debate and decide as it chose – and, for better or worse, change its collective mind from day to day. The executive arm, the strategoi, was directly accountable to the Assembly – literally so, since the strategoi had to explain and justify their expenditure. Pericles was often accused of dictatorship by his enemies, but though he certainly had immense authority, he had no institutionalised power: he led by virtue of persuasion, conviction, and the accumulating power of his reputation. Even the courts were popular institutions, with juries of two hundred or more, making bribery or intimidation almost impossible. The state arm was virtually non-existent: prosecutions were initiated and conducted by private citizens, and the nearest thing to the police was a force of 'Scythian archers', who were actually slaves from various foreign parts, mainly employed as heralds and chuckers-out for the Assembly: when

Athletes cleaning themselves with strigils (scrapers). Pottery painting, about 460 BC. Musei Vaticani.

the citizens were summoned to attend, the 'archers' literally roped them in, moving across the agora with a long, red-paint-soaked rope that left a tell-tale smear on the laggards.

How well did it work in practice? The highest praise of Athens and her democracy was given by Pericles himself, in a speech delivered to commemorate the men who had fallen in the first year of the Peloponnesian War. According to the historian Thucydides he said:

We live under a form of government that is not copied from the institutions of our fellow men but rather provides a model for others. It is known as democracy because power is exercised in the interests of the many, not the few. But while the laws give all men equal rights in their private disputes, public honours are paid to an individual on the basis of his personal qualities, not his rank or family connections; nor does poverty disqualify a man of low birth if he is capable of useful public service. We conduct ourselves as free men in our private lives too, avoiding mutual jealousies and suspicion; if our neighbour chooses to live after his own fashion, we do not resent it, or scowl at him in a manner that may be ineffective but is still unpleasant to look at . . . in public life we are chiefly restrained from lawlessness by feelings of awe and fear; we take heed of those who speak with authority, and we obey the laws – especially those enacted to assist the downtrodden, and those unwritten laws which all men regard it as shameful to break.

Opposite bottom
Greek foot soldier (hoplite). Pottery
painting, about 560 BC. British Museum,
London.

Opposite, top
Hoplites piped into battle: a pottery
painting that vividly suggests the close-
knit infantry lines that defeated the
mighty Persian army. About 640 BC.
Museo Nazionale di Villa Giulia, Rome.

Right
Bronze statue of a young man throwing
a ball; like many surviving Greek
bronzes, it escaped being melted down
in later times because it was lost at sea.
About 340 BC. National Archaeological
Museum, Athens.

But there were other points of view, especially once war-weariness set in. Twenty years after Pericles' speech, the comic dramatist Aristophanes was writing a scene in which the dead Aeschylus asks about those currently in charge of the city: presumably they are the kind of men they ought to be – honest, able, patriotic and so on? The assumption is enough to make everyone on stage fall about laughing – and was presumably intended to have the same effect on the audience. The political philosophers also tended to disapprove of democracy, which to them meant rule by the 'senseless mob'. Then, as now, interpretations differed according to bias: sympathisers called democracy 'rule by the people', would-be oligarchs preferred to talk of 'rule by the poor', whom they saw as plundering the rich. Near-contemporaries were harsh in their comments on the demagogues who swayed the Assembly, especially since their influence was thrown against peace on the several occasions when, even towards the fatal close of the Peloponnesian War, Athens might have had it. But retrospective criticism is always suspect: had the war taken a different turn, opinion would have promoted the demagogues to statesmen. A more telling accusation was that the Assembly was impulsive and unstable, too often taking wild decisions and then revoking them. This was particularly true as the war went on, and hopes and fears intensified. One famous incident has an aura of grim farce. After a revolt at Mytilene, on Lesbos, the Assembly decreed that the male population should be executed and the women and children enslaved. Then tempers cooled, and the order was cancelled. The ship carrying the original decree had already left for Mytilene, so a second ship had to be despatched in break-neck pursuit; its exhausted crew arrived only just in time to prevent the massacre. Later, there were no cancellations: when Thrace was threatened by the Spartans and the city of Scione revolted, the population was put to the sword or sold into slavery; and in 416, as the Cold War intensified during the truce of 421-414, the same savage treatment was accorded to the

island of Melos, which had never been in the Athenian sphere of influence. At home, the greatest injustice committed by the democracy was the trial and execution of the victorious commanders at the battle of Arginusae, who were charged with failure to rescue their shipwrecked men. Neither trial nor sentence was legal; they illustrated the perils of direct democracy, in which an inflamed sovereign people can all too easily override not only the laws but justice itself.

On the other hand Athenian democracy survived personal ambitions and party rivalries with remarkably little in the way of disturbances. The most violent single act in the great years of the democracy was the assassination of Ephialtes, the democratic leader who had dared to strip the Areopagus of its power; and that was an isolated murder whose only effect was to substitute Pericles for Ephialtes as leader of the dominant democratic party. An institution peculiar to Athens may have played a part in reducing political tension: ostracism, devised by Cleisthenes, was a kind of unpopularity contest that painlessly reduced the numbers of faction leaders. Any year, if the Assembly so decided, every citizen wrote on a sherd of pottery – an ostracon – the name of a man he wanted to see banished. If there were at least six thousand votes, the 'winner' was exiled for ten years, but without dishonour and without forfeiting his property or other rights.

Political decision-making has been a crude business in most societies: a particular point of view has generally prevailed after its adherents have murdered the people holding other points of view. So perhaps one should not be too critical of ostracism, while admitting that many of Athens' most distinguished men suffered by it. Themistocles, who master-minded the victory over the Persians at Salamis, was ostracised a few years afterwards; incredibly, he ended his life in Persian pay, as governor of the Asian Greek city of Magnesia. And at least one anecdote about ostracism indicates that human perversity has changed little over the millennia.

Earlier in Themistocles' career, he and his chief political rival, known throughout the city as Aristides the Just, were rival candidates for ostracism; and one citizen who intended to vote against Aristides remarked that he was simply sick and tired of hearing Aristides called 'the Just'. According to the story, this citizen was in fact talking to Aristides himself, whom he had not recognised; and, being illiterate, he asked the stranger to scratch 'Aristides' on the ostracon for him. Which Aristides, maddeningly just as ever, promptly did. He *was* ostracised, though perhaps not by one vote.

For all its shortcomings, democracy was the chosen political system of Athens in her greatest age. It withstood a century of almost continuous warfare before succumbing to the short-lived oligarchy of 411-410, set up in the mistaken belief that a more conservative system would bring Persia into the war on Athens' side. And even defeat and loss of empire failed to discredit democracy in the eyes of the Athenians themselves, who rapidly ejected the pro-Spartan Thirty Tyrants of 404-403. For Athenians democracy had evidently become a way of life, and they adhered to it while Athenian independence remained a reality.

Sparta was an oligarchy, and the champion of oligarchy throughout Greece, but her consitution and whole way of life was unique. There were *two* kings who had very limited powers (presumably whittled away in the course of the Dark Age), but who still led the Spartan army into battle, as Leonidas did at Thermopylae. Five ephors exercised most of the executive powers. However the oligarchic centre of power was the Council of Elders, twenty-eight men over sixty years old, who were elected from a limited number of noble families. Unlike the Athenian Council of Five Hundred they were permanent and prestigious; and they must have developed a strong *ésprit de corps*. The advice they gave the magistrates must have been compelling, and their influence over the Assembly (males over thirty) must have been immeasurably strengthened by the fact that debates, amendments and counter-propositions were not allowed: the

Council's proposals could only be accepted or rejected – and rejection is psychologically difficult to carry out where no alternatives are known to exist. Even the voting procedure at Sparta had an archaic flavour: every man in the assembly roared his Yes or No, and assessors stationed at a distance decided which side had the majority – or the louder voices.

Sparta's institutions were peculiar because they were partly archaic and partly adaptations to a special situation; legend attributed them to a law-giver called Lycurgus who was probably a composite or mythical figure. The institutions almost certainly reached their final form by the end of the seventh century, which had given the Spartans some bad moments. A serious defeat by Argos and a fierce, protracted revolt by the helots of conquered Messenia were evidently sufficient to convince the Spartans that permanent mobilisation and constant vigilance were necessary for Sparta to hold down her large subject population and wide territories. Not only the institutions but most other aspects of life became fixed; change was unwanted, and so, since the world changed, the world had to be shut out. The entire content of Spartan life was determined by this fundamental decision: the 'Spartan' education in endurance; the militarisation of the whole male citizenry; the fixed distribution of land; the prohibition of money, the exclusion of foreigners and contempt for trade; and the cultivation of an austere, taciturn, duty-conscious, unimaginative character-type in marked contrast to the more erratic, eloquent and creative Athenian.

Too much attention can be paid to political history and political institutions: most men in most societies have only a minimal contact with politics except as victims. But, as should now be apparent, this was not true of life in ancient Greece, where the mild climate and small scale of organisation encouraged a wide and direct involve-

Left
Boy wearing a cloak. Parian marble statue from Tralles in Caria, after a Greek work of about 270 BC. Arkeoloji Müzeleri, Istanbul.

53

ment that was quite different in quality from participation in a modern 'representative' democracy. There was no sharp distinction between public and 'everyday' life: indeed, the citizen idly shopping in the agora might find himself moments later swept along to the Assembly to discuss a military expedition in which he would have to serve, or the dispatch of a ship on which he would take an oar. When we turn to everyday life, in its normally accepted meaning, we find the same mingling of public and private, even in childhood.

EDUCATION AND EXCELLENCE

The Greek idea of education was *arete* – 'excellence', but excellence of a particular sort, which would enable its possessor to live the good life within the framework of the city-state. Introspection and special skills were not included in it: what counted were the qualities of the socially effective all-rounder, as we should expect in this intensely sociable society. The product of a good education would be physically active but dignified, quick on the uptake, eloquent, and able to hold his own at drinking, performing on the lyre at a party, or scoring points in debate. The Greek tendency to identify physical, moral and intellectual qualities is revealingly shown in descriptions of Socrates, in which the philosopher's virtue and brilliance are made to sound rather surprising in the light of his paunchy satyr-like appearance and lack of physical grace.

There is no way of knowing how many Greeks received any formal education. The pasting up of laws and, in Athens, the practice of ostracism, imply that all the male citizens were literate; and Athenian law did in fact require it. But it seems unlikely that the children of the poor spent long at schools, which were all fee-paying. Their education, insofar as it existed at all, must have been education at work, as apprentices. In better-off homes the first teaching was imparted by a household slave, the pedagogus. Then, at about six, the boy was taken to school by the pedagogus – or rather to schools, since he attended each of the three separate kinds in the course of a day: the grammar school for academic, and primarily literary,

Opposite top
Playing with a hoop.

Opposite bottom
Child playing with a yo-yo. Pottery painting. Staatliche Museen Antikenmuseum, Berlin.

Above
The Muse Terpsichore. Detail from a work by the Peleus Painter. Pottery, about 440 BC. British Museum, London.

education; a music school; and a training school or gymnasium for dancing, exercises and sport. Some girls may have gone to school, but (if so) at separate establishments.

Boys learned to write, using a stylus and a tablet of soft wax on which letters and words could be scratched and then 'rubbed out' so that the tablet could be used again and again. But Greek culture still had a marked oral bias, and boys who stayed on at school were required to memorise long pas-

sages from the poets. Above all they were soaked in the works of Homer, so thoroughly that in later life his words would spring to their lips on all sorts of occasions, providing striking examples, apt comparisons and authoritative pieces of wisdom (which an opponent in debate would be expected to cap with equally striking examples on the other side of the argument).

The emphasis on musical education reflects the Greeks' conviction of its profound influence for good or evil.

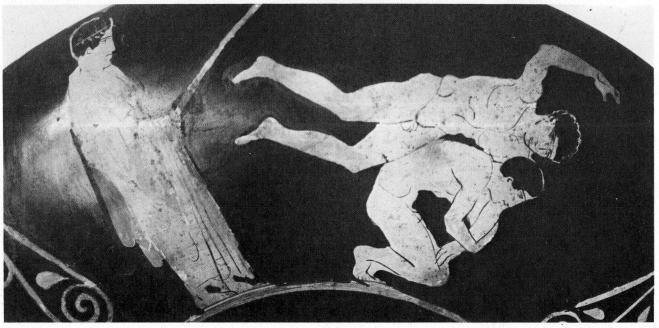

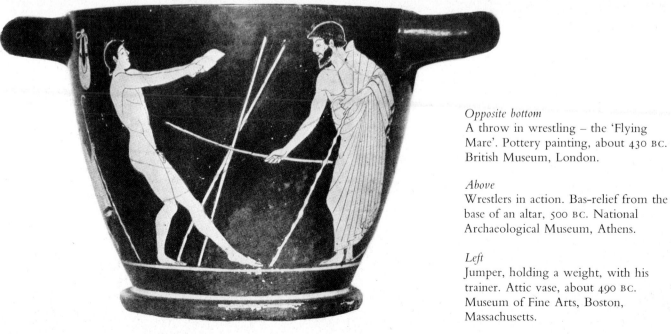

Opposite bottom
A throw in wrestling – the 'Flying Mare'. Pottery painting, about 430 BC. British Museum, London.

Above
Wrestlers in action. Bas-relief from the base of an altar, 500 BC. National Archaeological Museum, Athens.

Left
Jumper, holding a weight, with his trainer. Attic vase, about 490 BC. Museum of Fine Arts, Boston, Massachusetts.

Bad music could corrupt: in his Utopia *The Republic* Plato declares that effeminate music must be banned, and only sober, inspiring modes permitted. And singing and playing were important not only during leisure, but on many civic and religious occasions. At school, therefore, a boy learned the flute or, more often, the lyre, a stringed instrument used as the accompaniment to a song; 'lyric' poetry originates in such songs. The importance of athletics in Greek life is well known; its various forms and its larger implications are discussed in the next chapter.

There were no universities or equivalent institutions, but many roving teachers called sophists appeared in fifth-century Greece, offering to instruct paying pupils in the arts of success. Above all this meant the art of persuasion, so vital in the Assembly and courts of law: the art of marshalling evidence, drawing inferences, conducting arguments – and making the best of a bad argument by false reasoning, fine words and appeals to emotion; this last aspect of their teaching is all that remains of 'sophistry' in English usage. Some fifth-century sophists, however, taught other subjects including mnemonics and political theory, almost always with a view to practical application. In the fourth century a number of permanent teaching institutions were set up, notably Plato's Academy (so named after the gymnasium outside Athens where the school was founded). Though now remembered as a school for philosophers, this was intended to be a school for statesmen; and although the curriculum included geometry and other high-mindedly irrelevant subjects, men did come from all over Greece to study at the Academy.

As in most things, Sparta was different from the rest of Greece. Everything was sacrificed to the creation of a hardy military race. Spartans continued to follow the archaic custom of exposing sickly babies on a mountainside so they perished. At seven, boys were taken from their parents and joined a group that has aptly been compared to a boarding school – though few boarding schools would be happy about the comparison. The

'headmaster' and his assistants imposed savage discipline, assisted by chosen older boys for whom the younger 'fagged'. Boys wore a simple tunic in all weathers, and bathed in the cold rushing waters of the River Eurotas. Their bedding consisted of reeds which the boys themselves tore from the river, and their food of variations on porridge, so meagre as to deliberately encourage stealing, which was only disgraceful if the thief was unskilful enough to be caught. According to one famous story – famous because it enshrined an admirable action – a young Spartan stole a fox, hid it under his tunic, and allowed it to gnaw away his stomach rather than own up. Athletics and brutal games

Above
Woman admiring herself in a mirror. Attic pottery painting. Antikenmuseum, Berlin.

Opposite
A splendid amphora (storage jar) decorated with a rather disconcerting domestic scene: husband stabs unfaithful wife while lover runs away. Corinthian, about 560-550 BC. Musée du Louvre, Paris.

Opposite
Hippodameia, Queen of the Lapiths, about to be carried off by centaurs. Figure from the west pediment of the Temple of Zeus at Olympia. Archaeological Museum, Olympia.

Above
Young women washing. Attic pottery painting, about 450 BC. Staatliche Antikensammlungen und Glyptothek, Munich.

Left
Persephone seated at the foot of her husband's couch. British Museum, London.

seem to have dominated the syllabus, along with dancing – which was, however, the occasion for drilling. Such learning as they acquired seems to have been patriotic fare, including the laws of Sparta and militaristic verse; but even in Sparta a certain amount of Homer was learned by heart. Finally, Spartan education ended with the military training and militarised life for which it had always been intended as a preparation. One beneficial side-effect of the Spartan obsession with health and efficiency was that even girls were given a vigorous athletic education; and indeed women were rather freer in Sparta than in most Greek states. Other Greeks professed to be shocked by the girls' short tunics and occasional wrestling matches with the boys; the Athenian Euripides – admittedly writing at the height of the Peloponnesian War – held that their education led to unchastity, whereas Aristophanes portrays them as hopelessly provincial muscle-women.

WOMEN, MARRIAGE AND SEX

The Greek woman was emphatically inferior in status to men, both in custom and law. As a girl she owed perfect obedience to her father; he decided whom she would marry; and after the wedding she found not independence but merely a change of masters. In most states she could not own property, let alone take part officially in any but the most trivial commercial transactions (Sparta was one of the exceptions); her husband could do what he liked with her dowry unless he decided to divorce her, in which case her father could claim it back. Greek men married late, and the age-gap between an oldish man (say thirty) and a teenager must have reinforced the authority of the male. A wife was expected to spend most of her time at home, supervising the domestics if the family was well off and in any event making sure that the necessary housework was done, the food cooked, and the family clothes and other fabrics spun and woven. When friends (who would always be male friends) came to dinner, she had to retire to the women's quarters, which were as inviolable as a harem; no respectable woman ate with anybody

but members of her family. Apart from attending certain festivals, she would make no significant public appearances except for shopping expeditions to the agora. By contrast, her husband might be sociable and mobile; and if his mobility took in more or less serious sexual adventures, she was expected to put up with them, though her own peccadillos were regarded with less indulgence.

Put in these legal and social terms, the Greek woman's lot was an unhappy one; and many writers have so described it. But if so it was an unhappiness shared by most women in the West down to the twentieth century, and even now by many women in Southern Europe and the Islamic world. This is not to defend inequality, but to point out that the position of the Greek woman was

much the same as that of civilised women at most times and places. And that means that married life was probably much the same too – that there were sly wives and domineering wives as well as downtrodden and submissive ones; and that people valued domestic happiness but, if that was not available, they settled for comfort and

Above
Marble altar showing the sacrifice of Alcestis, Queen of Pherae, who – according to legend – gave her own life to save her husband Admetus. Museo Archeologico, Florence.

Opposite
Domestic scene with a lady, Hegeso, commemorated on a marble stele. Shortly before 400 BC. National Archaeological Museum, Athens.

compromise. There is little evidence in Greek literature that women were despised. Homer can sympathise with a noble and touching woman like Hector's wife Andromache, doomed to widowhood and slavery, and also with a charming girl whose mind is beginning to dwell on men, like Nausicaa, the princess in the *Odyssey* who discovers the shipwrecked Odysseus salt-caked and fascinatingly naked, and would clearly be willing to take him, properly cleaned up, for her husband. Greek drama has its heroines too, including Queen Alcestis, who in Euripides' play gives her life so that her husband may live. It also has a number

of fatal women: Queen Phaedra, who enacts the story of Joseph and Potiphar's wife with her stepson; Medea, abandoned by Jason, who murders her children by him and poisons her rival; and the female devotees of Dionysus, who tear their king apart when he tries to calm their frenzy.

In the great age of Athens there seems to have been more interest in the ordinary life of women and the home. Tender domestic groups appear as memorials on tombstones, and women and household scenes are frequently the subjects of pottery paintings. Literature too makes more of women. But the conventional ideal remained the Little Woman: in his funeral oration, Pericles lays it down that 'the greatest glory of a woman is to be talked about as little as possible by men, whether the talk is complimentary or critical'. In fact Euripides, who created such a splendid gallery of women characters, was widely regarded as a mysoginist, apparently just because he showed women as capable

of passion and action. The strongest indication that Athenian women were far from nonentities comes from the comedies of Aristophanes, the chief source of all our information about the less formal side of Greek life. In *Lysistrata,* the women of Greece withdraw their sexual favours to force their husbands to end the war. The men are consistently outwitted and eventually capitulate, but it is clear that abstinence is as difficult for the women as for the men – especially for those couples who love each other. It would be unwise to draw too many conclusions from Aristophanes' mixture of farce and fantasy, but it at least suggests that the mutual satisfactions of family life were as important in the fifth century BC as at any other time – and, incidentally, that most men cannot have got their main satisfactions from homosexual relationships or the services of courtesans, as is sometimes suggested. Aristophanes' *Thesmophoriazusae* is an even wilder farce in which Euripides' father-in-law is disguised as

Above
The theatre at Ephesus, the greatest of the Ionian Greek cities on the coast of Asia Minor (modern Turkey).

Right
Boy helping drunken man to be sick. Pottery painting, 490–480 BC.

Opposite
Terracotta figure of a dancer. Early second century BC. Museo Nazionale, Taranto.

a woman and spies on a festival from which men are excluded. The women are furious with Euripides – the 'mysoginist' – but mainly, it seems, because he has found them out: thanks to his influence, Athenian husbands now lock the doors of the women's quarters, keep guard dogs to scare off other men, and even lock up the larder (presumably to stop their women tippling and subsidising their boy-friends). The women are such bold hussies, Euripides' father-in-law implies, that they will commit adultery under their spouses' noses, and may even do away with them if their presence becomes too inconvenient. Unequal or not, it was a rich full life.

Prostitution flourished in ancient Greece, though probably no more so than in other societies. The most interesting practitioners were the *hetairai*, who closely resembled the traditional Japanese geisha girls or the poetically named *grandes horizontales* of Parisian society in the 1890s. Hetairai were skilled musicians, good conversationalists (who could, not being respectable, dine with the men) and also, presumably, stimulating lovers. Whether they were quite as cultivated, shrewd or golden-hearted as they were reputed to be must remain an open question: by the fourth century BC Greek writers were already glamorising the oldest profession. Hetairai were emancipated slaves or foreigners; the most famous, Pericles' mistress Aspasia, came from the city of Miletus in Ionia. She, at least, seems to have lived up to the legend, since she was a friend of Socrates as well as a 'friend' of Pericles, who divorced his wife and went to live with her. Having sponsored the law which restricted citizenship to those whose parents were both Athenian citizens, he later had to get round it so that his own son by Aspasia could be admitted as a citizen. As Aristophanes' plays – and common sense – suggest, prostitution can hardly have been more than an occasional substitute for marital relations; and the famous hetairai must have been purely upper-class luxuries.

The situation is less clear in the case of male homosexuality, despite the ancient Greeks' notorious addiction to it. It was widely accepted, as a wealth of lyric poems, inscriptions and other

references testify; and there were writers to argue that the love of man and boy was on a higher plane than love between man and woman. In this idealised version of homosexual relationships the older man stood *in loco parentis*, lovingly guiding his young friend towards spiritual and intellectual maturity. At this level of discourse there seems to have been some doubt whether full sexual relations should take place; but we may imagine that most relationships, on whatever waveband, were rather less problematic and high-toned, as surviving paintings on pottery make abundantly clear. But though homosexuality was accepted, it was not necessarily widely practised. It may well have been mainly aristocratic, and was probably most popular at Sparta, where the all-male boarding-school and barracks atmosphere must have favoured the development of intense male relationships (though curiously enough homosexuality is absent from the equally masculine world described by Homer). In this context there was nothing 'effeminate' about homosexuality, though transvestites were known at Athens: in *Thesmophoriazusae* Aristophanes has two characters who dress in women's clothes; one, the tragedian Agathon, who was a real person, also has wigs for day and night-time and is disliked by women – because he takes their customers from them. The atmosphere in Aristophanes' plays is unmistakably heterosexual (though there are plenty of seemingly good-natured references to homosexuality among the copious exchanges of bawdy); and it is possible that democratic Athens was not much inclined to the Spartan-aristocratic mode when it came to sexual tastes.

HOUSE, HOME AND MARKET

At Athens and other leading cities, the houses in which people lived must have looked mean and insignificant by comparison with the splendid public buildings on the acropolis and elsewhere. At the very height of Athenian power there seem to have been some six thousand houses in the city proper, chaotically huddled together in crooked streets and holding about 36,000 people. Many more must have lived within the walls at the Piraeus, or close to the city; and during the long periods in

Above
Women at work with wool. British Museum, London.

Top
Night visit to a hetaira. The suitor, offering apples at the girl's window, is an old man; his slave looks on. Pottery painting. British Museum, London.

Opposite
Girl using a carved chest. From Locri, in southern Italy. Museo Nazionale, Taranto.

kylix

oenochoe

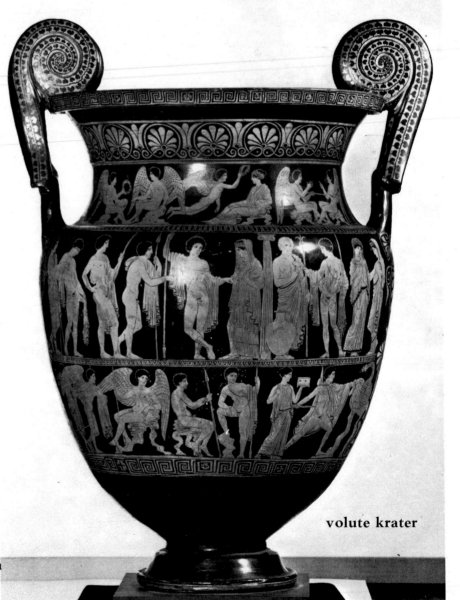

volute krater

amphora

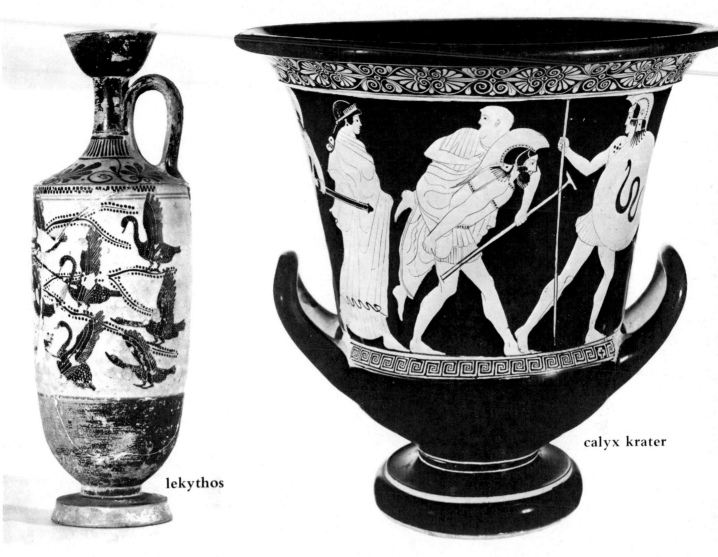

lekythos

calyx krater

the Peloponnesian War when the Spartans were ravaging Attica the population of the city was swollen by rustic refugees and their livestock. In normal times a majority of the people probably lived in the country; and in less commercially oriented places than Athens even the city-dwellers may often have gone to work in the countryside every morning, reversing present-day commuting habits.

The contrast between public and private building extends to materials: the temples were built of stone, houses (even wealthy men's houses) of baked

Opposite and above
A few of the many types of pottery vessel made by the Greeks: the *amphora*, a tall two-handled jar for storing wine or oil, and the *oenochoe* for pouring; two kinds of mixing bowl, the *calyx krater* and scroll-handled *volute krater*; the shallow *kylix* for drinking; and the narrow, delicate *lekythos*, a storage jar often used for funeral ceremonies.

clay bricks, topped with terracotta tile roofs. The walls were lime-washed on the outside and plastered inside. Furniture was sparse and holes in the roof served as chimneys; on a cold night when the wind was in the wrong direction, the inhabitants of a Greek house must have been faced with a choice between freezing and choking.

In houses of any size the basic layout was one that has often been seen in Mediterranean lands: an uninviting, small-windowed façade looks on to the street, while the true centre of the dwelling lies at the back, where rooms cluster round an inner courtyard. The layout could be adapted to every kind of private and commercial purpose, containing workshops, shops and offices in the ground-floor street front. Most of the private rooms served the functions we should expect, but in addition there was one or more room set aside for the womenfolk, where they probably did their spinning and weaving and to which it was com-

pulsory for them to retire when there was male company. Here and in the kitchen, at least, the wife was supreme.

Many Greek households must have been nearly self-sufficient, making clothes from wool supplied by the master's farm outside the city and bringing in food from the same source. However, the market seems to have had something for everyone – scent and probably cosmetics, fine fabrics and other ladies' luxuries as well as fish, cheese, oil, corn and so on; there were even moneylenders doing business at twelve per cent interest with the optimistic or unlucky. As so often, it is Aristophanes who has given the liveliest picture of the proceedings, including a snapshot of a vainglorious army officer clanking about in his armour between the vegetable and crockery stalls before going home with an omelette carefully packed into his helmet.

SOCIETY, WORK AND SLAVERY

Here as elsewhere, fifth-century Athens is easily the best-documented of the Greek states, and therefore stands as the type of them all. There is an unavoidable element of distortion in this, just because Athens was more articulate and prosperous and imperial than the rest: most of them must in fact have been simpler and more 'old-fashioned' and rural in organisation and outlook. Still, other Greeks may have complained of Athens' tyranny, but they never referred to her as a freak; so the distortions are perhaps no worse than those of most metropolitan-biased social descriptions.

The influence of the aristocracy on Athenian life never entirely disappeared; we have seen that for most of the fifth century aristocrats led the various factions in the democracy. The wealthy businessman had no trouble in being accepted as a member of the upper class, and was not necessarily expected to give up his business interests in order to make a public career; Nicias, chief commander of the disastrous Sicilian expedition, was an immensely wealthy man who hired out a thousand slaves to work in the Athenian silver mines at Laureum. But there was some feeling that – as in nineteenth-century Britain – the unemployed gentleman of private means was the most suitable person to run a state in which many of the highest official positions were unpaid. Aristophanes is a typical conservative in his attitude towards the radical democrats who exercised most influence at Athens during the last years of the war. He always refers to them as lining their pockets at the expense of the state – with how much justification it is now impossible to say. By contrast, the richest thousand or so citizens were expected to help the community by paying for certain important items, notably the fitting out of state shipping and the production of plays.

Below this level, fifth-century Athenian citizens fell into two social groups: hoplites and thetes. The former was a military classification, comprising all the male citizens – farmers, traders, craftsmen or whatever – who could afford the armour and weapons needed to serve as a hoplite. The thetes were the poorer classes–

mostly small farmers and the poorest craftsmen who hired themselves out by the day; they served in the army as auxiliaries or manned the fleet. From the meagre information provided by local government registers and army and religious fraternity lists, it looks as though hoplites and thetes were very roughly equal in numbers; the size of the hoplite class confirms the general impression that at Athens wealth was quite widely distributed among the citizenry. The military classification persisted, thanks to Athens' many wars and imperial commitments, and at times formed the basis for political groupings. As the strength and survival of Athens came to depend increasingly on the navy, the thetes gained previously-denied political rights; eventually, though there was no change in the law, they were tacitly allowed to hold most offices, including membership of the Council of Five Hundred, and small daily payments made regular attendance at the Assembly and the law courts a practical possibility for the less well-off. (However, the payment was never so generous as to encourage thetes to devote themselves to politics rather than work for a living, although conservatives inevitably claimed that it was.) Significantly, the destruction of the Athenian fleet in Sicily, which was a blow to the prestige of the navy, and therefore to the influence of the thetes, was followed by the oligarchic reaction of 411, apparently supported by the hoplites; one of the first actions of the new régime was to disfranchise the thetes and abolish payments for civic attendance. The oligarchy fell mainly because the Athenian navy based on Samos remained adamantly

Opposite
Boy, wearing a cloak and carrying a crook; probably a shepherd. Tanagra figure found at Myrina. Third century BC.

Above left
Servant girl carrying a box. Tanagra figure, probably second century BC.

Left
Sleeping slave. Terracotta figure from Cyprus. Third century BC. British Museum, London.

Above
Girls at a fountain. Pottery painting.
Second century BC. Musei Vaticani.

Above right
Men harvesting olives. Attic jar, about
540-530 BC. British Museum, London.

Opposite
Potters and pottery painters at work.
Pottery painting, about 430 BC.
Ashmolean Museum, Oxford.

pro-democratic; and after the great naval victory over the Spartans at Cyzicus, the pre-eminence of the navy was fully re-established and all the rights of the thetes were restored.

The metics (foreign residents) lived and worked outside this socio-political hurly-burly. As non-citizens they could not vote and were not allowed to own land, so they could never put down roots in the community. They were liable to military service, though it seems unlikely that they were called upon except in emergencies, or perhaps for material contributions. In communities like the Greek city-states, where kinship, ownership of land, political activity and membership of religious associations were so large a part of life, the metic was an anomaly – a free-floating individual in a closely bonded world. On the other hand, there seems to have been no social discrimination against metics, who appear on an equal footing with citizen guests at banquets and on other social and business occasions. A great many of them must have been merchants, and they may well have formed substantial colonies only in a few commercial cities such as Athens and Corinth.

The proportion of slaves to the rest of the population was probably higher in such cities too. In the Dark Age, and later still in many places, slave-owning on any scale was not particularly attractive: an extra worker also meant an extra mouth in hard times, while there was not much to be done with a surplus in a good year. The introduction of money and the growth of trade changed the situation – and above all at Athens, where farming for the market and a booming foreign trade created a demand for cheap labour. Most estimates put the slave population of Athens in 431 BC at 80-100,000, between a quarter and a third of the population as a whole.

At first sight the attitude of the ancients towards slavery is puzzling. In the *Iliad*, the Trojan hero Hector tells his wife Andromache that his own inevitable death in battle troubles him less than the knowledge that she and her children will pass into bondage in a stranger's land; and there are many similarly heart-rending passages in Homer, Aeschylus and other authors, lamenting the chances and changes of life that lead to enslavement. There is, in other words, just the imaginative sympathy we expect to find in great literature; but there is no note of outrage and no expression of protest. Evidently there is only one explanation: to a Greek or Roman it would have been as pointless to condemn slavery as to condemn death: both were simply in the nature of things. Few writers thought it necessary to attempt a defence of slavery, though the philosopher Aristotle did something of the sort by equating slaves

with barbarians who, unlike the Greeks, were slaves by nature – a feeble enough argument since, as Aristotle knew very well, many Greek prisoners of war had been enslaved, while perhaps an even larger number of Greek women and children from captured cities had been sold into bondage by the Athenians and other inflamed imperialists.

Many of the slaves at Athens were probably non-Greeks – Thracian victims of the Greek colonists established along the coast, or Asiatics specially purchased in the great slave markets of the East. It is not possible to be more precise: only slaves, perhaps, would have been interested in discriminating between places of origin, and their point of view was not put on record. Bearing this qualification in mind, it seems that the slave's lot was a relatively happy one in fifth-century Athens. He had some legal rights: he could not be killed, or violently assaulted without provocation –

though all experience in similar situations indicates that such rights were hard to enforce in a world run by property owners. Of more practical importance was the mild tone of Athenian society, created by its small-scale, domestic nature. Very few men owned large numbers of slaves: the norm was the family unit with two or three slaves – a man or two to help the master in the fields or workshop, and a nurse or maid working in the house. In this kind of atmosphere, a certain degree of affection and companionship flourished, and there is certainly no evidence that the Athenians feared the slaves all around them as the Spartans feared their own helots. In so far as slaves appear in Athenian literature it is as amiable rogues – pretty much the standard ruling-class literary version of serfs and workers for the next two-and-a-half millennia. The atmosphere was so relaxed that slaves were hired out by the day to other people, and even allowed to set up in business on their own, in separate premises from their masters'. Under this remarkable arrangement the slave merely paid over one-sixth of his income to his owner; the rest belonged to him, and if he was successful he might save enough to buy his freedom. How often this happened – and how often a master gratuitously gave a slave his freedom – is not known; freedmen certainly played no notable part in the public history of Greece, in marked contrast with the freedmen of Rome.

Greek slavery was relatively mild – but only relatively. The well-treated slave might be cuffed when his master was bad-tempered, sold when his master got into debt, and tortured (to make sure his evidence was not biased by loyalty) when his master got into trouble; and if he was really unlucky he was sent to work in the Athenian silver mines. On one occasion, at least, the slaves voted with their feet: in 413 when the Spartans took more or less permanent control of the Attic countryside by setting up a fortified camp outside besieged Athens, 20,000 slaves fled to join them. The details of the incident are obscure, but the slaves' sentiments are clear enough.

The small scale of production was not incompatible with vigorous activity and rapidly expanding trade. Most farming land in Attica consisted of small family-owned or -leased plots, though there may have been larger estates before the reforms of Solon and Pisistratus (who also seem to have suppressed the demoralising practice of share-cropping). Much of the land was turned over from cereals to olive trees and vines; the oil and wine produced could be sold in the city for local consumption or export. The need for thousands of storage jars caused pottery to become a thriving trade; the fifth-century Attic masterpieces of pottery were the splendid side-effects of a craft largely devoted to producing sound but commonplace jars in great quantities. The existence of an export trade must have given opportunities to develop all sorts of new lines with which to impress barbarians or the less sophisticated 'colonial' Greeks. Athenian metal-

Opposite
The *Charioteer of Delphi*. Bronze sculpture from the sanctuary of Apollo at Delphi, about 470 BC. Archaeological Museum, Delphi.

Above
Heracles banqueting with the gods Hermes and Athena. Pottery painting from the Andokides workshop. 525–500 BC. Staatliche Antikensammlungen und Glyptothek, Munich.

work has been found as far away as central Europe, and there were probably other, perishable, export goods we know nothing of. The most active merchants had agents in several ports; but even so their business was a high-risk, high-profit one, as for that matter it remained down to quite recent times.

Manufacturers in Athens itself were also small: the largest workshop in the city, owned by a metic from Syracuse, employed some 1,200 slaves making shields. Even a very wealthy man like the father of the orator Demosthenes owned a variety of small properties and concerns rather than one large one; and the great buildings on the Acropolis were not the work of teams but of a host of independent craftsmen and small contractors.

We know of only one really large industrial enterprise in the whole of Greece: the silver mines at Laureum, on the southernmost coast of Attica. These mines played a decisive role in Athenian history. They made it possible for the city to mint its own coinage without indebtedness to other states, and even to export silver to places where oil and wine were not sufficiently in demand. But even more crucial was the rich new vein struck in 483, and used on Themistocles' advice to build a great fleet of triremes; it was this fleet that smashed the Persians and effectively created Athens' seaborne empire. The mines were state-owned, but the working was contracted out; the hiring prices of slaves – hardly more than the purchase price – suggest that the working conditions must have been, to say the least, health-destroying. Anything up to 30,000 slaves worked in the mines of Laureum.

The economics of everyday life are hard to make sense of because the evidence is so fragmentary. The silver drachma was the main unit of currency, but there was a smaller silver coin, the obol, six of which were equal in value to a drachma. Athenian coins were stamped with the head of Athena, patron goddess of the city and goddess of wisdom; her special bird, the owl, appeared on the reverse side. In the fifth century an unskilled manual worker could earn two or three obols in a day, a skilled man perhaps twice as much. There were some extremely wealthy individuals who left 80,000 drachmai or more on their deaths, but most 'middle-class' Athenians were not grotesquely better off than the poorer citizens; one convincing estimate puts ninety per cent of the

Above
Aspects of leisure on a Corinthian vase: a banqueting scene in the upper band; a procession of riders in the lower. Early fifth century BC. Musée du Louvre, Paris.

Opposite top
Wool being weighed and dispatched under the supervision of a king or merchant. Spartan pottery painting, 565–560 BC. Musée du Louvre, Paris.

Opposite bottom
This coin is one of the earliest decadrachms of Syracuse. The obverse shows the head of Arethusa. The reverse shows the type of racing chariot first adopted at Syracuse.

population in an annual income group of 180-480 drachmai. Prices are even harder to set out usefully, and a sample must do. A decent workaday pot could be purchased for less than an obol; a decent workaday slave cost around 150 drachmai (the price would vary enormously, depending on the age, health and skills of the slave, who might, for example, be a labourer, a mason, a goldsmith, a clerical worker, or a schoolmaster); a good upper-middle-class town house cost 3,000 drachmai. For ease of calculation, a hundred drachmai was called a mina, and sixty mina comprised a talent. These terms were mostly used in trade or government finance; Athens, for example, had an emergency fund of a hundred talents that was spent on building a new fleet after the Sicilian disaster. But at least one example from a somewhat later period indicates that the inflated values of show business are nothing new: the famous fourth-century actor Polus is said to have received no less than a talent for only two appearances.

THE SPARTAN SYSTEM

At Sparta the need to maintain the dominance of a minority shaped the entire social system. Spartan life had not always been philistine and militaristic, as the seventh-century poems of Alcman and the fine early pottery of Sparta indicate; but after the Messenian helot revolt, security became the overriding need: Spartans concentrated on being soldiers and nothing but soldiers. When he was twenty, the young Spartan's education ended and he enrolled in one of the fraternities into which the community was divided; he roomed and ate with the members, even after his marriage (which was not permitted until he reached the age of thirty). There were no serious distractions from military life: no Spartan farmed his estates; they were worked by helots who gave up a fixed proportion of their produce, which the Spartan contributed in turn to the mess of his fraternity. Every effort was made to fix the social order and protect citizens against temptations: each man inherited a portion of land that was inalienable; helots could not be gambled, given away or emancipated, since they belonged to the

state, not the individual whose land they cultivated; money was prohibited (iron was the closest thing that existed to currency); and since luxury was frowned upon, trade remained a fringe activity undertaken by a few licensed non-Spartans. For at least 250 years the system produced a high degree of social cohesion; despite the oligarchic functioning of their political machinery, the Spartans happily called themselves 'the Equals', not without social justification.

The helot was the economic basis of the Spartan system – far more so than the slave in democratic states. This form of serfdom occurred in some other places – in Thessaly, Argos and Crete, for example – but the only information of any substance comes from Sparta. On the face of it there was not much to choose between being a slave and being a helot in Sparta. The slave could be bought, sold and moved about at will, whereas the helot was at least secure on his land; but on the other hand a slave, unlike a helot, might hope to buy or win his freedom. In reality, helots seem to have been worse off: we hear of revolts by helots, not slaves, and numerous stories describe the ill-treatment meted out to the helots by their Spartan masters. On one occasion the Spartans are said to have encouraged those helots who believed they had served Sparta well to claim their freedom; those who did so were formed into a triumphal procession which filed into a temple – and was never seen again By this kind of ruse the Spartans made sure they thinned the ranks of the boldest and, therefore, potentially most dangerous helots.

Opposite bottom
Pottery painting of a bathing scene.

Opposite top
Figure of a banqueter, probably from Dodona. Late sixth century BC. British Museum. London.

Above left
Young men at their ablutions. Vase from Capua. 510–500 BC.

Left
Achilles and Ajax playing a game. Pottery painting by Exekias. About 540–530 BC. Musei Vaticani.

Other sources claim that the Spartans privately but officially declared war on the helots at the beginning of each year, so justifying their excesses to themselves; and young Spartans are even said to have gone in for helot-hunting as part of their training. Not being a literary people, the Spartans left no account of their way of life, but most of the stories about their treatment of helots come from sources fairly sympathetic to them; though possibly exaggerated, they must represent the essential attitudes of the Spartans. However, there must have been helots *and* helots, since large contingents served with the Spartan army and seem to have been conspicuously loyal to their masters; some, for example, fell with the Three Hundred at Thermopylae. The explanation of this apparent contradiction may be that the loyal helots came from the Spartan 'home' territories in Laconia, which seem to have been more docile. The Messenians, to the west, had been a free people whom the Spartans had conquered and amongst whom they had no roots; on two occasions the Messenians were the mainspring of revolts that almost overthrew the Spartan system. This was finally accomplished from outside by the Thebans, who not only defeated the Spartans in battle but destroyed their economic base by liberating Messenia.

Left
Engraved bronze mirror cover showing Aphrodite playing dice with Pan. Fourth century BC. British Museum, London.

Above left
A young man watches the performance of a girl acrobat; she is almost certainly a slave. Vase from Apulia, southern Italy, fourth century BC. Museo Archeologico di Pegli, Genoa.

Opposite
A young man being sick after drinking; a hetaira helps him. Pottery painting. Martin von Wagner Museum of Würzburg University.

LEISURE, PLEASURE AND FASHION

The Greeks were as sociable in their leisure hours as they were in their public and working lives. Eating and drinking and bathing were most fully enjoyed in company; and, as we shall see in the next chapter, so were piety, literature and philosophising.

The Greeks ate three meals a day which corresponded fairly closely to our breakfast, lunch and dinner. Breakfast was 'continental' – a hunk of bread soaked in wine – and lunch, though more substantial, was equally functional. Dinner, however, was a festive and luxurious occasion for those who could afford it: men invited their friends home and were invited in turn, or they joined dining clubs which used the subscriptions to hire premises and pay for meals. (Such dining facilities, provided by emancipated slaves, were the nearest thing Greece offered to restaurants in this period; otherwise there were only vendors of snacks and wine in the market-place, reputedly all cheats or poisoners.) In some circles, the guests brought their own food and the host simply provided the drink. On his arrival, a guest removed his sandals and a slave washed his feet. Then tables laden with food were brought in and the diners were arranged around them on couches; like the Romans later on, they lay on their sides, leaving one hand free to pick at the food; knives and forks were not used, though there were spoons for consuming liquids. At Athens meals became more elaborate in the course of the fifth century, but oriental imports, like so many refinements, only became common later on, in the Hellenistic age.

In a well-ordered banquet, serious drinking began after the meal: libations were poured, a hymn was sung, and the company got down to business. Often there was a Master of the Banquet who laid down the proportion of water to wine: the thick, sweet Greek wine was always watered but, as pottery paintings show, had all the usual effects in the long run. Sometimes the company provided its own entertainment; and here the ability to sing to a lyre was an asset. Riddles were propounded, jokes told, verses recited; and on occasion – perhaps not so often as the literature suggests – the banquet turned into an earnest

Bottom left
Toy tiger with movable jaw, found at Thebes. About 1000 BC. British Museum, London.

Top left
Man and boy playing with a ball. Carving from a stele found at the Piraeus. Fifth century BC. National Archaeological Museum, Athens.

Above
Pottery portrait of a young man called Leagros, out riding. About 510 BC. Staatliche Antikensammlungen und Glyptothek, Munich.

Opposite top
Young man and woman playing a ball game. Pottery painting. British Museum, London.

Opposite bottom
Girls playing knucklebones. Terracotta group from Capua, about 300 BC. British Museum, London.

exchange of views. (The Greeks called a drinking party a *Symposium*. Plato's dialogue *The Symposium* features Socrates, Aristophanes and others debating the nature of love – whence the modern, intendedly non-alcoholic, application of the word to joint scholarly productions.) Professional entertainment could be laid on too, usually by specially trained troupes of slaves hired out for the evening: musicians and dancer-acrobats who might later be called on to provide more intimate services.

There were a number of daytime social centres where a man could meet more casual acquaintances to exchange news and gossip. One was the barber's shop – or rather the hairdresser's, since styling rather than shaving was the professional service the customers looked for. Others were the gymnasium changing-room and the public baths. The baths had already become quite sophisticated places offering facilities for cooking, steaming and cooling the body in a leisurely progression; however, though important in Greek social life, they were to become more important (and more sophisticated) in the Roman period. The Spartans, predictably, bathed in river water.

The most popular games involved simple, easily replaced equipment: marbles, draughts, five-stones (now a children's game, involving throwing the 'stones' into the air and catching them on the back of the hand), and various dice and ball games. Bets were laid on cock-fights and other animal combats. And the popularity of wine made *cottabos* a national late-night sport, since it involved flinging wine-dregs at a target. Significantly, none of these were team games: at play, as in all things, the Greek had an obsessive desire to shine.

Both men and women were intensely conscious of their physical appearance, and in spite of their limited equipment and attire they created and competed in following fashions. As a rule men wore beards, though they nevertheless patronised hairdressers who trimmed, styled and perfumed their locks. But even before the Persian wars, aristocratic young men were adopting a style that doubtless outraged their elders – wearing their hair

very long, dressing in prettily decorated linens, sporting jewellery, and even carrying flowers. Women too could be very elegant: in Aristophanes, references to their saffron robes, perfumes and dainty shoes are frequent and mock-disapproving, in the style of a man who mocks without the slightest hope (or perhaps intention) of reforming the practice mocked. Clothing did not lend itself to much in the way of fashionable variation, since it remained basically a simple tunic, consisting of an oblong of material folded and wrapped round the body, short for men, full-length for women; in cold weather or on formal occasions a cloak might be worn over it. Women did not appear bare-breasted, let alone nude: in this respect the artistic record can be misleading. The same applies to men: the Greeks do seem to have been completely unself-conscious about nudity, and their appreciation of male beauty led them, for example, to dispense with the wearing of loin cloths for certain kinds of athletic contest; but most of the time they wore clothes for obvious practical reasons. (An interesting example of artistic licence is the pottery-painting convention that showed the Greek soldier fighting naked, whereas in reality he of course wore armour; his nudity, like a uniform, distinguished him from any foreign soldier in the same scene.)

If clothes were relatively unexciting (though no doubt there were still fashions in the materials, colours and lengths, and in the hang of drapes) women could and did wear their hair in a wide range of styles. They also used as many accessories and beauty aids as most modern women: jewellery, wigs, hair-dyes, curlers, perfumes and cosmetics could all be bought in the agora.

Apart from the 'dainty shoes' of the women – perhaps reserved for festivals – Greeks wore sandals, if they wore anything on their feet; much of the time, like Socrates, they went barefoot. Hats were worn only as protection for travel, but walking sticks were standard equipment outdoors.

MEDICINE, DISEASE AND DEATH
The Greek attitude towards illness was part-superstitious and part-scientific.

The average countryman had his store of herbs and remedies which were the familiar mixture of useful and useless, magic, common sense and common nonsense. But those who could do so, sought advice – from a doctor, or from a doctor-priest and the god he served.

The god was Asclepius, better known by the Roman form of his name, Aesculapius. This son of Apollo was widely venerated, and had temples and shrines all over the Greek (and later the Greco-Roman) world; the most famous were at Epidaurus in the Peloponnese and on the island of Cos. At such places the afflicted gathered in large numbers to consult the priests and implore the god for assistance. The most favoured way of securing this was to sleep within the precincts of the temple, in the hope that one of the snakes sacred to Asclepius would come out during the night and effect a cure by licking the afflicted part; or that the god would send his answer to the prayers in a dream. (As a matter of fact the 'temple dream' was a widely used method of eliciting advice and information from the gods on a range of topics from the fate of empires to the location of a missing ring.) Like their modern equivalents, a good many devotees of Asclepius claimed to have experienced miraculous cures, and left grateful inscriptions to proclaim the fact.

The earliest physicians in independent practice may have learned their art from the temple priests; the reputed 'founder' of scientific medicine, whose oath is still sworn by practitioners at the beginning of their careers, was Hippocrates, who came from the Asclepian centre of Cos. He seems to have lived in the second half of the fifth century – in spite of which, almost nothing is known about him. The large collection of documents associated with his name originates from various periods of the fifth and fourth centuries, and does not even represent a single point of view or tradition; like the Spartan legislator 'Lycurgus', Hippocrates is an example of the Greek

Opposite
Woman wearing a himation (cloak) heavily draped over her chiton (ankle-length tunic). One of the Seasons: fragment of a bas-relief. Musei Vaticani.

Left
Asclepius, god of medicine: relief.
National Archaeological Museum,
Athens.

Above
Hunting scene from the Alexander
Sarcophagus from Sidon. Marble relief,
about 310 BC. Arkeoloji Müzeleri,
Istanbul.

Opposite top right
Elegant ladies wearing dyed and
embroidered clothing; one carries a fan,
the other wears bangles and an elaborate
headdress. British Museum, London.

Opposite left
Tomb sculpture in memory of a young
man. National Archaeological Museum,
Athens.

Opposite right
Physician and patient. Stele dedicated to
a physician and his son. British
Museum, London.

Above
'The Rites at the Tomb of a Hero': the heroes of mythology had a role in Greek life comparable to that of saints: daily offerings might be made to them in the hope that they would intercede with the gods. Pottery painting from southern Italy, about 330 BC.

Above right
Man on horseback. Fragment from a funerary stele, sixth century BC. Museo Barracco, Rome.

Opposite
Mourners lamenting over the body of a dead man. A moving scene despite the schematised painting style, which has only just developed from pure geometry. National Archaeological Museum, Athens.

tendency to personify the past. However, the Hippocratic collection does reveal a profession that has shed any idea of illness as divine retribution, and concerns itself chiefly with the search for natural causes and cures. It includes a large number of carefully-recorded case histories which are, however, rather depressing reading, since most of the patients died. There is also plenty of practical career advice. The physician must appear well-set-up and healthy, for people are prejudiced against doctors who seem unwell; and he must look thoughtful but not gloomy. And 'Hippocrates' lays great emphasis on cultivating the ability to predict the course of a disease, which a cynic might describe as substituting omniscience for success.

In most cases the general practitioner seems to have prescribed the medicines that have become the standbys of his profession; rest, quiet, harmless herbal remedies and a sensible diet. The doctrine that nature is the best healer was already known, though not universally held. However, since operations were obviously dangerous and horribly painful (there were no anaesthetics), even the more 'active' practitioners generally confined themselves to cupping and bleeding – a cure-all which was almost universally accepted right down to recent times.

Before the Hellenistic period the physician seems to have had about the same status as a superior craftsman; he set up shop in a town, employed assistants and solicited for business; he was not licensed or otherwise subject to social control. By the fifth century there also seem to have been municipal surgeries in some towns, but little is known about them. As always, the spectacularly successful attracted

most attention. In the late sixth century the outstanding physician of his time was (according to the historian Herodotus) Democedes of Crotona in southern Italy. The tyrant Polycrates of Samos paid Democedes two talents a year – a huge salary, if not quite in the class of Polus the actor. After curing the Persian king and queen of serious illnesses Democedes was even more lavishly rewarded. But Darius would not allow him to leave the country; so Democedes, being a Greek, preferred to abandon his barbarian gilded cage and flee back to his native city.

When the patient died, custom and the gods took charge. The corpse was washed, perfumed, dressed in white, and laid out on a herb-strewn couch at the front of the house, where it was visible from the street. An obol was placed in the dead man's mouth so that,

once in the underworld, he could pay the ferryman Charon to take him across the River Styx to the land of the dead. A bottle of oil was put beside the corpse and accompanied it to the grave. Relatives and friends visited the house during the day to lament the death and console the family; as they left they purified themselves from the taint of death, using water from a jar placed at the entrance.

The funeral took place on the following day, beginning with a procession. The corpse was carried on a litter, or drawn along in a carriage, depending on the wealth of the family. The family and close relatives dressed in dark clothes, lamenting loudly, weeping, beating their breasts and clutching their heads; the volume and intensity of the performance were increased by old women specially hired to make the display of grief more

impressive; various legal prohibitions at Athens and elsewhere make it clear that no great encouragement would have been needed for mourners to gash their faces and arms and tear their clothes to shreds. At the rear of the procession walked a flautist, playing a melancholy dirge.

The dead man was entombed with his coin and bottle, and also with a range of grave-goods indicating some belief that he would need these in the afterlife: cups, pots, plates, lamps and so on. After the funeral a wake was held, and days of sacrificing and mourning followed. At this point we are in the world of specifically religious beliefs and practices – the most important area of Greek life we have not yet discussed, both as a spiritual and a civic phenomenon.

Religion, Drama and Reason

GODS, MYTHS AND CRITICS

It is hard for most of us to take Greek religion very seriously. The first barrier is the sheer multiplicity of the Greek gods: Zeus, lord of all; his wife Hera; his brothers Poseidon, the sea god, and Hades, king of the underworld; his daughter Athena, patron goddess of arts and crafts, and of Athens; Artemis, virgin goddess of the chase; Aphrodite, goddess of love; Apollo, god of light, medicine and music; Dionysus, god of intoxication, both mystical and vinous; Ares, god of war; Hermes, the travellers' god; and many more, often with conflicting or overlapping functions.

The gods themselves stand at the centre of a great body of myths, some of which have a beauty and archetypal resonance that has led writers and artists to re-use and reinterpret them for century after century. There are also rather primitive stories of the creation of the world and the genealogies of the gods: while Uranus (the Heavens) is having intercourse with Ge (the Earth), their son Cronus cuts off Uranus' genitals and throws them in the sea; later still, *his* son, Zeus, overthrows and imprisons him to become king of the gods. An even larger group of stories involves the gods' quarrels and intrigues with one another, often displaying them in a ludicrously discreditable light: Zeus setting a vulture to tear eternally at the eternally self-renewing liver of the demi-god Prometheus, who had stolen fire from the gods to give to man; the lame blacksmith-god Hephaestus catching his wife Aphrodite making love with Ares, and hauling the guilty couple

up to the ceiling in a net; and so on. Finally, there are the interventions of the gods in the world of men, which are almost always erotic or arbitrary: Zeus, lustfully intent on a succession of human girls, changes himself into a bull, a swan, a shower of gold; and in Homer's account of the Trojan War the gods take sides and join in the slaughter like spiteful schoolboys, motivated by their own rivalries or by petty resentments against the human actors.

Below the gods come a group of human heroes who became the objects of cults, notably Theseus, king of Athens and slayer of the Minotaur, and Heracles (in his Roman guise Hercules), the strong-man whose twelve Labours included cleaning the Augean stables. Myth shades off into history of a sort with the Trojan War, and perhaps with the Theban cycle of Oedipus and his children, and the story of Jason and the Golden Fleece. And in addition to gods and heroes there are nymphs and satyrs; half-human, half-animal creatures such as centaurs; giants; and a whole gallery of monsters from the Furies (dog-headed ladies who plague and pursue the guilty) to the Sirens whose voices lure mariners on to the rocks.

There are several probable reasons for this fascinating confusion. Greek religion had no Bible, no prophet or lawgiver, no dogmas, and no church in the organisational sense. Myths were at the mercy of popular imagination and the poets, who could vary their details or invent or reinterpret them at will. Indeed the earliest coherent information about gods and myths comes from

Homer (written down in the late eighth century) and from Hesiod, a Boeotian poet whose *Theogony* of about 700 BC relates the genealogy of the gods.

The sheer antiquity of the gods and myths must have increased the likelihood of changes and accretions: many of the gods' names occur on the Linear B tablets of the Mycenaean age, at least five hundred years before Hesiod. The Olympians (the chief gods were supposed to live together on Mount Olympus) probably represent a fusion of two religions, Zeus and other sky gods – perhaps brought by the Dorians – taking over from an older earth-goddess and fertility-cult religion but absorbing some of its features. There is plenty of evidence that Athena, for example, was a pre-Dorian goddess; and, significantly, Athenians claimed that their city had never been occupied by the Dorians. According to one myth, Athena and Poseidon engaged in a contest to see which should be Athens' patron; Athena won, but in historical times Athenians in fact paid exceptional attention to Poseidon too. The obvious conclusion is that in this case the old goddess held her own against the new god – but that ever afterwards the citizens hedged some of their bets. Many quarrels between the gods must have a similar explanation.

Other myths – perhaps the ones we find most satisfactory – are more obviously attempts to explain the world; in such cases, however, the story often represents a later, rationalised version of a less obviously 'meaningful' myth. At a very basic level are the geographical explanations:

Left
The goddess of love and her son: Aphrodite and Eros. Terracotta group from Cyrene. First half of the fourth century BC. Musée du Louvre, Paris.

Top
The contest of Ares and Hephaestus, watched by Hera. The figure on the left is wearing a theatrical mask. British Museum, London.

Above
The hero Heracles as an infant, killing snakes sent by the goddess Hera. Coin from Crotona, southern Italy, 350 BC.

Above left
Bronze statue of Zeus or Poseidon:
either the king of the gods hurling a
thunderbolt or the god of the sea
flinging his trident. About 460 BC.
National Archaeological Museum,
Athens.

Left
Athena, protecting deity of Athens.
Bronze statue, fifth century BC. National
Archaeological Museum, Athens.

Opposite
Hermes, the messenger-god, is
unmistakable on this terracotta plaque in
his winged boots and broad-brimmed
travelling hat. The overall meaning is
unclear, though Hermes' bearded
solemnity suggests that he is acting here
as guide to the shades of the dead. From
Locri, about 470-460 BC. Museo
Nazionale, Taranto.
Below: two fine coins in the British
Museum, London. The one on the left
comes from the Greek island of
Peparethus; the coin on the right, from
Syracuse in Sicily, shows the head of a
goddess or nymph surrounded by
dolphins, and is stamped with the name
of the designer, Euaenetus. Museo
Nazionale, Taranto.

Left
An episode from Homer's *Odyssey*: one of Odysseus' companions, tied to the underside of a ram in order to escape from the cave of the blinded Cyclops. Archaeological Museum, Delphi.

Above
The Greek hero Heracles slaying an Amazon, one of the tribe of fierce women warriors. Relief from the Temple of Hera at Selinus. Museo Nazionale, Palermo.

Left
Zeus, king of the gods, was an indefatigable amorist with a taste for disguises. On this coin he is descending on Europa in the shape of an eagle.

Above left
Corinthian goddesses, possibly the mother and daughter Demeter and Persephone. British Museum, London.

Top left
Relief showing the Earth goddess Persephone with her husband Hades, Lord of the Underworld. Museo Nazionale, Reggio Calabria.

Above
Mount Olympus, home of the Greek gods.

observed, but Ethiopians worship black gods and Thracians red-haired ones. For Xenocrates there was only a single god, which he seems to identify with the universe itself. Many Greeks in fact spoke of experiencing the presence or inspiration of 'God' or 'the God', often without specifying further. By the fifth century, some writers felt it necessary to apologise for the gods. The great lyric poet Pindar indignantly denies that the scandalous tales about them are true. Aeschylus, the father of tragedy, ignores the tales in his trilogy on the death of Agamemnon and Orestes' vengeance: in this, Apollo insists on righteous revenge, while Athena ensures that justice is done – significantly, against the opposition of older deities, the Furies (sprung from the blood of castrated Uranus), who represented both superseded notions of religion and of justice done by recourse to blood-feuds. Other thinkers were more radical in their rejections. One, for example, propounded a version of the very modern notion that religion was 'the opium of the masses' – a set of fictions devised to keep the people in order. The philosopher Plato even recommended the deliberate creation of myths to shape the minds and emotions of citizens in his ideal society. And there were those, too, who sought to grapple with the problem that has puzzled all serious religious thinkers: the problem of how to reconcile a good and just god (or gods) with the existence of a manifestly unjust and often wicked world. From one point of view, the whole effort of Greek philosophy – which we shall be examining later – was to make natural and ethical sense of a world inadequately explained by gods, myths and rituals.

EVERYDAY RELIGION

Most of these moral and rational preoccupations were probably remote from the thoughts of the ordinary Greek. We can be quite certain that his religion satisfied him, since there is plenty of evidence that it was an intimate part of his everyday life and thoughts. There were altars in his home, herms (bronze or marble figures of the gods) set up outside the houses in the street, and shrines here and there in the city in addition to the temples

rivers run dry in summer because Poseidon became angry with the river-gods and never quite got over it; volcanic islands are the prisons of giants overthrown by the gods and still struggling to escape; and so on. At the highest level explanation and poetic symbolism combine, as in the story of Persephone. Hades kidnapped her and carried her off to his underground

kingdom; only after her mother Demeter, the corn goddess, had brought famine to the earth by refusing to let crops grow, did Zeus relent and force Hades to release her. But Persephone has to spend a third of the year in the Underworld, during which time the crops do not grow. During her Underworld sojourn it is, of course, winter time in the world above.

The Greeks anticipated most of the moral and logical criticisms we might direct at their religious beliefs. Having no theologians to blame, critics like Xenophanes blamed Homer and Hesiod for portraying the gods as indulging themselves in all the pastimes that were condemned in men – theft, adultery and treacherous dealings. Xenocrates, an Ionian writing in the late sixth century, is already contemptuous of gods created in the image of man: not only do the Greeks make their gods resemble themselves, he

Opposite
Woman burning incense. Relief on a side panel of the 'Ludovisi Throne': this figure of housewifely piety complements the naked girl flautist (p. 113), the two representing different aspects of Aphrodite, goddess of love, Museo Nazionale Romano, Rome.

Above
Mythical beasts on a Greek vase: the winged horse Pegasus and a rather skittish centaur, half-man, half-horse. British Museum, London.

on the acropolis. Every feast began with a sacrifice, every drinking-session with a libation. Great decisions were influenced by omens, portents and oracles; ordinary events, such as starting a journey or setting up shop, were prefaced with a prayer. Literature and art were largely inspired by religion or answered religious needs. And, above all, a host of annual festivals – great and small, solemn and verging on the frivolous – gave a religious turn to every aspect of a man's life, as an individual, a worker, and a citizen.

Inevitably, it is Athens we know most about. There, at least fifty festivals were celebrated every year. The virgin goddess Athena presided over rites in which phallic and other sexually powerful objects were paraded about to ensure the fertility of men, beasts and fields. By contrast (or as a result), the Apaturia was a family event – a great three-day gathering of the kinship groups (phratries) into which the whole citizen body was divided; children born since the previous year were introduced into the group, young men who had reached the age of eighteen were registered as adults, and men who had married put the fact on record. Women had their own festival, the Thesmorphoria, and so did each of the important crafts and each parish (deme).

Not all festivals were restricted to groups of citizens. At Athens the two major events were holidays for all – metic, freedman and slave as well as citizen. In March the City Dionysia was held (there was also a Rural Dionysia); the festival was introduced quite late by the tyrant Pisistratus, who doubtless wished to maintain his popularity as well as to proclaim the greatness of Athens. The Dionysia was essentially a fertility ritual, whereas the Panathenaea in July was a harvest festival dedicated to Athena and held at night. It was even grander once every four years, when a Great Panathenaea was held. Then, an endless procession of chariots, sacrificial animals and celebrants brought the goddess a new robe, draped on the mast of a ship that rumbled along on wheels: the scene has become immortal, recorded in stone on the famous frieze of the Parthenon. The Dionysia and the Panathenaea, like many other festivals, were celebrated with displays of lyric choral singing, dancing, athletics, recitations of Homer, and – the unique contribution of the Dionysia – drama; almost all were organised, in typical Greek fashion, as competitions, engaged in with intense rivalry.

MYSTERIES, ORACLES, ATHLETICS

The sentiment that seems to be absent in all this is the longing for immortality: virtually the whole of Greek religion is a celebration of the here and now, an expression of desire or gratitude for good fortune, an effort to avert calamities, an aspiration to approach the godlike in power and beauty while time and light remain. Such an attitude explains why the Greek conceived his gods as superhumans, addicted to human pleasures and vices, and liable to punish toofortunate mortals; their real advantage over man lay in the fact that they could enjoy eternal life – on earth. If there was any sort of life after death,

it was out of the light of the sun, in Hades' underground kingdom where the twittering souls of the dead were no more than bat-like wraiths. The intensity of the Greek love of life is perfectly expressed in a scene from Homer's *Odyssey* in which the slain hero Achilles tells his old comrade-in-arms, Odysseus, that he would rather be the vilest beast-of-burden labourer alive than lord it as king of the dead.

We know of only one important exception to this attitude – that of participants in the Eleusinian Mysteries, who do seem to have experienced and treasured some ecstatic intimation of immortality. The Mysteries took place at Eleusis, a town about twenty kilometres from Athens, but they attracted devotees from far beyond Attica; these gathered at Athens and, white-robed, set out at dusk with flaring torches along the Sacred Way to the Eleusinian sanctuary of Demeter and Persephone, patrons of the mysteries. But despite this impressive public spectacle, the ritual involved esoteric knowledge that was confined to initiates; and only seconddegree initiates were admitted to the very heart of the mystery. The ultimate nature of the revelation remains what it was intended to be – a mystery. It evidently involved the contemplation of a sacred ear of wheat, with all its obvious connotations of rebirth; but whether the ecstatic experiences undergone by initiates were produced by

Left
The head of a Gorgon. Anyone who looked at one of these monsters was turned to stone. Musée du Louvre, Paris.

Above
Bronze mask of a marine creature with wings in its hair; possibly Scylla, who preyed on sailors. British Museum, London.

Opposite top
Vase given as a prize at the Panathenaea; appropriately, the painting shows an athlete receiving the victor's crown. Athenian, 500 BC.

Opposite bottom
Relief of a banquet at which offerings are being made. Musée du Louvre, Paris.

intoxication, illusionism or faith remains in question.

Greek festivals and cults were local in origin, but a number of them, such as the Panathenaea, became more widely celebrated and attracted participants from outside. Two centres, and the festivals associated with them, were revered by all Hellenes and accessible to all of them, even in wartime. Delphi and Olympia became in effect sacred cities – complexes of splendid temples, 'treasuries' erected by the various states to house their offerings to the god, and votive statuary, with a tiny permanent population periodically swollen by devotees and supplicants. Delphi, situated in a high valley on the slopes of sacred Mount Parnassus, had been a holy place long before the god Apollo became its patron; in legend it was the centre or navel (omphalos) of the earth. Here dwelt the famous oracle that men came from all over the Greek world to consult. Individuals brought their prob-

lems to the oracle, and it was the ultimate authority on religious affairs. But the most astonishing fact about it – to the modern mind – is that Greek states regularly sent deputations to Delphi for prophecy and advice. The questions were put by a priest to a priestess, the Pythia, seated on a tripod. She answered in some kind of ecstatic trance whose exact nature remains unknown; it may have been induced by fasting or by drugs, or (an older but less plausible suggestion) caused by intoxicating fumes rising from a cleft in the ledge on which the ceremony took place. The priest then interpreted the wild words of the Pythia, often versifying his response – an impressive if somewhat suspect performance. Yet the Greeks had such faith in the oracle that when it seemed to prophesy wrongly they blamed themselves for misinterpreting its answers. These were indeed often ambiguous, whether through human prudence or the divine sense of play. In the most

747

Left
Hebe, cup-bearer to the gods; pottery painting in the Museo Jatta, Ruvo.

Above
The Eleusinian Mysteries were experienced only by initiates, and this relief – showing Demeter and Persephone with the young hero Triptolemus – conveys an appropriate sense of intimacy. National Archaeological Museum, Athens.

Opposite top
Delphi, dramatically sited in a hollow on the slopes of Mount Parnassus; hence the Greeks regarded it as 'the navel of the earth' and a specially holy place.

Opposite centre left above
The omphalos of Delphi: navel-stone reflecting the Greek belief that the holy site was the centre of the earth. This is a later replica, found near the Temple of Apollo. Archaeological Museum, Delphi.

Opposite bottom left
Earth goddess, probably Demeter, holding a pomegranate bud. Terracotta half-figure found at Delphi. Museum of Fine Arts, Boston, Massachusetts.

Opposite right
The god Dionysus and his wild following of satyrs and maenads. Pottery painting. British Museum, London.

notorious instance, Croesus, King of Lydia, is supposed to have asked the oracle whether he should go to war with Persia. The oracle told him that if he did so a great empire would be destroyed. He did, and it was: his own empire. The story is almost certainly apocryphal (Lydia was not even a Greek state), but it exemplifies the Greeks' attitude towards the oracle as well as their characteristic delight in sheer cleverness. Whether Delphi survived the centuries because its priests were shrewd and well-informed, or whether because the priestess genuinely experienced prevision – or a bit of both – depends more on one's wider convictions than historical knowledge.

The other major religious centre was Olympia in the Peloponnese. (This was far away and quite distinct from Mount Olympus, the highest mountain in Greece, which was the home of the gods, 'the Olympians'.) Olympia was the main cult-centre of Zeus himself, reaching a climax of magnificence in the fifth century with the building of the great temple of Zeus, which held a colossal seated gold-and-ivory statue of the god. It was also the site of a four-yearly festival whose high point was the Olympian Games – the series of athletic contests which provided the name and inspiration for the Olympic Games of modern times. If a record compiled at Athens is to be believed, the games originated in 776 BC with foot races; later, jumping, wrestling, boxing, throwing the javelin and discus, and horse and chariot racing appeared. As we have seen, cultivation of the body and athletics were part of everyday life; and almost all festivals included athletic contests, sometimes held by torchlight to increase the excitement. But the Olympian Games dwarfed them all in importance. For five days men and boys competed furiously for supreme glory. Contestants flocked to the Games from far and wide; the cities of Greater Greece, always struggling against inferiority feelings because of their 'provincialism', were proud to send their men, and treated them as semi-divine when they won. Other Greeks, even the most 'metropolitan', felt the same: at Athens, victors were given free meals for life. Even modern

Left
Emblems of Delphi and its famous oracle sacred to Apollo: the god himself, slaying the snake Python, and the tripod on which the priestess – the Pythia or Pythoness – sat to prophesy.

Above
The Tholos at Delphi; the standing columns of this well-known monument were re-erected in modern times. Delphi was one of the major religious centres of Greece, mainly dedicated to the cult of Apollo.

Opposite
The Athenian treasury at Delphi, which housed the city's offerings to Apollo.

pop and football superstars have nothing like the same aura, since the ancient champions carried away something of the numinous quality associated with Zeus, and their exploits were subjects for celebration by the poets; many of Pindar's choral odes (i.e. hymns) were written to celebrate victories at Olympia. True, the odes were commissioned – by patrons from as far apart as Syracuse, Rhodes, Corinth and Athens; but for all their technical elaborations they are unmistakably sincere meditations on the theme of life's supreme moments, that time when a man is touched by god-like greatness; and it is specifically victories at the Games that occasion the theme.

DRAMA, THE GIFT OF DIONYSUS
Perhaps the most remarkable thing that Greek religion brought into the world was an entirely new art form: the drama. Shakespeare, Molière, Schiller, O'Neill and Bernard Shaw owed the medium of which they were masters to the city of Athens; and more specifically they owed it to the god Dionysus.

Dionysus had had to force his way into the company of the Olympians. His worship involved darker, more dangerously ambivalent emotions than theirs, and in historical times there were still vivid folk-memories of his female followers, known as maenads, tearing to pieces animals and even human beings. In time Dionysus settled down in the Greek pantheon as a more or less respectable fertility god; later the Romans called him Bacchus and exploited his association with the vine so that he sometimes figures as little more than a god of boozing. But in late sixth-century Athens his cult could still occasion a vigorous mixture of obscene play and poignant emotion; and this was the starting-point of the world's drama.

We have seen that the tyrant Pisistratus founded the greatest Athenian festival dedicated to the god, the City Dionysia; and it may have been the newness of the festival that made another innovation possible. This was the addition of a speaking actor to the ritual singing and dancing performance of the Dionysian chorus; the actor became involved in verbal exchanges with the leader of the chorus, and the drama was born. The innovation is attributed to one Thespis, who had established it firmly enough to be awarded a prize for his work in about 534 BC; none of it survives, and Thespis is now remembered simply as the first 'Thespian'.

A second actor was introduced by the tragedian Aeschylus, the first dramatist whose works have survived – those performed in his last years, from 472BC. In less than twenty years a third actor was added, and that was the limit: if there were more parts than three, one or more of the actors had to double – a feat made easier by the fact that all the participants wore masks. Obviously no scenes could be written in which more than three speakers were on stage at the same time. The chorus continued to play an important part. In tragedy they commented on the action in the guise of courtiers, citizens or other groups, expressing the conventional man's moral values and common-sense spirit of compromise in the face of the principals' heroic compulsions. In comedy their role may well have been closer to the Dionysian original, with rollicking fantastic impersonations of frogs, birds or wasps, as in Aristophanes' plays.

The first true theatre was built in the open air on the southern slopes of the Acropolis, next to the temple of Dionysus – presumably because the new form of entertainment was so popular that special arrangements had to be made to allow everybody to see it. 'Entertainment' is not really the right word for a spectacle that remained so closely associated with Dionysus and the city: after a day of sacrifices and processions the young men brought the cult-figure of the god into the theatre so that he could see the performance; and before it

Opposite
Dionysus, god of wine and religious
frenzy, often portrayed as a young man.
Musée du Louvre, Paris.

Above
Mosaic showing musicians, by
Dioscourides of Samos; it comes from
the Roman city of Pompeii and is
probably a copy of a third century BC
painting. Museo Archeologico
Nazionale, Naples.

Left
Apollo and Heracles fight to possess the
tripod of the Delphic oracle. Pottery
painting. British Museum, London.

began there were solemn civic displays. The theatre of Dionysus was originally build of wood, so a description of some parts of its layout can only be a matter of educated guessing. The audience sat on benches arranged in a semi-circle on the slopes; below, the chorus chanted, sang and danced in a circle (the orchestra), while the actors performed on a low, raised platform behind, with some kind of raised structure (the skene) representing a palace or similar setting. Later, wood became stone; the orchestra contracted to a semi-circle, neatly dovetailing with both stage and seating; and painted scenery was introduced. The best-preserved of ancient Greek theatres is not the theatre of Dionysus at Athens, but one at Epidaurus, now restored and actually in use again.

By modern standards the performances were gruelling tests of endurance. Except in wartime, when the programme was curtailed, there were five days of solid dramatic fare. On each of the first three days, three tragedies by a single dramatist were

presented; and this was followed by a satyr play (a sort of parody of the tragic theme) by the same author. On the fourth day, no less than five comedies were put on. If, as seems likely, many people sat through the whole festival, it is hard to believe they could have done so without suffering from emotional exhaustion. After all, some of the greatest figures in world literature were writing for this audience, at times simultaneously. Aeschylus (525-456) had all his surviving plays staged in the lifetime of his younger contemporary Sophocles (c. 496-406); and the third of the great tragedians, Euripides (484-406), also began his career before Aeschylus' death.

Aeschylus' plays have a magnificent set-piece quality – more oratorio than opera, so to speak, though to contemporaries their introduction of a second (and later a third) actor would have made them seem intensely dramatic by comparison with anything they had seen before. Sophocles was the master-craftsman of Greek drama,

creating believable characters and situations, and developing them to inevitable, harrowing climaxes; he also gave expression to moral conflicts of permanent importance – in *Antigone*, for example, the conflict between religious and political loyalties. In Euripides' tragedies the atmosphere is less nobly remote: there is more realism, more ordinary human passion and weakness, and also more melodrama; the myths are ruthlessly remodelled and implicitly criticised, yet Euripides has a special taste for ending his plays with a *deus ex machina* – the 'god out of a machine' (literally a machine: a theatre crane) who resolves the conflicts of the plot and foretells the future. Though contemporaries such as Aristophanes considered Euripides a cynic and mysoginist, his works actually seem to be a curious, rather enigmatic mixture of mythic, 'modern'-realistic and personal-religious attitudes.

The great comic writer Aristophanes (c. 448-c. 380) was a younger contemporary of Sophocles and Euripides, and lived to see the collapse of the

Opposite
Greek theatre at Pergamum,

Above
Farcical scenes from plays. As these pottery paintings indicate, the flagging abilities of old age were considered a great source of amusement. (Left) Musei Vaticani, (right) British Museum, London.

Left
The theatre at Epidaurus is the best preserved of all Greek theatres. The sound of a coin dropped in the orchestra can be heard from any of its 14,000 seats. Fourth century BC.

Athenian empire and the recovery of the city, albeit as a solitary independent unit. His plays are a mixture of knockabout farce, wild poetic fantasy and political satire – in which respect they were absolutely up to date: in *Lysistrata*, for example, the women seize the Acropolis and secure the emergency fund with which the Athenians at that very moment intended to build a new fleet and carry on the war.

These writers are the only ones whose plays survive from the great age of Athens – some of their plays: only about forty-three in all. They *are* Greek drama, except for the late-fourth-century Athenian Menander, who introduced the comedy of character-types, and a large number of fragments from lost works. However,

Left
Athena equipped for war; the owl sacred to the goddess appears on her shield in this Etruscan pottery painting. British Museum, London.

Above
The Arcadian Way and the theatre at Ephesus, chief of the Ionian Greek cities in Asia Minor (modern Turkey).

Opposite
Performance of a tragedy showing the palace setting. Pottery painting fragment from Tarentum (now Taranto) in southern Italy, about 350 BC. Martin von Wagner Museum, University of Würzburg.

great though the losses are, it is clear that Aeschylus and the others were known to be the greatest masters of the drama: so our picture of it may not be too distorted.

One of the archons ran the Dionysia on behalf of the state. He chose which playwrights should be represented, but the cost of the performance was borne by a wealthy producer, the choregus; the job was usually taken by people with political ambitions who hoped to win popularity by putting on a good show, though it was possible to appoint a reluctant rich man who was felt to be lax in contributing to the general welfare.

Many conventions of the Greek theatre must have derived from its sheer size and open-air setting. Performers had to be seen and identified at distances of almost a hundred metres, and from many different angles; and so masks, strongly paterned and brightly coloured costumes, large formalised gestures and intelligently pointed dialogue were necessary; at a later date tragic actors started to wear thick-soled buskins to make them taller, which eventually turned into platform boots twenty centimetres or so high. Such conventions determined the limits of the drama; they made certain intimate effects impossible, even if dramatists had been inclined to abandon or modify their mythical-epic material. For this reason Greek drama never

entirely broke with its ritual origins and dispensed with the chorus, awkward though it was to fit the prescribed alternation of dialogue or choral song into many stories.

Actors and chorus were all men, which must have made for even more conventionalised effects than in the English theatre of Elizabethan times, where boys played the female parts. In the Greek drama one of the functions of a mask was to conceal the sex of the wearer; and costumes were adapted to the same purpose: in the theatre, unlike everyday life, they were long-sleeved and ankle-length. The actor's chief instrument must have been his voice, and presumably the finest performers could project their voices to the farthest edge of the auditorium while convincingly imitating the emotions and tones of both sexes. In the earliest plays the author himself is said to have taken the main part, but the special skills of the actor were recognised by 449 BC at the latest, when prizes began to be awarded for the best performances. By the later fourth century, actors had become stars in the modern sense, their presence often more important than the quality of the play.

The price of admission to the theatre for the day was two obols – most of a poor man's day's wages; but from the time of Pericles the state paid it for them. The theatre of Dionysus must have seated at least 15,000 people

(Plato says 30,000), and evidence of various enlargements suggests that it was often packed to capacity. As the fame of the Athenian theatre spread, not only citizens and metics but also foreign visitors flocked to the Dionysia; women, children and slaves may have been admitted in some circumstances, though perhaps only in the company of influential or privileged men. These included priests, officials and ambassadors, all of whom had stone seats – not mere benches – at the front of the auditorium. Not much is known about the behaviour and responses of audiences at tragic performances: it is perfectly possible that they appreciated nice points of verse technique and dramatic irony; but it is equally possible that most of them responded on a simpler level – to awe-inspiring enactments of legends that were common property. Some tragedies did deal with contemporary events, though only one has survived: Aeschylus' *The Persians*, set at the Persian court as it awaits the news from Salamis. However, Aristophanes' comedies are full of broad, impudent contemporary references which presuppose a politically aware and appreciative audience as well as an extraordinary licence granted to the author, who is forever poking fun at the sexual aberrations and political grafting of prominent writers and politicans. Again audiences may have enjoyed the knockabout fun rather than the lyrical beauty of Aristophanes' choruses, but there is no record of their disapproval – though we know that when they disliked a comedy they showed it by taking out their packed lunches and eating them noisily, presumably crunching down as hard as they could on their onions. There were evidently connoisseurs too, or at least fans: not content with a single performance of each new play, they followed the 'company' as it toured the rural Dionysia celebrated by the parishes of Attica in December. These, incidentally, were the only repeat performances given of the fifth-century masterpieces in their authors' lifetimes. So great was the prestige of Aeschylus that revivals of his tragedies began shortly after his death; but Sophocles and Euripides were not revived until the fourth century.

Like so many public events in Greek life, the dramatic festival was a competition, with prizes for the best tragedy and comedy as well as the best actor. Careful precautions were taken to prevent corrupt verdicts – which is both typically Athenian and indicative of the ferocity of the Greek competitive urge. However, there were other forms of literary activity, at Athens and elsewhere.

POETRY, HISTORY AND BOOKS

Down to the fourth century, Greek poetry was a largely public art, primarily intended to be recited or sung to an audience. The introduction of writing made literary composition easier, and provided a permanent record of it; it also ended the cumulative composition and adaptation that characterised the oral tradition and produced the Homeric epic. But solitary reading of books was rare, though there are occasional references to book collectors, and the dramatist Euripides is supposed to have lived in a book-lined cave by the sea-shore. The book (a roll of papyrus) was a 'script' rather than an object of private study. This applies even to the wealth of poetry written between Homer and Hesiod and the fifth-century Athenian drama. Alcman wrote lovely choruses for Spartan girls to perform; Sappho of Lesbos and other poets of simple, personal emotion composed their verses as lyrics, to be accompanied by a lyre or flute; the epitaphs of Simonides are public memorials (of the dead at Thermopylae: 'Tell the Spartans when you see them, passer-by,/At their command, obedient, here we lie.'); and the odes of Pindar are works of public celebration, commissioned and paid for as such. This wealth of poetry, falling between the impersonalities of Homer and the drama, constitutes the first great outburst of directly stated emotion and opinion in literature; but – typical of the Greeks – it is very much emotion on display, whether recorded and shaped for a small circle of friends or the world at large.

Efficient prose, as always, developed later than poetry – though in the modern world, where poetry is very much a minority taste, that fact seems

Below
The birth of the goddess of love, Aphrodite, from the sea. Marble relief from the 'Ludovisi Throne'. Museo Nazionale Romano, Rome

Opposite
Girl playing the flute. Relief on a side panel of the 'Ludovisi Throne', perhaps the greatest surviving sculptural work from the Greek colonies in Italy. Museo Nazionale Romano, Rome

almost paradoxical. Among the Greeks, prose became the medium of a reasoned search for the truth, about man, society and the universe itself. In history, natural science and philosophy the inquiry began in Asiatic Greece and culminated in Athens (as might also be said of literature, if anything after Homer could properly be labelled a culmination); but in philosophy at least, Italian 'Greater Greece' made its most substantial contribution to intellectual history.

The first Greek prose writer whose work survives is Herodotus, though he must have had predecessors whose efforts have been lost, since part of his purpose was to correct them. He was born at Halicarnassus (modern Bodrum, in Turkey), travelled in Egypt and other lands, spent some time in Periclean Athens, and by about 440 had settled at Thurii, an Athenian foundation in Greater Greece. His *History* is no mere compilation: the material, for all its diffuseness, is skillfully related to the grand theme of the Greco-Persian wars and the triumph of Athens in particular. However, although Herodotus is not entirely uncritical, he is above all a collector and teller of wonderful stories with human interest rather than analysis as his chief concern. Within less than a generation the Athenian Thucydides had brought the writing of history to a level of accuracy and impartiality never again equalled in Antiquity. Thucydides served as a general in the Peloponnesian War until 424, when he failed to save the city of Amphipolis from the great Spartan general Brasidas; as a result he was sent into exile and only returned to Athens twenty years later, dying soon afterwards. His history of the war is therefore contemporary history, but written from the sidelines and with a massive attempt at fairness despite Thucydides' evidently passionate attachment to Athens. It is also the first piece of sustained historical research, based on documents and eye-witness accounts which have been carefully examined and compared with one another. With its tense, compressed style and narrative excitement, Thucydides' history ranks as a masterpiece of both literature and history. At his death Thucydides had brought his

history down to 411 BC. It was continued and completed by Xenophon, an Athenian aristocrat disillusioned by post-war Athens who spent part of his later life as a pensioner of Sparta. Xenophon had little of Thucydides' historical rigour. His best book is the *Anabasis*, a splendid eye-witness narrative of war and adventure, about the fighting retreat from Babylon to the Black Sea undertaken by 10,000 Greek mercenaries in order to escape from Persia. where they had been involved in a civil war; Xenophon himself was one of the leaders.

In the early sixth century – well over a century before Herodotus – Ionia gave birth to what may be called philosophy with a natural-scientific bias. A series of Ionian thinkers (whose works survive as no more than enigmatic fragments) were asking such questions as: what is the primal stuff from which the universe is made? by what process did this change and diversify into the world as we know it? or are change and diversity mere illusions? Thales of Miletus held that water was the primal substance, whereas his fellow-citizen Anaxamines believed it was air. Heraclitus of Ephesus stated that 'all is in flux'; the first Southern Italian philosopher of distinction, Parmenides of Elea, argued that since the One can never become the Many, real change is impossible; and Empedocles the Sicilian attempted to reconcile their conflicting views by positing a universe made of Earth, Air, Fire and Water, set in motion by the operation of two forces he called Love and Discord.

The extraordinary thing about these speculations is that they made no concessions to the cosmological myths and religious beliefs which we know pervaded Greek life. There is no entirely convincing explanation of this development, though part of it may lie in the commercial prosperity which brought the Ionian cities into extended contact with Egypt and Western Asia. Apart from acquiring mathematical and astronomical skills from abroad, the Ionians may have developed a certain scepticism through realising the infinite variety of gods worshipped in their world. Certainly the earliest Greek philosopher, Thales, and two of his successors, Anaximander and An-

aximines, were citizens of Miletus – an immensely prosperous and powerful city down to 494, when it was destroyed by the Persians in retaliation for its part in the Ionian revolt.

Little is known of the lives or teaching methods of the early philosopher-scientists. We have a fuller picture of Pythagoras – supposed discoverer of the famous theorem – though the evidence is largely based on tradition and legend. He was born on the island of Samos, off the Ionian coast, but about 531 settled at Croton in Southern Italy. There he founded a school, or rather something approaching a religious order with an austere rule of life – in spite of which it is said to have governed Croton for some time, with notable success. Pythagoras thus introduced two elements into philosophy that were very influential on later Greeks: the idea of philosophy as a way of life, and the idea of philosophers as proper persons to rule a state. Pythagoras is also credited with a belief in the transmigration of souls (reincarnation) and with the discovery that musical intervals could be expressed as mathematical proportions. Mathematics remained an important element in Pythagorean beliefs, which long survived the master's death; numbers were valued for their mysterious properties and relationships, which seemed to reflect some absolute, unchanging order of things. This quality appealed not just to the Pythagoreans but to many Greeks. One of the most striking features of the Greek mind, apparent in all the philosophers we have discussed so far, was a taste for all-embracing theories rather than an acceptance of multiplicity – let alone the modern scientific attitude of adopting partial and provisional explanations while busily collecting facts; even in medicine, the most empirical of Greek sciences, theories about the four 'humours' of which the body was supposed to consist were to bedevil treatment throughout Antiquity and almost into modern times.

At Athens the natural-science-philosophical outlook seems to have been introduced by another Ionian, Anaxagoras, who became a friend of Pericles. His true successors, however, were not Athenians but Leucippus and Democritus, who put forward an

atomic theory of matter more than 2,300 years before its correctness was demonstrated. At Athens, philosophy was dominated by ethical and political concerns in the teaching of Socrates (469–399) and Plato (*c.* 427–348), as was perhaps inevitable given the intensity of Athenian public life. Socrates seems to have been interested in natural science as a young man, but most of his career was devoted to ethical problems. The oracle at Delphi is said to have told one of his friends that Socrates was the wisest man in Greece –

and Socrates, all too conscious of his ignorance, concluded that his wisdom lay in the fact that he *knew* that he knew nothing. He therefore adopted his celebrated habit of cross-examining everybody he met, exposing the flaws in their thinking and the unjustified assumptions on which it rested. Although he had done the state good service, fighting bravely as a hoplite in several Peloponnesian War battles, in 399 Socrates was accused of impiety and corrupting Athenian youth, sentenced to death, and, following

Philosophising in the open air: mosaic showing Plato's Academy in session. Museo Nazionale, Naples.

Athenian custom, given the poison hemlock to drink. Though his questioning of accepted beliefs may have irritated some people – he called himself the city's gadfly – Socrates was probably condemned on political grounds, as one who had associated with many of the recently defeated oligarchic party.

Socrates' great contribution to philosophy lay in subjecting the whole field of human conduct to the test of reason. More than that it is difficult to say, since he appears to have written nothing. If he had any positive doctrines, they cannot now be distinguished from those of his disciple, Plato, who makes Socrates the hero of many of his writings, and often no doubt attributes his own views to the older man. In return (so to speak) Plato made Socrates immortal; for Plato was a great literary master and one of the most influential philosophers in history. He invented his own literary form, the dialogue, which was admirably suited to portray philosophical conversation and Socrates' long chains of critical reasoning. As a thinker he initiated one of the main philosophical traditions, based on the conviction that every object, thought or concept in the universe is the imperfect shadow of pure, unchanging Forms which are the true reality, knowable through reason and contemplation. The Forms are also known as Ideas, and this type of philosophy is called Idealism – rather confusingly in view of the modern everyday meaning of the words.

Plato's dialogues show Socrates debating and teaching in quite ordinary social circumstances; *The Symposium*, for example, with its famous disquisition on the nature of love, is set at a drinking party whose members include the rising young politician Alcibiades and the comic dramatist Aristophanes. But Aristophanes, in his *Clouds*, presents Socrates as running a school in his own house, with pupils boarding there; and Plato, as we have seen, set up his Academy as a permanent institution (in one form or another it survived for *nine hundred* years). Both men evidently intended to exercise influence, on the leaders if not the citizen body, and both had students who became men of power; Alcibiades

attached himself to Socrates, and Lycurgus and Phocion, the chief figures in the struggle to maintain Athenian independence against the growing threat from Macedon, both studied at the Academy. To what extent they regarded such studies as more than a course in persuasion and analysis, useful to their careers, is another matter. And since Plato lived in an age when the city-state was dying as an independent institution, neither he nor his pupils achieved more than temporary practical success. Paradoxically, these Greeks – characteristically obsessed with public and contemporary effectiveness – exercised their deepest influence posthumously.

Opposite bottom
Oedipus encounters the Sphinx, whose riddle he succeeded in answering. Pottery painting, about 470 BC. Musei Vaticani.

Opposite top
Perseus fleeing after beheading the Gorgon Medusa; he carried out the operation without being turned to stone, since, without looking at her, he watched her reflection on his polished shield. British Museum, London.

Above
Helios, the sun, drives his chariot across the sky in this pottery painting. British Museum, London.

Greek Art and Architecture

Mycenaean art

When the Greeks appeared in the Aegean around 1900 BC, the area had already produced some notable art and architecture. The Cycladic islanders had traded their pottery up and down the Mediterranean, and had mined their native marble to fashion smooth, beautifully balanced little figures. And, on a larger scale, the Minoans were engaged in creating an opulent palace culture with colourful decorative styles and a range of skilled craftwork. The impact of Cretan styles and skills on the Mycenaeans is evident from the sixteenth-century treasures recovered from the shaft graves at Mycenae itself. Many of these were items that rarely survive the centuries, since they are usually melted down or destroyed: the gold masks used to cover the faces of the dead; gold ornaments – hammered, granulated, engraved and drawn into wire patterns; engraved and inlaid bronze swords and daggers; and vessels of carved rock crystal. The ornamental subjects are different in spirit from the festive scenes of Cretan art, for the Mycenaeans delighted in hunting and warfare, decorating their metalwork and pottery with sieges and sea battles, and carving war chariots on their stone grave-markers – the earliest Greek sculptures. A few later finds, such as the Vaphio cups from a tomb near Sparta, indicate that Mycenaean art was developing a virile individual style; and occasional examples of weapons, armour, ivory and jewellery have come to light. But only pottery, as usual, survives in any quantity

from later centuries, thanks to its peculiar combination of qualities – it is cheap and easily broken, but almost impossible to destroy completely. Greek pots, with stylised or pictorial decorations, have been found in many places between Italy and Syria, bearing witness to the scope of Mycenaean trade at its height. Equally, the feebler decorative treatment of later times is a symptom of the decline of Mycenaean Greece and the closing-in of the Dark Age.

Fragments of wall paintings from Pylos and elsewhere suggest that Greek work in this art was also derived from the Minoans. But the layout and construction of Mycenaean buildings are related to a different, though widely diffused, tradition. The great citadels of Mycenae and Tiryns consist of large irregular stones, closely fitted together so that they hold in place – and could hold off attackers – without cement; later Greeks, understandably awestruck by the gloomy grandeur of these sites, believed that they were the work of the Cyclops, one-eyed giants of myth; and this type of masonry is still called 'cyclopean'. The 'beehive' tombs of the Mycenaeans, which were

Left
Marble Cycladic figure carved about 2000 BC. British Museum, London.

Opposite
Attic vase in the Protogeometric style of decoration, which eventually developed into the denser Geometric shown elsewhere in this chapter. About 1000 BC. British Museum, London.

actually more common than the shaft graves, were also built in this way. The roofs were not made on the arch or lintel principle, but by overlapping stones inwards from the sides until they met; this procedure (known as corbelling) is crude, but lends itself to ruggedly impressive effects, as in the famous tomb at Mycenae miscalled 'the Treasury of Atreus'. Inside the citadel lay the palace, made of a timber framework filled in with rubble and plastered over. At its heart was a large rectangular room which must have been where the king sat in state; his throne was on one side of the room, which had a hearth in the centre surrounded by four columns. Here, perhaps, kings and heroes feasted, Homeric-style, seated at long tables; but this is mere speculation. The palaces survive only as archaeological sites, not as buildings; they – and, presumably, most of Mycenaean art – were destroyed in the general collapse before the Dark Age.

OUT OF THE DARK AGE
Pottery provides the main evidence of cultural revival in the three hundred years between about 1,000 and 700 BC. To begin with, Athenian potters and painters started producing wares decorated with bold concentric circles, semicircles and other abstract patterns, precisely applied with compass and rule. The style spread over most of Greece; but within a hundred years or so this impressively simple 'Protogeometric' developed into a full-blown 'Geometric' style in which the vase was covered with dense ornament in horizontal bands. Painters elaborated a range of new motifs – zigzags, swastikas, meanders squared off into key patterns – and crammed them on to every inch of the surface, even filling the interiors of the patterns with hatchings to minimise the empty spaces. By about the eighth century little human and animal figures were appearing in some of the bands, though they are treated geometrically and as silhouettes, often repeated with the regularity of paper cut-outs. Later still, huge vases used as memorials in Athens' cemetery carried action scenes – most often, for obvious reasons, funeral processions.

It is interesting to note the domi-nance of pattern in these indigenous Greek wares. The humanity of Greek art is its most famous quality, yet the stimulus to it came from outside. In pottery this is identified with 'Orientalising', apparent in the eighth century and no doubt connected with the establishment of the first Greek trading post in Syria around 800. The horizontal bands disappear; new patterns and images are taken over from the East – floral patterns, free curving lines, winged monsters; and experiments are made with outline drawings of the human figure, executed with greater freedom and realism.

Eastern influence also seems to account for the revival of metal-working techniques and miniature craft work such as ivory carving. But the next major advance involved working on a substantially larger scale.

ARCHAIC ART: SCULPTURE
In art, the years 700-480 BC are conventionally known as the Archaic period. This faintly derogatory term suggests that Archaic art was no more than a prelude to the 'Classical' art which was created immediately afterwards; but for some years it has been realised that Archaic art is of interest in its own right. Trained by modern art movements, the twentieth century appreciates, as the nineteenth rarely could, the aesthetic appeal of 'primitive' and stylised forms, understanding that they are not failures of realism – even when they are moving towards realism – but alternative modes of communication.

Monumental sculpture in Greece seems to have been directly inspired by Egyptian art. Before about 650 BC – when the Greeks established a trading post at Naucratis on the Nile delta – small pottery and bronze figures had been made, and so had statuettes cut from soft limestone which reflect the Syrian influence on Greece. In the later seventh century life-size and over-life-size figures appear, cut from marble quarried at Naxos and other Greek islands. The most characteristic types were the standing figures of young men and women, put up as dedications in temples or monuments on graves; whatever the purpose served, each wore the distinctive 'Archaic smile', faint and – to modern

Above
Archaic bronze statuette of Apollo. Museum of Fine Arts, Boston, Massachusetts.

Opposite
Two examples of the Geometric style in Attic pottery: a wine jug (oenochoe), ninth to eighth century BC (British Museum, London); and a jar (amphora) used as a cinerary urn, about 900-850 BC (Kerameikos Museum, Athens).

eyes – disturbingly ambiguous. They were made all over the Greek Aegean area, but yet again Athens provides the best evidence – this time through the sheer chance that when the Persians sacked Athens they destroyed the buildings on the Acropolis and threw down the votive statues; the Athenians reverently buried the remains, which were therefore preserved without further damage or re-use.

In the course of the Archaic period, sculpture became increasingly realistic. Even the earliest standing figures are rather more human and less intimidating than their Egyptian prototypes; but all the formal emphasis is on symmetry and frontality, as of figures just emerging from a wall behind them. Gradually the young man (kouros) steps forward with a new suppleness; the parts of his naked body are rendered with increasing detail and accuracy; and finally he loses contact with the 'wall' and stands in a natural, relaxed pose with his weight on one

foot. His female equivalent (kore) presents a different line of development: she was always shown clothed, so in her case the sculptor made his chief innovations in the treatment of her tunic (chiton), scoring a pattern on the smooth surface to indicate drapery and making the folds progressively more emphatic and natural-looking. Relief sculpture, unhampered by problems arising from the need for three-dimensional treatment, advanced towards realism even more quickly; by the early Classical period even a colonial town in Greater Greece could afford and appreciate a masterpiece such as the *Ludovisi Throne*, with its subtle and moving carving of the birth of Aphrodite. At each stage in this development sculptors sought to achieve a balance between patterning and the intended degree of realism; and the sense of form found in the kouroi and korai was taken over into Classical art and formed an important component of it.

TEMPLES OF STONE

Most Greek houses were relatively humble places throughout the Archaic and Classical periods; time, money and skill were lavished on public buildings, and above all on the temples that embodied the religious and the civic spirit of the polis. In a sense, architecture was the queen of the arts, to whom the others paid tribute. Most sculpture was for or associated with a temple in the form of votive statuary, relief carvings on the great friezes at roof level and free-standing figures for the pediments (triangular gables) at each end of the building. The important commissions of the great fifth- and fourth-century painters were panel and wall paintings for temples – famous in their own time and for centuries afterwards, and carefully described by Roman connoisseurs such as Pliny, but long since vanished. Even pottery was widely used for dedications to the gods and for burial with the dead, though, of

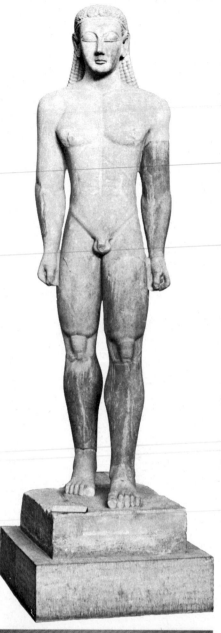

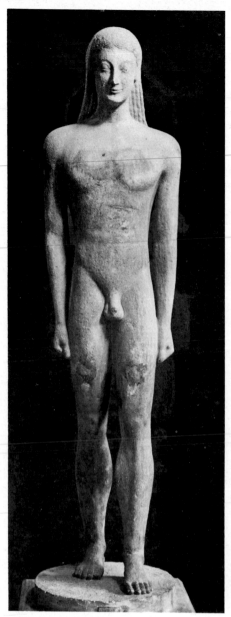

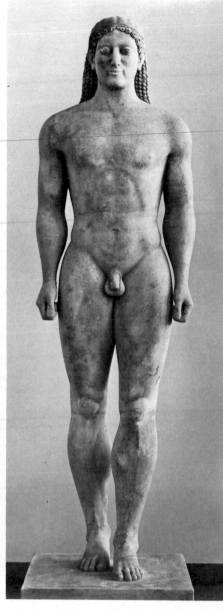

Above
Three stages in the evolution of the
standing male figure (kouros) from a
highly conventionalised, wall-backing
figure to a realistically detailed, moving
human being. National Archaeological
Museum, Athens.

Left
Attic vase decorated in Geometric style;
however, schematised figures in
silhouette have now been allowed into
the design. National Archaeological
Museum, Athens.

Above
Archaic marble statue of a young
woman (kore) from the Athenian
Acropolis. Notice her characteristic faint
'Archaic smile' and the use of paint on
the figure. Acropolis Museum, Athens.

Above
The Euthydicos Kore. Marble figure of
a maiden, about 500 BC: the elaborate
drapery is in marked contrast to the
conventionalised treatment of the figure
on the left. Acropolis Museum, Athens.

course, it had equally important secular functions in the kitchen, on the table and (the finer pieces) at drinking parties and other occasions for display.

This public art would have been much more colourful than we can easily imagine: the buildings and statues that survive represent Greek art after the paint has worn away and the accessories have been destroyed or looted. Apart from mural decorations, many of the mouldings and other architectural details of buildings were brightly painted; statues had coloured clothes, hair, eyes and lips: polished bronzes with inlaid eyes, lips and nails flashed with yellow brilliance in the sunlight; and the three-dimensionality of reliefs was emphasised by the now-vanished earrings the figures wore, the spears they carried, the bridles attached to their horses. The Acropolis of Athens and the sacred cities of Delphi and Olympia must have been strikingly colouful patches on the Greek landscape, worthy of strangers' awe.

The Greek temple was not a place of worship in which believers would expect to gather and hold services: it was a house for the god or goddess, presided over by a cult figure of the deity and looked after by his or her priests; public ceremonies took place outside, at an altar in front of the building. But although the splendour of the temple was naturally felt to reflect the splendour of the god, the Greeks began to build in stone remarkably late: not on any scale until about 640 BC, although they then started producing master-works almost at once.

Like the Egyptians before them, the Greeks built in a simple lintel-and-pillar style, presumably derived from wooden buildings, in which vertical posts held up a roof of horizontal beams. They had no use for such devices as arches and vaults, and indeed their engineering feats went little further than widening the distance between the internal columns needed to support a large building. The subtle beauty of the Greek temple was created from very simple elements: a rectangular structure with a pitched roof, surrounded by a colonnade. Architectural improvements were aesthetic rather than constructional: the use of entasis, a slight swelling in the body of

Opposite bottom
The architectural orders: the plain Doric style, with a distinctive 'cushion' capital at the top of each column.

Above
The architectural orders: the Ionic style, with its sculpted frieze and a distinctive scroll (volute) capital at the top of each column. (*opposite top*) Huge volute from an Ionic capital.

a column that prevented it from appearing to shrink in the middle; the slight inward inclination of the colonnade, also for optical reasons; and so on. One great advantage of this relative simplicity was that public works could be sub-contracted without difficulty, involving large numbers of independent craftsmen with the project. This, rather than forming a tightly disciplined mass of men permanently under orders, was a way of doing things in the true Greek spirit – an interesting example of the general outlook of a culture prescribing its technical procedures.

In seventh-century Greek buildings, two main decorative styles developed, based on the treatment of columns and of the frieze-cornice area running round the building above the colonnade. The styles – called orders – were the Doric and the Ionic. The easiest way to identify them is by their columns: the Doric is massy and powerful, culminating in a large cushion-shaped capital beneath the lintel; the Ionic is more slender and more ornate, with a distinctive capital swelling out into two large scrolls (volutes). The Ionic probably came from the East and predominated in Asiatic Greece and the nearby islands: it was used on three great temples, two of them on the island of Samos and one at Ephesus – the colossal Temple of Artemis, which ranked as one of the Seven Wonders of the An-

Left
The Moschophoros, marble statue of a herdsman carrying a calf. About 560 BC. Acropolis Museum, Athens.

Above left
Head of a man: the paint, which has disappeared from most Greek statuary, gives an impression of Greek art and life that is rather different from the received one.

Opposite left
The Vix Krater, a huge (164 cm high) bronze mixing bowl discovered in a tomb at Vix in France. About 520 BC. Musée Archéologique, Chatillon-sur-Seine.

Opposite right
Corinthian jug (oenochoe) of about 600 BC. British Museum, London

cient World. All three have perished, as have the earlier buildings in the Doric style that spread over mainland and Greater Greece; the few temple columns standing from ruined Corinth are the best remaining examples.

POTTERY: ART, CRAFT, WEALTH

Meanwhile, the 'minor' arts were helping to create the wealth that financed the great building and sculptural projects of the fifth century. With the new refinement of gold and metalworking techniques, Greek craftsmen produced statuettes, decorated armour and jewellery for export as well as home consumption. A large bronze wine-making bowl has been found in a Celtic royal tomb at Vix in northern France; Scythian gold objects in the native 'animal' style, found in the Crimea, are often the work of Greek craftsmen.

At Athens, where olive oil and wine exports were so important to the economy, there was a concomitant need for containers; so potters were assured of a steady demand for utilitarian wares between commissions calling for more sophisticated potting and painting skills. Few workshops can have been highly specialised; even many individual painters seem to have worked as potters too, presumably specialising later in life as their talent became apparent and opportunity offered. It is doubtful whether they even expected or received any recognition as artists, though they might be known and respected as citizen-craftsmen who had made a success in life; but their own opinion is clear from the fact that they often signed their best pieces as potter and/or painter.

By about 600 an entirely new style of painting was developed: the black-figure style. This was pioneered by Athens' commercial rival, Corinth, but its very popularity encouraged the Corinthian potters to over-produce and lower standards; the Athenians took it up and by the mid-sixth century were dominating the export market. The new style still involved using silhouettes, but now the figures were larger, fuller and more realistic, painted in black against the unpainted reddish-buff background of the fired clay. Internal details of figures and objects – drapery, musculature, etc. – were drawn in by scratching through the paint to the clay; other details were sometimes touched in with red and white paint. With their high Attic glazes, black-figure vases are superbly distinctive works of art; scenes of war and death on them have a sinister intensity (if only through colour association), but the range of subjects is already very wide, from myth to bibulous merrymaking. Around 530 BC a new technique was introduced at Athens and quickly superseded the black-figure everywhere; for well over a century or more, Athens' supremacy as a producer of fine pottery remained unchallenged. The red-figure technique was the reverse of the black-figure: the painter filled the areas *around* his figures with black, leaving the figures themselves in unpainted reddish-buff. Internal details could now be painted in, with an immediately noticeable gain in freedom of drawing; the main disadvantage was the starker overall effect created by red-on-black. Greater freedom

Opposite
The *Discus Thrower*, by Myron of
Eleutherae, reveals the mastery of
movement achieved by Greek sculptors
since Archaic times. Roman copy.
Museo Nazionale Romano, Rome.

Above
Relief of riders, from the frieze on the
west side of the Parthenon. About
435 BC. Part of the 'Elgin Marbles' in
the British Museum, London

Left
The god Apollo: marble pediment
figure from the Temple of Zeus at
Olympia. Archaeological Museum,
Olympia.

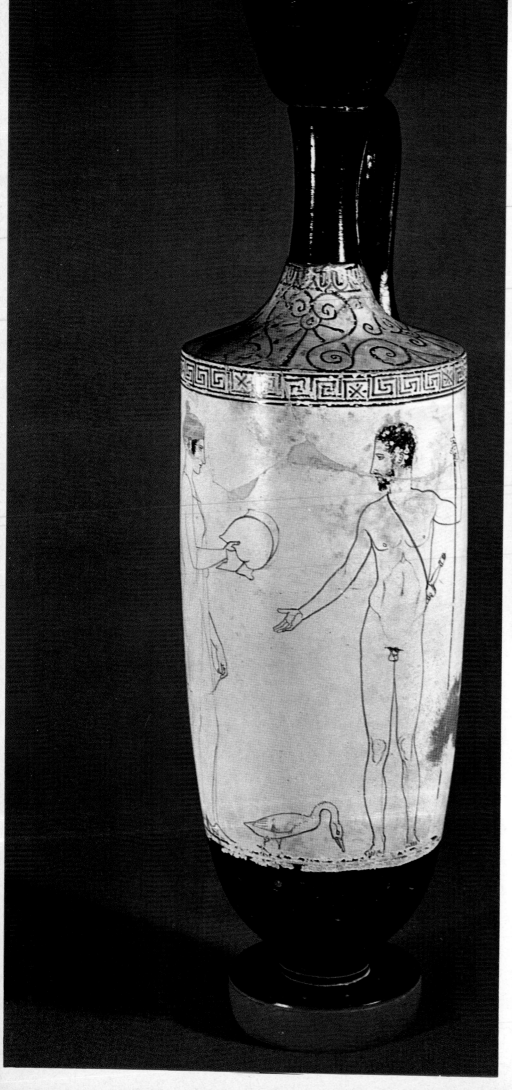

Left
Vase (lekythos) with painting in brown, black and red on a ground of white slip – an attractive though relatively uncommon alternative to the black- and red-figure styles. In this scene by the 'Achilles painter', a woman is handing a warrior his helmet. About 440 BC. British Museum, London.

Above
The Parthenon, on the Athenian Acropolis. Viewed from the Propylaia.

Opposite left
Black-figure amphora showing Theseus and the Minotaur.

Opposite right
Red-figure style. The upper register shows the rape of the daughters of Leucippus; the lower register, Hercules in the garden of the Hesperides.

encouraged greater realism: three-quarter views, eyes shown in profile instead of frontally (Egyptian-style), and a variety of movements and gestures were mastered over the following decades; and apart from its own merits, Athenian pottery is used as the main visual source for information about Greek painting, which, in terms of drawing techniques at least, was meeting and overcoming the same problems.

THE CLASSICAL AGE

The Classical age is usually defined as the years between 480 and 323 BC; that is, between the victory at Salamis (which effectively ensured Greek independence) and the death of Alexander the Great (when the Greek world encompassed the eastern Mediterranean). In art, the period witnessed the sculptor's achievement of full mastery over his material, and the collaboration of builders, sculptors and painters on the Parthenon and other great Athenian works – pre-eminent in their own generation, but now unnaturally isolated in their grandeur because most of their rivals, such as the Temple of Zeus at Olympia, have disappeared.

Early Classical sculpture – before about 450 – completed the development of the Archaic kouros and kore into naturally posed figures that could be viewed from any angle. Instead of standing foursquare, with only one foot advanced to suggest movement, the kouros began to raise his arms, turn his head, shift his weight. The female figure was still treated with greater reserve, but a new awareness of the female body is shown by the substitution of the heavy peplos – a cloak, following the contours of the body more closely – for the voluminous chiton. Such developments must have made this a time of intense excitement for sculptors, who revelled in their freedom to create never-before-seen stances and gestures in marble and bronze. The most famous, in his own day and since, was Myron of Eleutherae, who carved the *Discus Thrower* (Discobolus), a superb work even in the Roman copies by which it is known. The difficult posture and accurately rendered musculature seem a world away from the older standing

figures, and do in fact represent a new thing in the sculptural world; the fully active human figure, as convincing in its parts as in the whole. The other outstanding figures that survive are from the pediment of the Temple of Zeus at Olympia, notably the *Apollo* who stood in the centre of the west pediment; a more sober figure than the discus thrower, he stands with arm outstretched, decreeing victory for the lapiths in their struggle against the centaurs. The *Discus Thrower* and *Apollo* exemplify the survival situation as far as Classical and much later Greek art are concerned: most of the great individual works are known only by repute, by Roman copies (not always of a high standard), or from coins or engravings on jewels; the other remains are purely architectural and more or less fragmentary – reliefs or free-standing statuary for pediments, both intended to be admired not just for themselves but for the skill with which they were fitted into awkward shapes and integrated into the architectural whole. It says a good deal for the Greek achievement that even its broken and incom-

plete history has been taken as the 'Classical' norm by so many people.

The destruction of the Athenian acropolis by the Persians was a disaster of the first magnitude, even for the commercial-imperialistic power of Athens: apart from rebuilding the fortification wall of the citadel, the Athenians did relatively little to make good the damage for the space of a generation. Then, soon after 450 BC, ambitious plans were made for a group of splendid marble buildings that would celebrate Athens' imperial greatness and astonish Hellas. There is no doubt that Pericles master-minded the project, though it was of course approved by the Assembly and financed out of the Athenian treasury. It was carried out over the next fifty years (not without some economies) in spite of Pericles' death and in the teeth of war and defeat.

As everybody knows, the results are still visible in the ruined glory of the Parthenon, the Propylaea, the Temple of Athena Nike and the Erechtheum; in order to visualise the full splendour of the Acropolis in (say) 400 BC we should also have to conjure up a host of smaller shrines and votive statuary, with a processional throng winding up from the city during the great festivals. Just such a procession – the Panathenaic procession itself – was carved on the running frieze around the main block inside the colonnade of the Parthenon: an unorthodox Ionic touch on this greatest of all Doric masterpieces. The building itself was situated so that it dominated the city and even rose clear above the other Acropolis buildings when viewed (as the architects must have intended) from the north-west; and every optical refinement known to the Greeks was employed to enhance its beauty.

Not much is known about the architects of the Parthenon, Ictinus and Callicrates. Ictinus also designed the Temple of Apollo at Bassae in Arcadia, of which a notable feature was the appearance of a new order. The Corinthian order was a variant of Ionic in which the volute capital on top of the column was replaced by a mass of acanthus leaves; it was not much used by the Greeks, but became a favourite with the Romans.

Overall supervision of the Parthenon project seems to have been entrusted to the native Athenian sculptor Phidias, the universal genius of his time. (However, the architects' contribution cannot have been negligible: Ictinus is known to have written a book about his work on the Parthenon.) The building was carried out with incredible speed, taking only nine years (447-438 BC); both the building and its precious inhabitant, a colossal gold and ivory cult figure of Athena by Phidias, were ready for consecration at the Panathenaea of July 438. The pedimental sculptures took another six years to finish, probably from designs by Phidias. Inevitably, the cult figure of Athena Parthenos – that is, Athena the Virgin – has been destroyed, like

Opposite
The architectural orders: the Corinthian style, notable for the elaborate acanthus-leaf decoration of its capital.

Right
The *Spear Carrier* (Doryphorus). Marble statue by Polyclitus of Argos. Roman copy of the late-fifth-century original. Museo Archeologico Nazionale, Naples.

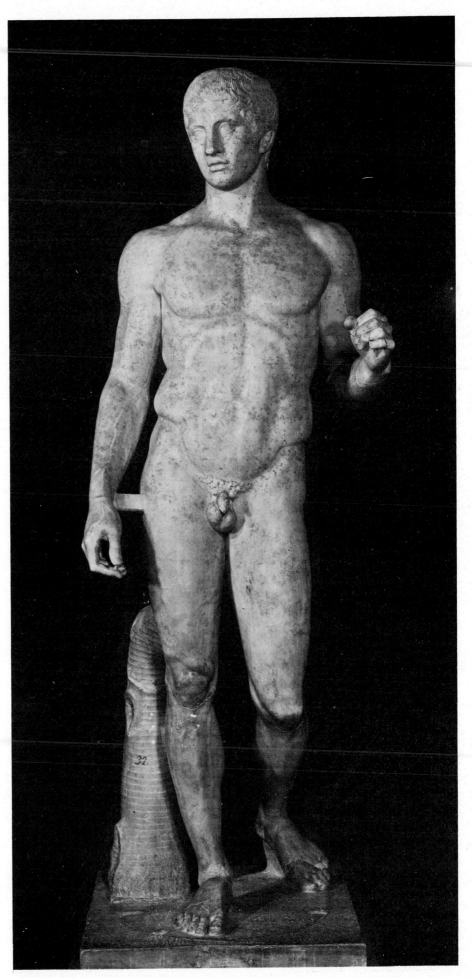

Above
The Temple of Athena Nike on the
Acropolis at Athens.

Opposite top
The Erechtheum on the Acropolis at
Athens.

Opposite bottom
The 'Maidens' Porch' with caryatids
(female figures as columns) on the south
side of the Erechtheum.

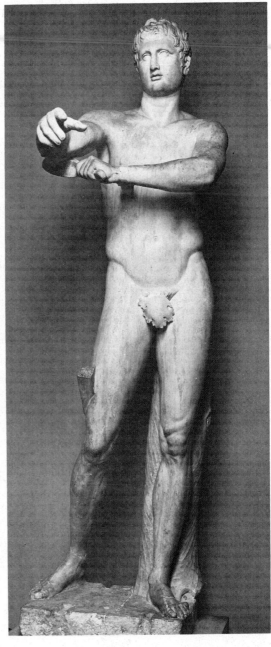

Phidias' colossal gold and ivory Zeus for the temple of the god at Olympia, which ancient commentators considered his masterpiece. The surviving reliefs and sculptures from the Parthenon have always been regarded as the climax of Classical art – men, gods and beasts superbly natural, noble and balanced, individually and as groups. But they represent something of a deviation from the realistic tendency of the earlier period, perhaps because the elevated subject matter encouraged a more poised, hieratic rendering even of battle scenes: the men and women of the Parthenon sculptures, whatever actions they are engaged in, have the unmoved serenity of the gods they are glorifying. It is possible, too, that this treatment reflects something in the mood of the late fifth century; for Phidias' most famous contemporary, Polyclitus of Argos, was said to have treated kouros-like subjects in a very restrained style; and his *Spear Carrier* (Doryphorus), known from Roman copies, confirms that he did so.

Of the other Classical buildings on the Acropolis, the small Ionic Temple of Athena Nike (Athena Bringer-of-Victory) was designed by Callicrates at about the time the Parthenon was begun. But construction of the Athena Nike was deferred until the 420s, by which time the design had to be modified to accommodate the Propylaea, the grand marble gateway to the Acropolis, built from 437. Finally, the

Erechtheum, though small, is one of the great masterpieces of Ionic. It housed the joint cults of Athena and Poseidon, as well as that of Erechtheus, a legendary king of Athens said to have been reared by Athena herself. (This joint household was doubtless specially arranged to mollify Poseidon – defeated in his attempt to become the city's patron – while ensuring that the victorious Athena was not offended by honours paid to her rival.) A curious feature of the Erchetheum, never fully explained, is the use of female figures as columns, their heads supporting the 'maidens' porch' on the south side of the building. The Romans occasionally copied the idea of using such figures

Left
Statue of Mausolus, governor of Caria; it reflects the growing taste for individualised – if still flattering – portraiture. About 350 BC. British Museum, London.

Above and opposite
Greeks and Amazons in battle. This relief, from the Mausoleum at Halicarnassus in Asia Minor, shows the developing taste for realism in depicting scenes of violence. British Museum, London.

(called caryatids); a British architect, more literal, applied a copy of the maidens' porch to St Pancras' Church in London, where a line of load-bearing Greek girls still confronts the Euston Road.

The other artistic achievements of the Classical age can only be summarised here. Below the Acropolis, on a hill in the city itself where it looks down on the agora, stands the Temple of Hephaestus, an unassuming Doric building begun in 449; its dedication to the blacksmith god was appropriate and intentional, since the temple itself was near the potters' and metalworkers' quarters. At Athens and elsewhere, civic architecture also flourished, including assembly and music rooms, theatres and stoas (shops and offices with covered colonnades). Athenian red-figure pottery continued to dominate the market, maintaining a high standard through the fifth and fourth centuries. However, many people prefer a special type, developed in the mid-fifth century, of which there are all too few survivors: the tall cylindrical oil jar (lekythos) used for funereal and other religious offerings. This had a white ground on which the artists drew in outline, broadly colouring the drapery and

other details in a much more 'painterly' manner than was possible with the black-figure or red-figure techniques. The often exquisite charm of the painted figures suggests more vividly than anything else what we have lost by the disappearance of Greek painting.

The art of the fourth century has also been depleted – a fact that makes it hard to appreciate the development of Classical sculpture away from the Parthenon style, which has so often been taken as the Classical norm. Sculptors now began to explore new subjects and to attempt representations of emotions and dramatic movements: the development is so emphatic that it must have been warmly approved – if not directly stimulated – by patrons, civic and private. The most immediately obvious change was a new interest in the female form, already provokingly semi-visible through the 'transparent' draperies of figures on a balustrade added to the Temple of Athena Nike at the end of the fifth century. By the 360s, Praxiteles was confidently sculpting divine Aphrodite in the nude; this, the *Aphrodite of Cnidus*, is known only through what seem to be quite poor Roman copies, but Praxiteles' *Hermes with the infant Dionysus* has survived to exemplify the

rather bland sensuality of his style. The other great fourth-century sculptors were Scopas, credited with introducing violently emotional facial expressions, and Lysippus, master of large-scale compositions involving dramatic movements and swirling draperies. Lysippus' skill was such that Alexander the Great allowed no other sculptor to portray him. Alexander's evident wish for a true (if possibly flattering) likeness marks the coming-of-age of portraiture, which had earlier been infrequent, idealised and often even posthumously executed. Self-assertion was combined with a new taste – for the colossal – as early as the mid-fourth century, when the Hellenising governor of a Persian province built a gigantic marble tomb for himself; the governor was Mausolus of Caria, in the south-west of Asia Minor, and his tomb was the Mausoleum, which has since become a type-name. This new sense of personal uniqueness and taste for the colossal, along with personal emotion, violence, realism and much else, became components of the new age ushered in by the career of Alexander the Great.

Alexander the Great and the Hellenistic Age

THE RISE OF MACEDON

While shifting alliances and temporary supremacies kept fourth-century Greece in a state of mild confusion, a new power arose on the northern marches of the Greek world. Macedon was large and populous, but so backward that most of the Greeks were reluctant to acknowledge kinship with its wild and woolly tribesmen. The Macedonians were hardened by their wars against the Illyrians, the Thracians, and other non-Greek peoples; and they were sunk so deep in the quasi-Homeric past as to give allegiance to a king, just as Persians and other barbarians did. But despite its negative consequences for the good life as conceived by the Greeks, kingship could be a source of great political strength if the right man was king.

Macedon found the right man in Philip II. He inherited a shaky throne in 359, efficiently disposed of his rivals, bought off and then fought off his barbarian neighbours, and finally turned his attention to divided Greece. At a time when citizens of the Greek states were beginning to prefer intermittently hiring mercenaries rather than fighting their own battles, Philip had distinct military advantages: a standing army of hard, disciplined, loot-hungry Macedonian soldiers, stiffened by the presence of permanently employed mercenaries. This military establishment was expensive to maintain, even with the proceeds from the gold mines Philip was lucky enough to possess; and the need for spoils provided an additional motive for aggression.

All the same, Philip moved slowly and carefully, combining devious diplomacy with ruthless use of force; his piecemeal aggression never alarmed enough of the Greek states for them to unite against him. His favourite tactic was to induce them to betray one another for short-term gains, confident that each state that did so would find itself friendless when the Macedonian army moved against it. Athens behaved no better than the rest, though Philip's aggressions were repeatedly denounced in the 'Philippics' delivered to the Assembly by Demosthenes, the greatest of all Greek orators; his speeches have often been likened to Churchill's pre-war orations against Hitler's Germany.

At the end of twenty years Philip had a firm grip on northern Greece. Then, belatedly, Athens and Thebes formed an alliance to resist further Macedonian encroachments. The battle of Chaeronea (338) was a turning-point in Greek history: the allies were defeated and the age of the city-state effectively came to an end. Thebes and other cities were garrisoned by Macedonian troops; Athens was allowed to make a separate peace, though she and the other Greek states had to join the new confederation organised by Philip, with himself as its 'elected' head.

The purpose of the confederation – the Corinthian League – was to march against the ancient enemy, Persia. Victory would crown Philip's efforts, and the loot of Asia would pay his mounting debts. Despite the enormous size of the Persian Empire and the overwhelming superiority of the Persian army in numbers, Philip's enterprise was less rash than it seems. Time and again in the past the Greeks had shown they were more than a match for the Persians, and the need for a war of liberation in Ionia – if not of wider conquest – was a commonplace of Greek political rhetoric; but its accomplishment had been indefinitely deferred by the Greeks' lack of unity.

Having imposed that unity, Philip was on the point of setting out when he was stabbed to death while taking part in a procession. The assassin was a man with a grievance, conveniently slain on the spot before he could implicate anyone else. The Persians may have been behind the murder, but it is equally possible that Philip's queen, Olympias, or his eldest son Alexander was responsible; Philip had put aside Olympias and had recently fathered a child by his new wife, making Alexander's position uncertain. Or, given his megalomaniac career as a world conqueror, Alexander may even have had his father removed before Philip left him no worlds to conquer.

THE CONQUESTS OF ALEXANDER

If Philip's successor had been an ordinary man, the history of the world might have been different. But the twenty-year-old Alexander was a military genius, decisive, inspiring and utterly dedicated to his own glory. Like other great generals he possessed the ability to act more swiftly than his opponents believed humanly possible. Before the Greek cities had finished celebrating the assassination of Philip, Alexander had marched into their midst and overawed them into electing him as his father's successor. While he was away campaigning against Macedon's barbarian enemies, Thebes broke out in revolt, besieging the Macedonian garrison in her citadel; Alexander returned to Greece, stormed the city, sold its inhabitants into slavery, and razed it to the ground. While destroying one of the most sacred of cities, he indulged in the sort of cultural-sentimental gesture of which autocrats are fond – he spared the house in which the poet Pindar had lived. Then, still only twenty-two, he crossed into Asia to make war on Persia.

After crossing the Hellespont with an army of some 40,000 men, Alexander was almost immediately confronted with a Persian army which he smashed at the battle of Granicus (334). Asiatic Greece was quickly liberated. Then, instead of pressing on into western Asia, Alexander struck into Syria, intending to cut the Persians off from the Mediterranean and protect his rear against the powerful Phoenician fleet by occupying its bases. Darius tried to stop him, unwisely choosing ground on which he could not make his superior numbers tell, and was routed so thoroughly that Alexander was able to capture the

Opposite
Silver coin of King Amyntas of Macedon, father of Philip II. Kabul Museum.

Right
Alexander the Great: Roman copy of a famous portrait sculpture by Lysippus; about 330 BC. Musée du Louvre, Paris.

Opposite bottom
Alexander the Great riding down a Persian. Relief from the Alexander Sarcophagus. Late fourth century BC. Arkeoloji Müzeleri, Istanbul.

Above
Men fighting a lion: pebble mosaic from Alexander the Great's birthplace, Pella in Macedon. About 300 BC.

Top left
Head of Alexander the Great from Pergamum in Asia Minor, an important Greek state in the Hellenistic age that followed Alexander's death. Arkeoloji Müzeleri, Istanbul.

Top right
Alexander in battle: detail from the mosaic shown above. Museo Archeologico Nazionale, Naples.

Opposite top
The battle of Issus, in which Alexander (left, on horseback) defeated Darius (in the chariot). This mosaic, found at Pompeii, dates from the first century BC but may well be an accurate copy of a fourth-century painting. Museo Archeologico Nazionale, Naples.

Great King's mother, wife and daughters; typically, Alexander treated them with generosity.

But, having achieved as much as any other Greek would have considered useful, Alexander refused Darius' offers of peace. He occupied Phoenicia and Palestine, and besieged the great port of Tyre, near-impregnable on its inshore island. The seven-month siege, persisted in while Sparta revolted and the Persians counter-attacked in Asia Minor, demonstrated that Alexander was more than just a brilliant cavalry commander; finally, with the help of Phoenician cities antagonised by Persian rule and jealous of Tyre, the city was stormed and destroyed. Alexander marched on into Egypt, where he founded Alexandria – easily the greatest of his many foundations, chiefly intended as strategically placed military settlements – and was hailed as the new pharaoh by the oracle at the oasis of Siwah. As pharaoh, and son of the god Ammon, Alexander was himself a god; and it seems possible that he took his promotion quite seriously.

In 331 Alexander resumed the assault on Asia, crossing the Euphrates and the Tigris. At Gaugamela, faced with a huge Persian army under Darius himself, Alexander outmanoeuvred the enemy and broke the flower of the Persian infantry with a brilliantly timed cavalry attack closely supported by pikemen. Darius fled again, only to be murdered by his own lieutenants

as Alexander's army moved inexorably from Babylon into Persia itself, taking the great cities of Susa, Persepolis and Ecbatana; at the ancient capital, Persepolis, Alexander captured the enormous gold reserves of Persia and burned the palace to commemorate his victory.

However, the war was far from over. The vast and mountainous area of east Iran remained unsubdued, and resisted Alexander for three years (330-327), during which time the Macedonian army had to besiege and capture one fortress after another in the most difficult terrain. Even when he had reached the limits of the empire, Alexander pressed on, overrunning the Punjab and apparently being prepared to go on to the end of the world – whatever that might be. However, his troops, weary of fighting and intimidated by the Indian war-elephants, simply refused to go on. In 325 Alexander was forced to turn back, though under his leadership even the journey became a hazardous land-sea exploration along the Persian Gulf which came close to disaster.

Back in Babylon, Alexander dealt ruthlessly with the governors who had got out of hand during his absence; many had never expected to see him again once he had disappeared beyond the Persian borders of the known world. He also pushed on with his plan to fuse Macedonians, Greeks and Persians into a single imperial race. After taking Persepolis he had ar-

ranged for some 30,000 young Persians to begin military training under Macedonian instructors; he had appointed Persians as well as Macedonians to govern provinces while he was campaigning; and he himself had assumed the title of Great King after the death of Darius, dressing in the Persian fashion and allowing his Eastern subjects to prostrate themselves when they came into his presence. Alexander's followers failed to understand his 'soft' policy towards the Persians, and many were disgusted by his adoption of a semi-divine monarchical style so alien to Greek tradition. There were mutterings and even conspiracies among some of Alexander's closest friends and lieutenants during his career of conquest, punished with more or less justice by executions and assassinations; but Alexander kept the loyalty of the army in the field, partly no doubt by the way he ostentatiously

Above
Tomb carving showing cavalrymen of the Hindu Kush; this mountain country at the far end of the Greek world (modern Afghanistan and Pakistan) was penetrated by Alexander's conquering army. National Museum of Pakistan, Karachi.

Opposite
Ptolemy, one of Alexander the Great's generals; after Alexander's death he became king of Egypt, founding a dynasty that lasted for 300 years. Ny Carlsberg Glyptotek, Copenhagen.

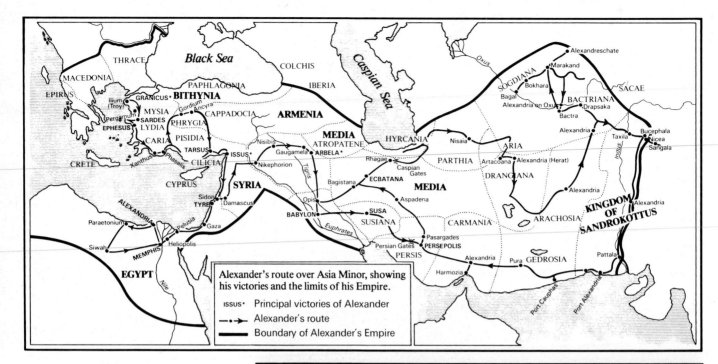

Alexander's route over Asia Minor, showing
his victories and the limits of his Empire.

ISSUS•   Principal victories of Alexander
-•→   Alexander's route
━━━   Boundary of Alexander's Empire

shared the hardships and dangers of his
men. Once back in Persia, however,
the army turned against Alexander's
integration of Macedonian and Persian
units: 'Go fight your battles with
your Persians and your father Ammon!' shouted the Macedonians. But
it was the army, not Alexander, that
capitulated after he threatened to dis-
charge them all. There followed the
famous 'marriage of East and West' in
which thousands of Macedonians took
Persian wives while Alexander himself, already possessed of one Persian
wife, married Darius' daughter. Alexander's policy has often been interpreted as an idealistic attempt to
reconcile East and West – a view that
ignores all the peoples in the empire
who were not invited to join in the
Greco-Persian reconciliation. But the
policy was a remarkable example of
realism, implicit in Alexander's decision to pursue the war beyond the
Tigris-Euphrates line: if he was to
capture the Persian Empire and control
its vast area permanently, he needed
a larger master-race than Greece alone
could provide. (The Persian kings had
had the same problem: the major
weakness of their empire had been the
insufficient numbers of the Iranian
master-race; so an enlargement made
good military-political sense.) Perhaps
too Alexander believed the Greeks and
Persians would work together more
harmoniously if united in worship of a
god-king: already the son of Ammon

in Egyptian eyes, he secured the Greek cities' recognition of his divinity in 324 – and died the following summer, aged thirty-three. His ultimate aims can never be known, but it says little for their moral grandeur that he was preparing yet another warlike expedition, this time to southern Arabia, when he was carried off by a fever.

THE HELLENISTIC WORLD

With the carelessness of one who believed himself immortal, Alexander had made no arrangements for the government of his empire in the event of his death, or for the safety of his posthumously-born son. Held together by the centripetal force of one man's authority, the empire fell apart as soon as the man disappeared.

In the ensuing scramble for power among Alexander's generals and his relations, the relations perished and the generals emerged as kings in the giant fragments of his empire. Two of them founded long-lived dynasties that were named after them: Ptolemy in Egypt, and Seleucus in western Asia. Macedon was less stable under a series of ambitious generals, but remained a great power, firmly in control of Greece. Immediately after Alexander's

Opposite bottom
Antiochus III, one of the Seleucid dynasty that ruled western Asia after the break-up of Alexander's empire. Antique copy of the third-century BC original. Musée du Louvre, Paris.

Above right
Greco-Buddhist art developed as a result of Greek cultural penetration into north-west India in the wake of Alexander's army. This moulded stucco female head comes from Hadda in Afghanistan. Fourth to fifth century AD. Musée Guimet, Paris.

Right
A Greek coin issued by the western Asian empire of the Seleucids. On it, King Antiochus IV identifies himself with Zeus as 'the god manifest' (obverse) and Zeus enthroned (reverse). Koninklijk Kabinet van Munten, Penningen en Gesneden Stenen.

death, Demosthenes led the Athenians and other Greeks in a new attempt to regain independence, but the rising was premature; the Macedonians, victorious on sea and land, dismantled Athens' democracy and hunted down Demosthenes, who took poison to avoid capture. From about this time mainland Greece went into a rapid decline. Theoretically independent though overshadowed by Macedon, the city-states remained irritably inclined to revolt but were less and less able to do so effectively. Exports fell catastrophically as their small-scale production of wine and oil failed to compete with the huge output of the Hellenistic kingdoms. International commerce was taken over by the eastern Hellenistic states, with Rhodes and Delos providing carriers and staging points. Economic decline led to a shrinking mainland population which reinforced the political insignificance of the old city-states. The great centres of the Greek world were now no longer in Greece itself. All three of the great new successor-states were ruled by Macedonian Greeks, with a Greek-speaking administrative structure and, for a long time, a mainly Greek army. Alexander's dream of a Greco-Persian fusion failed to materialise, but the lands he conquered became permeated with Greek culture – so much so that the age that followed, and the world of Greece, Egypt and the East, are simply described as 'Hellenistic' (not Hellenic, but Hellen*ised*). The Ptolemies remained a Greek dynasty right down to the reign of the last of them, the famous Cleopatra; they were munificent patrons of Greek scholars and scientists, and assembled the famous Library at Alexandria. In Asia, even after the Iranian and Indian areas of the unwieldy Seleucid empire won their independence, they continued to use the Greek language and issue coins with Greek inscriptions. The Hellenising process was generally confined to the cities and the cultural and political élites, but the effects could still be far-reaching: in north-west India, for example, Greek and native sculptural traditions were blended in the school of Gandhara, which produced the earliest statues of the Buddha, who therefore appears

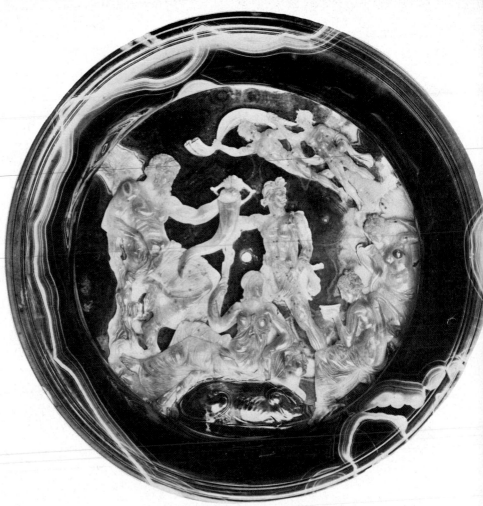

with features of 'Classical' handsomeness.

The East remained Greek even after most of it was incorporated into the Roman Empire. Later still, a strongly Greek-influenced milieu witnessed the birth of a new religion, Christianity, whose sacred books were written in the Greek *lingua franca* of the East. And ultimately the Greek portion of the Roman Empire survived the collapse of the Latin-speaking half, remaining a force in the world for almost another thousand years.

ALEXANDRIA

Though Greek in culture and outlook, the new great powers inevitably functioned in an atmosphere quite different from that of the city-state. In Greece and elsewhere, the city remained an important expression of municipal life, but it no longer acted as the focus of a man's existence; even Athens, which eventually recovered a precarious independence, turned into something between a tourist centre and a university town. The citizen ceased to be a member of a small, visible community, and

became an isolated individual in a state so large that it seemed no more than an abstraction. This condition resembles that of twentieth-century man (who, however, suffers more acutely from it, in his working as well as his social and political life); and the results were similarly paradoxical – individualism in philosophy and art, gigantic public works glorifying a state arm more powerful than anything imaginable in the Classical age, and an increasing nostalgia for that age. Big-city life in great imperial centres such as Alexandria and Antioch was more irresponsible, more consciously 'cultured', and far more comfortable for the better-off; palaces rivalled temples in size, and although the houses of the rich still followed the old Greek pattern, clustered round a courtyard that was now invariably colonnaded, the scale and furnishings indicated that luxury was no longer considered the prerogative of the gods.

The city of cities in the Hellenistic age was Alexandria, the Egyptian port founded by Alexander the Great and turned into an opulent cosmopolitan capital by Ptolemy and his successors.

Opposite
Hellenistic art in Egypt: the Farnese Cup. The interior glorifies the Egyptian queen Cleopatra I. Museo Archeologico Nazionale, Naples.

Above
Hellenistic art in Egypt: bronze standard lamp in the form of the god Eros, found in a tomb at Ballana. Egyptian Museum, Cairo.

Right
The Egyptian goddess Isis, Hellenised into a Greek-style divinity, as commonly occurred during the Ptolemaic period. Statue in Greco-Roman Museum, Alexandria.

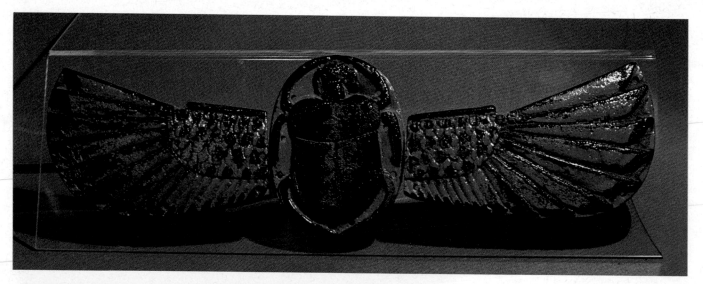

Left
Greco-Egyptian religious syncretism:
this bronze figure is composite in subject
(Heracles-Serapis, combining Greek hero
and Ptolemaic-Egyptian god) but purely
Greek in sculptural style. Kabul
Museum.

Above
Khephri, the Egyptian scarab god: late
Ptolemaic funerary object placed on the
breast of a mummy. Schimmel
Collection, New York.

Opposite top
Hellenistic gold diadem from southern
Italy. Third century BC. British
Museum, London.

Opposite bottom
Bust of a woman from Palmyra. It
illustrates the mingling of Greco-Roman
and Oriental elements. British Museum,
London.

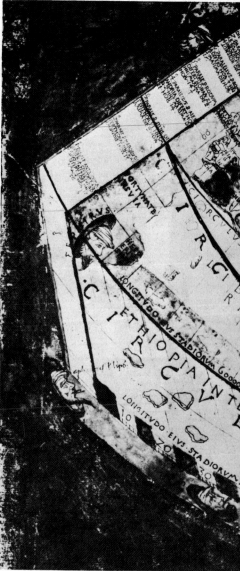

Left
Greek ladies; the one on the right, with the curious hat, is dressed for travelling. British Museum, London.

Above left
Greek terracotta statuette of a woman. Fourth to third century BC. Metropolitan Museum of Art, New York, Rogers Fund, 1922.

Opposite
Ptolemy of Alexandria's map of the known world: a copy of about 1460. British Library, London.

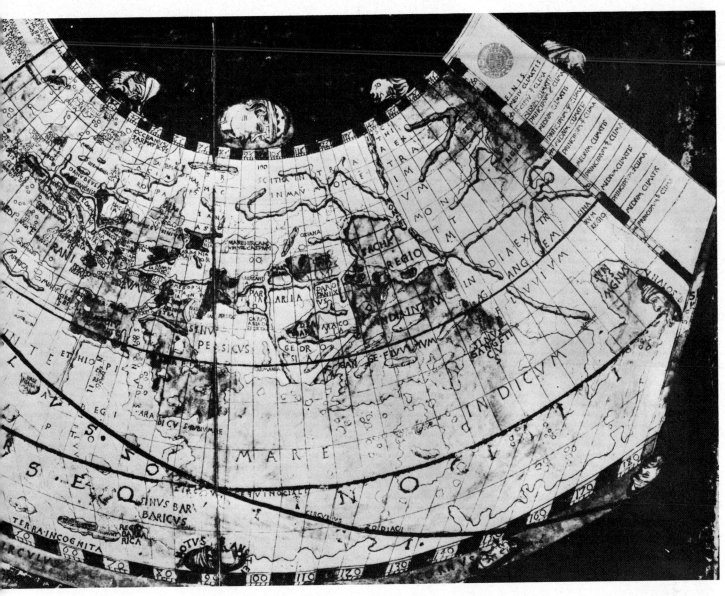

Unlike the old city-state, it housed an enormous mixed population – at the height of its prosperity perhaps as many as a million Greeks, Jews, Egyptians and others. The prosperity was firmly based on Egypt's super-abundant wheat harvests, which fed the city masses and ensured Alexandria's livelihood as an exporter. Papyrus for writing, fine fabrics, glass, perfumes, drugs and a great variety of craft and luxury objects were also traded through the port, which benefited in one way or another from almost every commercial transaction involving Egypt and the outside world.

Alexandria's advantages as a port were improved by human effort. The city was laid out on a stretch of coast with the island of Pharos immediately in front of it, sheltering the harbour. This was turned into a double harbour by the construction of a mole linking Pharos with Alexandria; and ships entering the great eastern harbour were guided in by 'the Pharos' – one of the Seven Wonders of the World, a lighthouse high enough for its fire to be visible at fifty kilometres.

The Ptolemies' choice of Alexandria as the capital of Egypt doubled its glory. A whole series of magnificent palaces grew up alongside the eastern port, since it became a tradition that each Ptolemy should build a new one for himself. The body of Alexander the Great himself, 'kidnapped' by Ptolemy I, was entombed alongside those of the new Greek pharaohs. All the standard amenities of Greek urban life were present at Alexandria: an agora, a theatre, an amphitheatre, and a gymnasium; also an artificial hill in the centre of the city, devoted to the cult of the god Pan; and also the Serapeum, the temple of the Egyptian god Serapis, whom the Ptolemies introduced into the Greek world.

The royal palace complex included the Museum (that is, a place dedicated to the Muses), where scholars, scientists and writers worked under royal patronage. Though to some extent foreshadowed by Plato's Academy, this was unique in being a self-regulating, tax-exempt corporation – not a museum in the modern sense, but something more like an endowed research institution. The most splendid of the facilities was the famous Library of Alexandria, which was built up in an astonishingly modern spirit. All the important works ever written in Greek were assembled in the most accurate texts available; with the royal blessing, librarians pursued original manuscripts all over the Greek world, often paying very high prices (and, inevitably, often

Opposite
Ruins of Ephesus, the greatest city of
Ionian Greece; one of the Seven
Wonders of the Ancient World, the
Temple of Artemis (Diana of the
Ephesians), stood just outside it. The
city became part of the Hellenistic state
of Pergamum, then passed to the
Romans, and was finally destroyed by
the Goths in AD 262.

Above
Women deep in conversation. The
Hellenistic artist's interest in everyday
life is evident in this little terracotta
made in about 200 BC, probably at
Myrina in Asia Minor. British Museum,
London.

Right
The Pharos of Alexandria, one of the
Seven Wonders of Antiquity: apart
from coins, this translucent green glass
vase found at Begram carries the only
representation of the great lighthouse.
Kabul Museum.

Left
Colossal marble head of a horse with bronze bridle and bit; one of the quadriga team sculpted by Pytheus and placed at the top of the Mausoleum at Halicarnassus. About 350 BC. British Museum, London.

Opposite top
The Laocöon, a Hellenistic sculpture on the subject of the Trojan priest Laocöon, who tried to prevent the fatal Wooden Horse from being carried into the city; he and his sons were killed by two sea serpents. Musei Vaticani.

Below
Sleeping Hermaphrodite. Antique copy of a third-century BC original; the mattress was added by the seventeenth-century Italian sculptor Bernini. Musée du Louvre, Paris.

being swindled). Original creative work was also done – most of it minor, but then the Hellenistic age was not one of great literary creativity anywhere, so far as it is possible to judge from surviving works. The outstanding poet was Theocritus, who introduced one of the most enduring of literary conventions. The pastoral celebrates the simple lives and loves of shepherds and their sweethearts – the kind of quasi-nostalgic subject that makes its appeal to city-dwellers in every age who feel their existence has become artificial and over-refined. Theocritus was a native of Syracuse, but failed to find a patron until Ptolemy II took him up; most of the poet's life seems to have been spent in Alexandria or on the island of Cos, at that time part of the Ptolemaic empire.

Ptolemy II had other records made in (or translated into) Greek, including the history of his own kingdom by the Egyptian high priest Manetho. He is also credited with arranging for the Greek translation of the Old Testament, called the Septuagint after the seventy-two scholars Ptolemy is supposed to have summoned from Jerusalem and set to work on the island of Pharos; however, textual analysis has shown that the Septuagint could not have been compiled at a single time and place, though it is almost certainly the work of Egyptian Jews.

As a centre of scientific and mathematical research, Alexandria became the home of Euclid, who systematised geometry, and of Aristarchus of Samos, who ventured to suggest that the earth revolved around the Sun. Eratosthenes, who became chief librarian, measured the circumference of the earth with surprising near-accuracy; he was a polymath – calculator, mapmaker, historian and even dramatic critic. And the great mathematician and engineer Archimedes is said to have studied at Alexandria, though he returned to his native Syracuse, where he invented the screw for raising water and drew appropriate conclusions from the bath water displaced by his own body – whereupon he gave his famous cry of scientific exultation: 'Eureka!' ('Got it!'). Alexandrian science, like Alexandrian commerce, continued to flourish in the Roman period, and the second-century AD geographer Ptolemy (non-royal) produced the most successful map of all time – a map of the universe, with the earth majestic and unmoving in the centre, which had authority over the European mind until the Copernican revolution of the sixteenth century. But when Hero of Alexandria discovered the principle of the steam engine he applied it to nothing more than the designing of mechanical toys: in a society with large labour resources – slave-power – there was no inevitable link between science and technology.

THE COLOSSAL ART OF THE GREEK EAST

The Seleucid empire had a splendid capital at Antioch, a royal library, even a school of poets of whom the best known was Meleager; but it never rivalled the cultural prestige of Alexandria. The very much smaller kingdom of Peragmum in Asia Minor was in many respects more successful. Her rulers maintained their independence in a world of great powers, and lavished the wealth of Pergamum's silver mines on beautifying the town and advertising themselves. All these great Hellenistic capitals had rational grid-design town plans, quite unlike the huddled accumulations that had gone to make up the city-state; and Pergamum was an outstanding example, skilfully laid out on the terraces of a hillside and culminating in the acropolis and royal palace. The grandest Pergamene monument was the Altar of Zeus and Athena, erected around 180 BC to commemorate the victory of Pergamum over Gaulish tribesmen who had ravaged Asia Minor. The victory is represented symbolically by the relief on the Altar showing gods fighting giants: the emotional tension and harsh energy of the struggle is typical of Hellenistic art, and a world away from the conscious restraint of the Classical age. Another famous Pergamene statue is *The Dying Gaul* (Roman copy), also highly emotional and exceptional in entering into the feelings of an alien enemy. The culture-conscious Pergamene kings made much of their devotion to Athens, and did in fact lavish gifts on the city. The greatest was the Stoa of Attalus (first king of Perga-

mum), a long colonnaded walk-cum-shopping area that has been restored in modern tines and now serves as a museum.

The cult of the colossal even spread to the islands. The famous Colossus of Rhodes – yet another of the Seven Wonders – was actually a statue of Apollo, about 32 metres high, which straddled two rocks in the harbour mouth, far enough apart for a boat to pass between the legs. Rhodes became a wealthy maritime state with the opening up of the East by Alexander, and like Pergamum she maintained her independence of the great powers and produced a flourishing art. Apart from the Colossus (destroyed in an earthquake towards the end of the third century), the best-known Rhodian work is the sculptured group of the Trojan prince Laocoön and his sons being killed by serpents. Its later history is of some interest. The Roman emperors eventually became its owners, and the Roman encyclopaedist Pliny the Elder considered it the supreme masterpiece of art. It disappeared with the Roman Empire, only to be dug up again on the Esquiline Hill in 1506, when its frenzied style profoundly impressed and influenced Michelangelo. Now it is in the Vatican Museum.

As well as portraying extremes of emotion, the Hellenistic sculptor broadened the subject matter of his art. Classical art was almost entirely con-

fined to gods and godlike men and women; Hellenistic works included children, battered boxers, the deformed, the old and the dying, variously in sentimental, pathetic and realistic vein. The colossal, emotional, dramatic, realistic, grotesque, sentimental: the common denominator of these apparently diverse characteristics is the virtuosity to which they gave free rein. It appears equally in the dramatic drapery of the *Winged Victory of Samothrace* and the slick mastery of a difficult posture in the *Crouching Venus*. The increasingly sensual and all-too-human aura of the Hellenistic Aphrodite was another sign of the times; some, however, like the *Venus de Milo* (that is, the Aphrodite of Melos), are self-consciously 'classical' in intention – rather forced attempts to achieve serenity on the part of artists in a more hectic and showy age.

Above left
Grotesques, like this one in ivory, became popular in Hellenistic art. British Museum, London.

Above
Hellenistic figure of a boy removing a thorn from his foot. British Museum, London.

Opposite
The *Winged Victory of Samothrace*, a Hellenistic sculpture now in the Musée du Louvre, Paris.

The other arts can only be mentioned briefly. Like earlier works, Hellenistic paintings have disappeared. Pottery painting no longer helps to preserve some kind of record: thanks to a radical change in style, Hellenistic pottery was either shiny black, with possibly a few abstract strokes painted on in colour, or decorated with applied clay reliefs. The few surviving mosaics are almost the sole remaining evidence of what was said to have been a great age of painting. Objects with gold and gems were skilfully fashioned but often over-worked for effect. Cameos, perfume and drug bottles and a variety of other knick-knacks were produced for the luxury market, but the discovery of glass-blowing in first-century BC Syria meant that glass objects could be made in quantity, and fairly cheaply, for the first time.

Like all virtuoso styles, the Hellenistic can easily be dismissed as hopelessly vulgar. Yet its technical accomplishment was astonishing; without the range of emotions and subjects it introduced we should be far less tolerant of the narrow limits of classicism; and it was mainly Hellenistic works that the Romans and later cultures took to be representative of Greek art and proceeded to imitate with such enthusiasm

DRAMA AND IDEAS

The Hellenistic combination of reverence for the past and virtuoso display in the present had mixed effects on the Greek theatre. The works of the great tragedians began to be regularly revived, and in 330 BC authorised texts were established at Athens (though a century later they had to be pawned to the culture-hungry Alexandrians when cash was needed to buy out the Macedonian garrison). Papyrus finds show that these 'classics' were widely

Left
The *Venus de Milo* – that is, the Aphrodite of Melos, found on the island in 1820; it has become the most famous of all Hellenistic statues. Late second century BC. Musée du Louvre, Paris.

Opposite
Crouching Venus. Historical and Archaeological Museum, Rhodes.

Above
Late Hellenistic pillar in the form of a comic actor. Arkeoloji Müzeleri, Istanbul.

Opposite
This splendid bronze head of a Berber exemplifies the wider artistic outlook of the Hellenistic period. British Museum, London.

read and performed. At about the same time, theatres were spreading all over the Greek world, and soon became *de rigeur* for any city that cared about its reputation; performances were given not only at Dionysia but during any other festivals and celebrations for which the financial backing was available. But if the theatre flourished, the drama went into a decline: thousands of plays must have been written, but they have vanished – and not entirely by accident, it seems, since contemporaries never considered them remotely comparable with fifth-century works, and quoted them far less often in their writings. It has been plausibly suggested that Hellenistic drama consisted of lifeless imitations of 'Classical' drama for highbrows, and otherwise of overblown set-piece 'scripts' which served as vehicles for the virtuosos of the theatre: the actors. The 'star system' was in full swing by the fourth century, and we have already seen that famous actors like Polus could command fortunes for a few performances. Hellenistic theatrical conventions encouraged 'performances' rather than serious drama: actors became grotesque giants, wearing padded costumes, built-up shoes and masks conveying wildly exaggerated emotions, looming above the orchestra on a three-or-four-metre-high stage.

Athenian drama flourished a little longer, however – in comedy. Menander (c.342–c.293) was the outstanding writer of New Comedy, so named to distinguish it from the Old Comedy of Aristophanes. (Scholars, following Hellenistic critics, identify a transitional Middle Comedy; but the late plays of Aristophanes are the only complete examples to have survived). Menander's works are recognisable ancestors of the Western comedic tradition. The chorus now takes no part in the main action, merely appearing between acts. The plots are full of love crises caused by unsympathetic parents or differences in the lovers' social status, foundlings who prove to be kidnapped sons or daughters of respectable parents, and elaborate confidence tricks staged by crafty slaves; the ending is always a happy one. The characters are mainly types: misers, garrulous cooks, soldiers who are cowardly braggarts, scoundrely ser-

vants. These durable elements reappear in Roman comedy, in the Italian improvised *commedia dell'arte*, in Shakespeare's *Comedy of Errors* and Molière's *Fourberies de Scapin*, still lively enough to hold the stage and win awards in Britain and America when adapted recently as *Scapino*.

Athens' other cultural distinction in the Hellenistic age was to remain the philosophers' capital; none of the major figures was born in the city, but all gravitated to it, evidently preferring freedom and congenial company to the fleshpots of Alexandria and Pergamum. The greatest of the philosophers, Aristotle (384–322), was not fully a man of the new age. Born at Stagira in the Chalcidice peninsula of Thrace, he came to Athens to study under Plato at the Academy; his early interest lay in zoology, and – characteristically – he left the Academy after Plato's death, when the philosophising became too unfactual for his taste. Later he became Alexander the Great's tutor, though whether Alexander's career owed much to Aristotle's philosophy is doubtful. Returning to Athens in 335, Aristotle set up a school in a grove sacred to Apollo Lyceius (whence Lyceum); however, his taste for discussion in the open air, while walking up and down with his pupils, led to the school being nicknamed 'the Peripatetic school'. He is said to have given two courses of lectures – one, in the morning, to a restricted circle of students, and another in the afternoon on topics such as politics, which a wider audience could attend. The distinction was probably the utilitarian one between advanced and general students, though the mystery and glamour of philosophy suggested to some later writers that esoteric and marvellous truths were passed on in the mornings to 'initiates'. It seems unlikely that Aristotle cast himself in such a Pythagorean role: he was one of the most fact-minded of the ancients, strikingly unlike his master Plato in preferring to discover and analyse realities rather than reason about perfect entities and how things ought to be. Though by no means always correct in his information and inferences, Aristotle possessed a brilliant and all-inclusive intellect, ranging over every subject of study from logic to

natural history, from metaphysics to rhetoric.

Aristotle's encyclopaedic learning made him the major non-religious authority of the European Middle Ages: he, Socrates and Plato are the greatest philosophical thinkers of ancient Greece. But some of Aristotle's contemporaries and successors had a far more direct influence on the way men lived in the centuries immediately ahead. Mentally, Aristotle lived in the age of the polis; his *Politics* describes and compares the constitutions of Greek states whose independence and importance were being destroyed for ever by his pupil Alexander. Diogenes, Epicurus and Zeno the Stoic spoke to men who needed a new kind of

philosophy, suited to an age when the ordinary citizen could no longer control events, was conscious of himself as an individual rather than as a member of a community, and consequently sought for individual or universal – not community – values. Some turned from the Olympian gods (who in their local aspects were identified with the city-state community) and embraced mystery religions or oriental cults such as Egyptian Serapis and Isis; others turned to the new philosophers.

The most radical of these was Aristotle's contemporary Diogenes of Sinope, a port on the southern shore of the Black Sea. Diogenes was the best-known of the Cynics, who were not the hard-headed materialists of

modern usage, but 'drop-outs' who believed in reducing their needs to a minimum, living according to nature, and detaching themselves from the world and its vanities. In legend, Diogenes' version of this secularised Buddhism included such eccentricities as living in a tub and rebuffing Alexander the Great; nevertheless his philosophy was a serious one and intermittently influenced the Greco-Roman world.

The Epicurean and Stoic philosophies had even greater influence, since they were more compatible with ordinary life in the world. Epicurus, though born on Samos, was the son of an Athenian and eventually set up his school in the city; he taught in

the garden of his house, and thanks to misunderstandings of his philosophy 'the garden of Epicurus' had become a by-word for private self-indulgence even in Antiquity. For Epicurus taught that pleasure was the only object of existence; however, he added that desire only bred greater desire – another Buddhistic point of view – so that happiness could not be achieved by the pursuit of pleasure in the ordinary sense. Instead, Epicurus recommended temperance, the enjoyment of friendship, and the cultivation of contentment. Above all, the wise man should have no fear of the gods: the universe was material, a collection of atoms as Democritus held, and if the gods existed they did not concern

themselves with the affairs of men.

Epicureanism became the philosophy of men able to retire from the world in modest comfort; Stoicism appealed to those who were compelled by circumstances or temperament to act or endure. Its founder, Zeno, was a Cypriot who taught in the shelter of an Athenian stoa, which gave the name to his philosophy. Stoicism held that the soul of man was a spark from the cosmic fire, to which it would eventually return if it was faithfully tended. This meant that a man must live according to nature and reason, which in practice involved virtuous, 'stoical' acceptance of fate and diligent performance of the duties appropriate to it; while acting as he should, the stoic remained

self-sufficient, cultivating a happiness that was independent of his circumstances. Stoicism was to be the philosophy most congenial to the empire-building people who gradually took over the Hellenistic world: the Romans.

Opposite
Mosaic of the Nile in flood, from Palestrina: a detail of the mosaic above affectionately recording the abundant wild life of the river and the huntsmen working out of a boat. Museo Archeologico Nazionale, Palestrina.

Above
Mosaic of the Nile in flood, from Palestrina: a glimpse of the bustling life of late Hellenistic Egypt. Museo Archeologico Nazionale, Palestrina.

Rome: Republic and Empire

ORIGINS, REAL AND MYTHICAL

The Roman Empire began with a group of hilltop villages, easily defensible against intruders who ventured into the marshy lowlands. The sites, later the famous seven hills of Rome, proved to have other advantages: they controlled the most convenient north-south route across the Tiber, and they were close enough to the sea to become an entrepôt for trade with Central Italy. By about 575 BC the villages had amalgamated into a city-state of modest importance, perhaps already influenced or dominated by her powerful Etruscan neighbours.

The two Roman accounts of the city's beginnings are more portentous. According to one, the brothers Romulus and Remus were left to die in the wilderness but were suckled by a she-wolf. They founded Rome and peopled it with fugitives and outlaws; then they acquired women for the community by stealing them from the neighbouring Sabines – the 'rape of the Sabine women'. Though the legend has a certain low-life plausibility, much of it must have been suggested by Greek myth; Romulus, a son of the god Mars, is himself eventually promoted to become the god Quirinus. A later, more glamorous legend attaches Rome directly to the world of Greek myth. Aeneas, one of the princes of Troy, evades the victorious Greeks and makes his way to Italy, where he marries the daughter of King Latinus and becomes a great warrior – and the ancestor of the Romans. The Greek elements in these stories are hardly sur-

prising, since the Greeks established themselves in Italy during the eighth century, and soon exercised a strong influence on the Etruscans, the dominant people in Central Italy.

According to later tradition there were seven kings of Rome from the time of Romulus. Several of them were probably Etruscans, and they seem to have introduced the earliest of the civic amenities for which Rome was to become famous: a system of public sewers including the Cloaca Maxima, and the Temple of Jupiter, Juno and Minerva on the Capitol – the acropolis of Rome. Both of these have been credited to the last king of Rome, Tarquinius Superbus, who is, however, better known as the rapist of the Roman matron Lucretia; this incident, which inspired much later literature including Shakespeare's narrative poem *The Rape of Lucrece*, is supposed to have sparked off the revolt led by Junius Brutus which drove Tarquinius from Rome. Thus in 510 BC (according to tradition: possibly rather later in reality) Rome simultaneously freed herself from Etruscan control and

became a republic. The word 'king' (*rex*) remained so odious to the Romans that even five hundred years later, when the state was again permanently ruled by a single man, a new terminology had to be devised to describe the situation.

THE CONQUEST OF ITALY

The new republic was created by and for the upper class of patricians, who alone elected and served as public officials. The chief executive power was vested in the two consuls, who were elected every year. In dire emergencies a special officer was chosen, the dictator, who held absolute power for the duration of the emergency and was expected to lay it down the moment the crisis was over. Legislation and leisurely-pondered advice was the business of a Senate of elders (*patres*), as it had been under the monarchy.

The patricians probably originated as the wealthy class, but if so they had hardened into an artistocratic caste by

Above centre
Romulus and Remus being suckled by a she-wolf. In fact, only the wolf in this bronze group is antique (either Greek or Etruscan); the children were added in the fifteenth century by the Pollaiuolo brothers. Museo Capitolino, Rome.

Opposite
The legend of Rome's founders begins with scenes carved on this altar panel: Romulus and Remus suckled by a she-wolf, and their discovery by shepherds. Museo Nazionale Romano, Rome.

Opposite
Numa Pompilius, legendary second king of Rome; he was said to have been a Sabine from Cures, and to have introduced the main features of later Roman religion. Forum Romanum, Rome.

Above
Aeneas, legendary Trojan ancestor of the Romans: relief from the Ara Pacis, Rome.

Above right
Terracotta head of a helmeted warrior; an example of the vigorous art of the Etruscans, that still-mysterious people who were the teachers and eventual victims of the Romans. From the site of Veii, about the fifth century BC.

Right
Roman bust, traditionally supposed to be of Brutus, founder of the Roman Republic. Museo Capitolino, Rome.

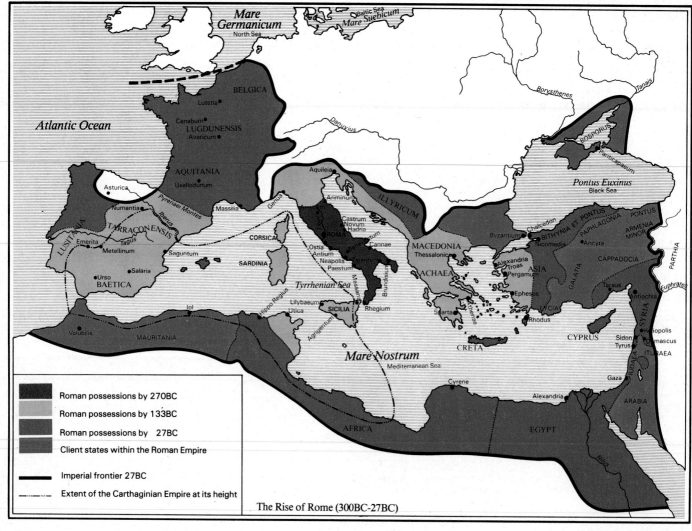

The Rise of Rome (300BC–27BC)

Legend:
- Roman possessions by 270BC
- Roman possessions by 133BC
- Roman possessions by 27BC
- Client states within the Roman Empire
- Imperial frontier 27BC
- Extent of the Carthaginian Empire at its height

republican times, unwilling to admit even the richest members of the lower or plebeian class *(plebs)* into their ranks. During the next 200 years the plebeians forced one concession after another from the patricians, who were dependent on their inferiors for military manpower even if, as seems unlikely, the use of slaves would have met their economic needs. Therefore, the main weapon of the plebeians was secession – the literal withdrawal of the plebeians *en masse* from the city, which apparently happened several times. Plebeian equivalents to patrician institutions were devised, notably elected tribunes and a plebeian assembly; the patricians were forced to accept their integration into the political system, giving the tribunes the power to veto most decisions while the plebeian assembly could pass resolutions (plebiscites) that had the force of law. In time plebeians gained admittance to all the chief offices, and a plebeian element appeared in the Senate. In theory at least Rome had become a

state in which the people ruled; in practice only the richer plebeians had much time for political life, and they soon coalesced with the patricians in a more broadly based ruling class. Reforms of the harsh laws penalising debtors, and new land made available by conquest or colonisation, largely alleviated the discontents of the poorer plebeians, leaving the Romans an impressively united people.

Despite these internal struggles, Rome slowly established a position of supremacy throughout the Italian peninsula, beginning by entering into a league with the neighbouring Latin-speaking peoples who shared the plain of Latium with her. Moving north against the Etruscans, the Romans captured the important town of Veii in 396, only to come up against a horde of Gauls – Celtic invaders from the north who defeated the Roman army and sacked Rome itself; the Capitol held out, but the Gauls marched away only after they had been paid off. The city had to be rebuilt, yet within a

few years Rome had reasserted her leadership of the Latin League and begun to turn her partners into subordinate allies. Etruria was gradually brought under Roman control, but half a century of warfare was needed to subdue the fierce Samnite tribes of the southern Apennines, who were never fully reconciled to their victorious enemies. Once more a Roman army sustained a humiliating defeat – at the Caudine Forks (321), where it let itself be trapped in a narrow defile and was forced to surrender – and once again Rome recovered.

It was Rome's power of recovery, not her military strength, that made her rise to empire inevitable. Other peoples might win victories; the

Opposite
Aeneas tended for a wound in his thigh; his mother, the goddess Venus, looks on sorrowfully, and his son Ascanius weeps. Pompeian wall painting.

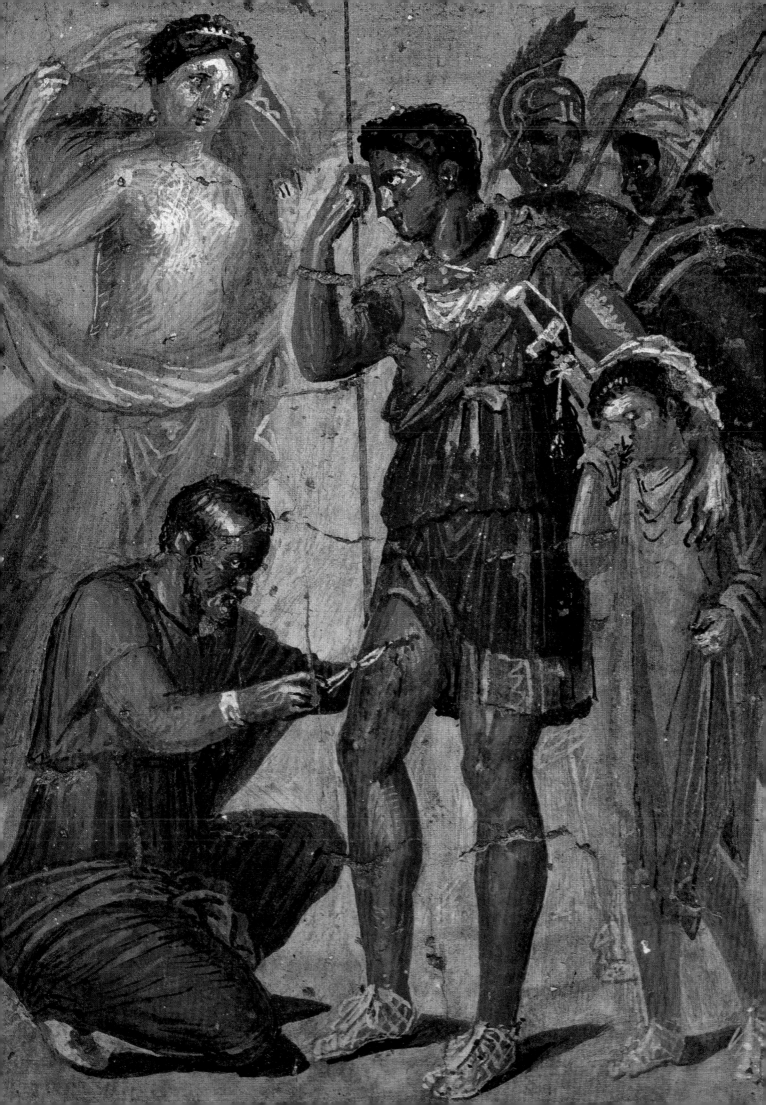

Romans won wars. Later writers looked back on the early centuries of the republic as a golden age of virtuous men, selflessly devoted to duty – men such as Cincinnatus, who was called from the plough to become dictator, saved the state in sixteen days, and then returned to his plough. A more material reason for Roman success was the relatively generous attitude adopted towards allies and defeated peoples. From as early as 380 BC Rome was extending citizenship rights to at least some of these, giving her victories a permanence unknown to the Greek city-state. Further extended by carefully placed Roman and Latin colonies, the population and territory of 'Rome' increased steadily, and with it the capacity to control the unreconciled. The policy was not applied as consistently or quickly as it might have been, but its value was to be proved by Italian loyalty to Rome during the long wars against Carthage, the great Phoenician power of North Africa.

First, however, Roman expansion brought her up against the Greeks of Southern Italy and into alliance with Carthage. As a great maritime trading power Carthage was in competition with the Greeks in the western Mediterranean, and had earlier allied with the Etruscans to restrain Greek ambitions. Centuries of Greek-Carthaginian warfare over control of Sicily had ended in a stalemate, with Carthage controlling the western and the Greeks the eastern half of the island. In 282, when Rome was drawn into an inter-Greek dispute that led to war with Tarentum, the Tarentines called in one of the leading military adventurers of the age, Pyrrhus, King of Epirus in north-west Greece; and the Carthaginian fleet came to the assistance of Rome. Pyrrhus' professional army twice defeated the Romans, but with such heavy losses that he retired to Sicily: he is said to have remarked 'Another such victory and I shall be ruined'. Despite these 'pyrrhic' victories he returned for one more attempt, which was even less successful, and then, having lost two-thirds of his army, sailed away and left the Tarentines to their fate. By 272 Rome was mistress of the Italian peninsula from the Arno to the Straits of Messina.

THE STRUGGLE AGAINST CARTHAGE Control of the Straits of Messina was the issue that brought Rome and Carthage into conflict. But war was probably inevitable, given Rome's new position as a Mediterranean power and virtual protector of the Sicilian Greeks. Messina was controlled by the Mamertines, Italian mercenaries who had seized the city after being brought to Sicily by Pyrrhus. When they were attacked by Syracuse they accepted a Carthaginian garrison; but they then appealed to Rome, and, on the promise of aid, expelled the Carthaginians and embroiled the two great powers in war.

The First Punic (i.e. Carthaginian) War was a hard-fought affair that lasted twenty-three years (264-241 BC). Rome's citizen armies performed well against the mercenaries employed by Carthage, but Rome had to become a naval power to win; she built several fleets, and developed new boarding tactics involving grapnels that enabled the legionaries to make their prowess felt. After its first surprise victory at Mylae, in 260, the Roman navy suffered some bad reverses; an expedition to attack Carthage itself turned into a disaster; and though the Carthaginians were pushed back in Sicily, the Romans failed to achieve a decisive result. Finally the Roman navy won command of the seas with a victory off the Aegates Islands and the two exhausted combatants made peace. Carthage ceded her Sicilian possessions to Rome and paid a war indemnity of 3,100 talents. Three years later, taking advantage of a mercenary revolt that had paralysed Carthage, the Romans used the excuse of an appeal by some of the mercenaries to seize Sardinia and Corsica; when the Carthaginians protested against this blatant aggression the Romans added insult to injury by extorting another large indemnity from them. The existence of possessions outside mainland Italy led to the first 'imperial' administrative measures a few years later, when two extra magistrates of the praetor class

were appointed, one to take charge of Roman Sicily, the other to administer Sardinia and Corsica. The 'republican empire' had begun.

The Carthaginians reacted energetically to their reverses, building up a new empire in Spain under Hamilcar Barca, his son-in-law Hasdrubal and Hamilcar's son Hannibal. This Barca family represented the Carthaginian 'hawks', bent on expanding the empire and revenging themselves on Rome; there was a peace party in the city too, led by a senator called Hanno, which argued that Carthage's future lay in Africa; but their influence seems to have prevailed only at the most unfortunate moments, when their lack of enthusiasm hampered military operations without ending them or conciliating Rome.

Beyond this, little is known of life at Carthage, though the bare facts about her oligarchic city-state constitution have been preserved. Her religion certainly involved human sacrifices to Baal and other gods; her art was imitated from the Greeks; and the only Carthaginian book worth translating was an encyclopaedic treatise on farming – though this 'fact', like the Roman phrase 'Punic faith' (meaning 'treachery') and much else,

may prove no more than the extent of Roman prejudice, through which most of our information has been filtered.

The forward policy of the Barcas in Spain brought on the war that decided the fate of the Mediterranean. According to a Roman-Carthaginian agreement of 226, Spain south of the River Ebro was recognised as the Carthaginian sphere of influence. But like most such agreements it left opportunities for discord if the parties to it were in the mood. In this case the opportunity for disagreement lay in the existence of a Roman ally, the city of Saguntum, on the Spanish coast, south of the Ebro. Hannibal tried to bring Saguntum under Carthaginian control; Saguntum refused and resisted; Hannibal besieged and captured the city; and the Romans declared war. Evidently both sides were spoiling for a fight.

Hannibal was one of the greatest generals of all time, and certainly the most dangerous opponent Rome ever had to face; while he was still a boy, his father, Hamilcar, had made him vow undying enmity towards the Romans. His power to command loyal service is all the more striking in that the majority of his men were mercenaries

with no permanent commitment to the Carthaginian cause; they were also of many nationalities (Numidians, Spaniards, Celts), each fighting in its native fashion and posing difficult problems of co-ordination. Hannibal mastered these and won victory after victory over the Roman legions, despite their advantages in being a citizen militia, produced by a single community and trained to fight together. Like most great generals, however, Hannibal moved fast and kept the initiative by doing the unexpected.

All this was apparent from his first campaigns. The Romans equipped armies to invade Spain and Africa, confident in their naval superiority and huge reserves of manpower; but instead of letting them choose their own ground, Hannibal decided to strike into Italy and raise the subject-cities of

Opposite
Roman remains at Timgad in Algeria.

Above
Roman theatre at Thugga (modern Dougga) in Tunisia.

Above
The Roman Forum. The Temple of Vesta stands in the centre, and the Palatine Hill on the right.

Opposite top left
Scipio Africanus, conqueror of Hannibal. Bust in the Museo Archeologico Nazionale, Naples.

Opposite top right
Terracotta vase in the form of a war elephant. Museo Archeologico Nazionale, Naples.

Opposite bottom and left
The Roman city in Africa: ruins of Leptis Magna.

Rome against their masters, reversing the balance of manpower. The Carthaginians marched through Spain and southern France, gave the slip to a Roman army based on Marseille, and crossed the Alps – an epic feat until modern engineers tamed the mountains with roads and tunnels; bringing an army over them was still heroic when Napoleon did it 2,000 years later. Early autumn snows made Hannibal's task even more difficult, and he came down into Italy with a force of only 26,000 men (about half the original number) and a much depleted train of elephants with which to disorganise and terrorise the elephantless Romans.

But the benefits of Hannibal's daring were rapidly felt. The Celtic inhabitants of the Po Valley, subdued by the Romans only a few years before, began to go over to the Carthaginians; and the Roman army in Sicily, on the point of sailing for Africa, had to be recalled to face the invader. When it joined the existing Roman forces in the north and attacked Hannibal in December 218 – only eight months after he had set out from Spain – he outmanoeuvred, ambushed and routed it at the battle of Trebbia.

An exceptionally severe winter gave Rome a breathing-space in which to raise fresh armies. But in May 217 Hannibal crossed the Apennines into Central Italy; and at the battle of Lake Trasimene, a pursuing Roman army allowed itself to be pinned between the hills and the lake, and was driven into the water with huge losses.

In spite of this brilliant success, the cities of Etruria and Latium remained loyal to Rome – the first setback for Hannibal's strategy and one of the fruits of Rome's enlightened policies towards subjects and allies. Hannibal therefore pushed on into Southern Italy, where he hoped to find more support among the less-reconciled Samnites and Greeks. The Romans appointed as dictator one of their elder statesmen, Fabius, who adopted 'Fabian tactics', trying to wear Hannibal's army down and buy time instead of fighting a pitched battle. To many Romans this policy seemed dubious, since the Carthaginians were able to march all over Campania and Apulia, looting and burning at will, and apparently demonstrating the impo-

tence of Rome to her allies. In 216, when Fabius had served the six-month maximum term as dictator, he was replaced by two newly-elected consuls, Paullus and Varro, who collected a large army and moved directly against the Carthaginians.

At Cannae in Apulia, Hannibal's army, though outnumbered, won the greatest of its victories; the Romans suffered their greatest-ever disaster. The legions forced back the Carthaginians in the centre, while Hannibal's African pikemen held the wings and his Spanish and Celtic horsemen drove off the Roman cavalry. The specially reinforced Carthaginian centre did not break; the Africans closed in from the sides; and the Spaniards and Celts completed the encirclement by attacking the Roman rear. The Romans were slaughtered, and one of the consuls, Paullus, fell. Soon afterwards, Capua and many other southern Italian towns declared for Hannibal, and Rome's situation appeared to be desperate.

This proved to be the high point of Hannibal's fortunes. Rome raised new legions, accepting even criminals into the ranks; but she returned to Fabius' policy of avoiding battle. Instead, she fought the Carthaginians and their allies wherever Hannibal was *not* present. Capua, Syracuse, Tarentum and other pro-Carthaginian cities were besieged and taken; Hannibal's brother, Hasdrubal, was defeated and killed in an attempt to reinforce the Carthaginians from Spain; and a new Roman general of genius, Scipio, finally drove the Carthaginians from Spain. With steadily declining manpower, Hannibal was forced back to Bruttium, in the toe of Italy. When Scipio invaded Africa and his victories threatened Carthage itself, Hannibal was recalled; he left Italy after sixteen years' campaigning, having failed to conquer it yet having never sustained a defeat.

In Scipio (later given the name Scipio Africanus), Hannibal met his match. At the battle of Zama in 202 BC, there was no successful ambush or outflanking, but a straight fight between the two armies – Hannibal's almost certainly without his veterans, most of whom it must have been impossible to transport from Italy to Africa. The outcome was decided by Scipio's

Roman and Numidian cavalry, who broke their opponents' ranks and then fell on the Carthaginian rear. After this defeat Carthage sued for peace, agreeing to dismantle her navy, give up all claims to Spain and pay an enormous war indemnity.

Although Carthage was now no more than a dependent ally of Rome, suspicion of her had become ingrained in the Roman mind. When Hannibal began to reform the Carthaginian government and economy, the Romans willingly believed the reports of his opponents in the city, who accused him of plotting a war of revenge with the Seleucids. Hannibal was forced to flee from court to court, seeking shelter from enemies or doubtful friends of Rome; when, in about 182, the king of Bithynia in Asia Minor decided to give him up to the Romans, he poisoned himself to avoid a more degrading and painful fate. Carthage survived untouched until 150, although her renewed commercial prosperity caused the fanatical Cato to end his every speech in the Roman Senate with the words *Carthago delenda est* – 'Carthage must be destroyed'. And destroyed it was, by a series of deliberately contrived incidents that finally provoked the Carthaginians into attacking one of Rome's allies. The Romans intervened and, after a three-year blockade, razed the city. The Senate grimly decreed that neither house nor crop should again rise on the site, which was ploughed and sown with salt; however, Carthage was so well situated as a port and entrepôt for the African hinterland that she rose again a hundred years later, as one of the most prosperous Roman cities in the Mediterranean.

EMPIRE AND CIVIL STRIFE
Rome now controlled the entire western Mediterranean. With so much new territory to organise, the Romans

Opposite
Carthaginian stele with a priest carrying a child to the sacrifice. Late fifth or early fourth century BC. Musée Bardo, Tunis.

Right
The military dictator Sulla; antique bust in the Musei Vaticani.

177

were reluctant to become involved in Eastern affairs, even though Philip V of Macedon had fought against them as an ally of Hannibal. When Rhodes, Pergamum and other Greek states appealed to Rome for help against Philip's ambitions, Rome did intervene and in 197 won a decisive victory; but though Macedon was stripped of her conquests, her fleet and 1,000 talents, Rome left the Greeks their liberties and actually withdrew her forces. The only result was to create a power vacuum that the Seleucid king Antiochus determined to fill. When he invaded Greece the Romans returned, defeated his army at Thermopylae (191), and themselves invaded Asia; after another defeat at Magnesia, Antiochus ceded his dominions in Asia Minor – nominally to Rhodes and Pergamum: though very much the protecting power, Rome still eschewed territorial gains. But after another war against Macedon and a series of Greek intrigues and squabbles, Macedon became a Roman province and the rest of Greece was cowed by the utter destruction of Corinth in 146. Thirteen years later, Attalus of Pergamum died, bequeathing his possessions to Rome, and the Roman province of 'Asia' (actually part of Asia Minor) was formed. Meanwhile, the tribes along the coasts of Southern France and Dalmatia had been subdued. With Egypt friendly and Seleucid Syria visibly in decline, the Mediterranean had effectively become a Roman lake.

The acquisition of such an enormous empire within a few generations put a terrible strain on the Roman political system and the Roman way of life. As in other rapidly enriched societies, there was irresponsible luxury, women were allowed more freedom in practice if not in theory, and the young became harder to control. 'Culture' acquired a separate and prestigious existence. The conquest of Greece led to a Greek counter-conquest of Rome in the spheres of religion, philosophy, literature and the plastic arts: like parvenus everywhere, the Romans paid cash down for statues, paintings

Right
The army in action: scene from Trajan's column, Rome.

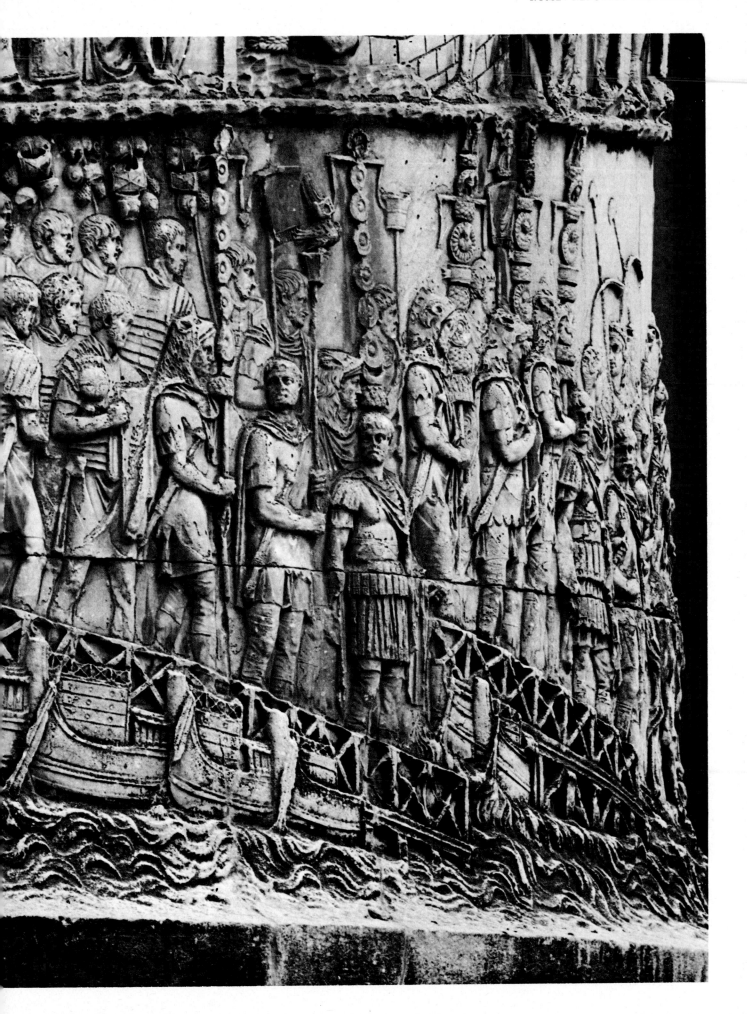

and lessons in philosophy and rhetoric; and like most impoverished artists and intellectuals, the Greeks willingly sold.

Conservatives inevitably complained that the new sophistication was incompatible with the ploughman virtue of Cincinnatus, and that luxury was enervating; but there were deeper causes for the upheavals that shook and finally destroyed the republic in the space of a century. In practice the old Roman system had been run by the Senate, though both magistrates and the plebeian institutions – the tribunate and popular assembly – had wide powers that were never brought into play. With the growth of empire there was discontent at home on several fronts. The new-rich businessmen and capitalists resented their exclusion from power by the aristocracy controlling the Senate. An ever-growing mass of landless proletarians crowded into the tenement blocks of Rome, mutely threatening the security of the possessing classes; they found themselves redundant in a world where the peasant could not compete against the products of mass slave labour on large estates. Many Italian cities had not yet been admitted to the privileges and profits of Roman citizenship, and began to grow restive. And the provinces of Rome's young empire felt that they were being fleeced by their governors and tax-gatherers, appointed by an administration that was still no more than an enlarged city-state government. The provincial's best hope was to be protected by a Roman general with larger ambitions than self-enrichment; and troops too developed a more personal loyalty, looking to their general for protection against sharp businessmen and other exploiters when their service was over and they had been settled on the land.

In the light of all this, the confused and violent history of the late republic becomes easier to follow; what remains astonishing is that Rome survived when she was so often simultaneously torn by civil war and engaged against foreign enemies. The first crisis occurred in 133-132, when the tribune Tiberius Gracchus proposed a drastic agrarian reform to limit the size of estates and use the surplus to re-create the smallholding class.

Since the conservative Senate opposed the measure, Gracchus persuaded the Assembly of the People to pass it – thus invoking the dormant sovereignty of the people but (in conservative eyes) violating the conventions of the constitution. When he sought re-election as tribune, a group of senators and their followers assassinated him on the Capitol; whether they acted through self-interest, or genuine fear that Gracchus was aiming to become a tyrant, remains an open question. The murder of Gracchus was the first act of violence in Roman political life, foreshadowing the epidemic slaughter of later decades.

Ten years later, Tiberius' younger brother, Gaius Gracchus, was elected to the tribunate and took up the reform programme again. He was even more radical, proposing measures to keep the price of wheat low, to recommence re-distribution of the land, and to tackle unemployment by a programme of public works and the establishment of colonies in Italy and abroad. Since they were designed to help the poor, the Assembly of the People readily passed them, though the Senate short-sightedly disapproved. But when Gaius proposed to extend citizenship to Rome's Latin allies, the people were easily persuaded not to share their privileges; Gaius failed in a bid to be re-elected, and shortly afterwards the Senate issued an emergency decree authorising the consuls to 'save the state' by massacring Gaius and his followers; Gaius himself committed suicide to avoid capture.

The Gracchi can be viewed as revolutionaries or reformers, or simply as faction leaders: they were, after all, members of the aristocracy, like most later chiefs of the Populares, or popular party, manipulating popular assemblies to make up for their inability to control the Senate. If the policy of the Gracchi seems too riskily idealistic to bear such a cynical interpretation, it is certainly true that Roman party politics soon became more a matter of personal ambition, political machinery

Opposite
Pompey the Great, perhaps the most successful of all Roman generals – until he quarrelled with Caesar. Antique head in the Galleria degli Uffizi, Florence.

and horse-trading than of genuine reformism; the party machines – families, 'clients' and gangs – fought and intrigued against each other in the city unless (or until) the army became involved.

After the death of Gaius Gracchus, however, the Optimates (the Senatorial party) ruled unchallenged. But their position was weakened by incompetent handling of a war against Jugurtha, King of Numidia, that dragged on for years. Against the wishes of the Senate, Gaius Marius, an officer of relatively humble birth, was given the command. He created a new kind of paid professional Roman army which in the event proved more loyal to its commanders than to the state. Jugurtha was defeated and strangled; then (102-101 BC) Marius won two bloody victories over the Cimbri and Teutones, Germanic tribes whose early successes in invading Italy had terrified the Romans. Marius was now a power in the state, with an enormous personal following including the veterans for whom he had obtained land grants. However, he had few political aims except satisfaction of his vanity, partly accomplished by numerous consulships; and when his clumsy manoeuvres upset both Optimates and Populares, a period of political confusion began.

Violence broke out again in 91 with the murder of Drusus, another tribune who had proposed extending the franchise. This time the Italian allies reacted vigorously to the disappointment of their hopes: they rose in arms, and fought so effectively that the war was ended by Rome conceding citizenship to all who were prepared to stop fighting; in effect, all free Italians became citizens.

This, the Social War, confirmed the military talents of Lucius Cornelius Sulla, who emerged as a rival of Marius. As consul for the year 88 he was given command of the army against Mithradates VI of Pontus, who had invaded Roman Asia and had received an enthusiastic welcome from a provincial population disillusioned by Roman exactions. Marius, jealous of Sulla and afraid of the threat to his pre-eminence, allied himself with the tribune Sulpicius, and was named by the assembly to replace Sulla.

Instead of giving up his command, Sulla simply marched on Rome, took it, executed Sulpicius and 'rectified' the political situation. Sulla's assault on Rome itself marked a new stage in the decline of respect for constitutional forms; he himself is something of an enigma – conservative champion of the Senate, bent on restoring the old ways yet ruthless and murderous in the means he used to do so. Leaving a precarious situation in Rome, Sulla marched east to deal with Mithradates. Marius, who had fled from Rome, now returned and indulged in an orgy of revenge on all who had offended him; before he could set off for the East he died (he was about seventy).

Sulla, an outlaw now that his enemies controlled Rome, defeated Mithradates but made peace with him in return for money and supplies, looted the cities of Asia, and then invaded Italy. He quickly crushed the Marians and by 82 BC found himself master of the Roman state.

Sulla then legalised his position by having himself elected dictator; wiped out every trace of opposition by posting up seemingly-never-ending proscription lists; and enacted a complete programme of reforms which made the Senate more representative (of the possessing classes at least), broke the power of the tribunes, and protected the state against the ambitions of generals such as – Sulla. While he lived – and could call upon his veterans, comfortably settled on lands confiscated from the Samnites and other enemies – Sulla's consitution worked, even after his retirement in 80; but most of his measures were scrapped within ten years of his death in 79.

Since his power was absolute with or without a constitution, Sulla must have been sincere in his traditionalist convictions. He apparently failed to realise that using violence against the state – whether to reform, rule or ruin it – was the most anti-traditional course of action it was possible to follow. More than most saviours, Sulla was a harbinger of doom.

POMPEY, CRASSUS AND CAESAR

Sulla's lieutenants Pompey and Crassus were responsible for sweeping away his constitution – mainly, no doubt, because neither was trusted by the

Opposite
Bust of the great orator Cicero. About
50-40 BC. Galleria degli Uffizi, Florence.

Above
The Appian Way, most famous of
Roman roads, lined with tombs.

Senate which Sulla had done his best to strengthen. For its part, the Senate was understandably suspicious of successful generals, with the paradoxical result that Pompey and Crassus, though fierce rivals, were more than once compelled to work together to achieve their political aims.

Crassus had the smaller military reputation, but more money: he had exploited his position under Sulla to become rich, and a series of later investments turned him into a multi-millionaire. His military services to Rome were probably as valuable as Pompey's more spectacular victories, for Crassus defeated a slave revolt that theatened the whole basis of Rome's existence. Its leader was Spartacus, a Thracian who led a break-out from the gladiators' school at Capua (gladiators were virtually prisoners) and gathered an army of runaway slaves. For three years (73-71) they plundered Italy and defeated Roman armies; if Spartacus' advice had been taken they could have marched out of the Empire to freedom, creating a disturbing precedent from the point of view of the Roman ruling class. Instead, Spartacus' army was trapped in Southern Italy by Crassus' troops and destroyed; enough prisoners were taken for it to be possible to crucify them the entire length of the Via Appia, the great highway stretching 375 kilometres from Rome to Brundisium, the main port for the East.

After this, Crassus had little opportunity to see action, and spent the next decade trying – not very successfully – to build up a political following with the help of his vast wealth. It was Pompey who seemed predestined to never-ending glory. As a young man he won victories in Africa that caused Sulla to give him the title 'the Great' (Pompeius Magnus), though with dry military realism Sulla styled himself 'the Lucky' (Sulla Felix). Pompey then spent several years hunting down the last of the Marian-popular party in Spain, returned to Italy in time to steal some of Crassus' credit for defeating Spartacus, and after a spell as consul received a special commission to clear the Mediterranean of the pirates infesting it. Having accomplished this, Pompey crowned his career with a victorious campaign in

Left
Gaius Julius Caesar, conqueror of Gaul and Roman dictator: statue in the Museo Capitolino, Rome.

Above
Statue of a Roman senator in his toga.

the East: Mithradates' kingdom of Pontus was destroyed, Syria was officially incorporated into the Empire, and the East was thoroughly reorganised. Pompey returned to Rome in 62 BC, still only forty-two years old, and laid down his command.

Meanwhile, Roman politics had become more tangled than ever. One of the most influential figures in the Senate was Cato, great-grandson of the Cato who had inspired the final destruction of Carthage; he imitated his ancestor's conservatism, and his rigid attitudes helped to make difficult any compromise between the Senate and powerful individuals such as Pompey and Crassus. A more moderate figure was Cicero, the greatest of all Roman orators: by birth a 'new man' like Marius, he nonetheless worked to save the state by bringing together the Senate and the equites in a centre party standing for unity, law and order against over-mighty individuals. (The equites, or equestrians, were the class of wealthy non-senators; they had been given a measure of politico-judicial influence by Gaius Gracchus.) Cicero's great moment came during his consulship in 63, when his defeated opponent in the election, Catiline, began plotting to seize power. Although lacking definite proof, Cicero excoriated Catiline so effectively in the Senate that on one occasion all those sitting near him began to move away, finally leaving him in guilty isolation. Eventually Catiline fled to join his supporters in Etruria while Cicero acted vigorously in the city, arresting Catiline's fellow-conspirators and persuading the Senate to sanction their immediate execution. Catiline was defeated and killed in battle, and Cicero was hailed – or at any rate hailed himself – as the saviour of the state. He later made a habit of reminding Rome of the fact on every possible occasion; which did not, however, increase his political influence.

Another political force was Gaius Julius Caesar, who as a young man narrowly escaped execution by Sulla because of his connections with the popular party (his aunt was Marius' wife). These connections served him well in his chequered career as a machine politician of doubtful aims; for much of the time he worked with

arrangements were made: Pompey and Crassus were to become consuls for 55 and then to have commands in Spain and the East; Caesar's command was to be extended for five years. During the next two years Caesar became the first Roman general to bridge the Rhine and penetrate the great forests of Germany, and the first to cross the Channel and fight the blue-painted Celts of damp and foggy Britain, who submitted to Caesar for the duration of his visit. Then a series of Gallic revolts began, culminating in a coalition under Vercingetorix that stretched Caesar's resources of manpower and genius to the limit. Vercingetorix was finally besieged and captured at Alesia in 52, and by the end of the following year Gaul had been thoroughly subdued.

THE CIVIL WARS

In the meantime the balance of power within the republic had been upset. Crassus had gone into action against the Parthians, the troublesome semi-nomadic people who had taken over the Iranian and Mesopotamian territories of Persia. Their tactics were unusual – fighting as archers on horseback, leading the enemy on but always staying out of range; and in 53 the over-eager Crassus had fallen into a trap at Carrhae (Harran) and had been killed along with most of his men. Pompey remained at Rome (he was an absentee commander in Spain) and gradually drifted towards the Senatorial party; whether he was motivated more by jealousy of Caesar's military achievements or fear of their consequences must be a matter for speculation. Pompey now became the champion of tradition and legality – belatedly, since he as well as Caesar had acted illegally on numerous occasions. Indeed, respect for the law had never been the same in Rome since the Sullan era, and great men like Pompey and Caesar openly took up illegal consulships or ignored the vetoes of their colleagues, while small men like the infamous Clodius operated as political gangsters and played up to the dole-fed mob which the city population was turning into.

Now, taking a legal but treacherous course, Pompey had his command

Crassus, whose money he needed.

After Pompey's return from the East in 62, the Senate proved reluctant to allot land to his veterans or ratify his Asiatic settlement – understandably so, since both were calculated to maintain Pompey's influence through an extensive network of patronage. Having laid down his military command, Pompey was forced into a new alliance with Crassus; Caesar acted as 'honest broker', thereby achieving near-equality with Pompey and Crassus for the first time. An irresistible combination of political and financial strengths, this alliance – the First Triumvirate – won effective control of the republic: Caesar became consul in 59, used his power to satisfy his partners, and took up a five-year command based on the Roman provinces on either side of the Alps (Cisalpine and Trans-alpine Gaul; Illyricum). As a politician-turned-soldier, the middle-aged Julius Caesar surprised the Roman world by displaying supreme military genius (a phenomenon repeated later by the middle-aged politicians Oliver Cromwell and Leon Trotsky). He rapidly conquered Gaul for the Atlantic to the Rhine, adding vast new territories to the Empire. When the accord between Pompey and Crassus began to show signs of strain, Caesar brought them together at the Conference of Luca, where new

renewed but allowed Caesar to be recalled. Rather than enter Italy powerless against Pompey's forces, Caesar broke the law by bringing his army with him; at the crucial moment, ordering his troops across the Rubicon river dividing Cisalpine Gaul from Italy, Caesar is said to have uttered his famous remark, '*Alea jacta est*' – 'The die is cast'.

The civil wars of the next nineteen years (49-30) ended by destroying the republic. Caesar's advance into Italy took Pompey by surprise, and he only just managed to escape to the East, where he was certain of support. Caesar overran Italy and defeated the Pompeians in Spain before crossing to Greece and facing Pompey himself. His attempt to blockade Dyrrhachium was repulsed, and the situation began to look serious until Pompey unwisely decided to give battle at Pharsalus; though outnumbered, Caesar's veterans were battle-hardened by ten years in Gaul, and they utterly destroyed Pompey's forces. Pompey fled to Egypt, only to be murdered by a reward-hungry soldier as he stepped ashore. Caesar arrived in hot pursuit, became involved in Egyptian politics, and finally placed his mistress, the twenty-one-year-old Cleopatra, in control of the country. After victories in Asia Minor ('Came; saw; conquered') and Africa (as a result of which Cato committed suicide), Caesar came closest to disaster during the last of his battles, at Munda in Spain, where he defeated Pompey's sons and his own sometime lieutenant Labienus (45 BC).

In four years Caesar had conquered the Roman world, intermittently returning to the capital to enact reforms: reducing the burdens of debtors, founding new colonies, limiting the use of slaves in agriculture, introducing the 365-day 'Julian' calendar. He had also accumulated as much power as (legally) the Roman system could confer. Though the republican forms were respected, Caesar went much further than Sulla in self-aggrandisement: he was voted dictator for life, his portrait appeared on Roman coins, and he wore a purple robe and other quasi-royal emblems. Contemporaries seem to have believed that in him Rome finally had found a new and

permanent master, different in kind from men like Marius, Pompey, and even Sulla, who had aimed at 'authority', a preponderant influence in the state based on prestige, wealth and a network of Roman and provincial 'clients'. Caesar himself never touched the formal structure of the republic and in 44 refused the title 'king'; but his style of government was autocratic, and prompted the conspiracy that led to his assassination, at the age of fifty-six, on the Ides of March, 44 BC. One of Caesar's most attractive qualities was his magnanimity: he generally spared captured opponents during the civil war, and often took them into his service. (This much-lauded clemency seems to have applied only to Romans: large numbers of defeated Gauls lost their right hands for resisting Caesar, and Vercingetorix, like Jugurtha and other foes of Rome, was strangled and flung down from the Tarpeian Rock below the Capitol). In the event it was Caesar's virtues, even more than his ambitions, that led to his death: the chief assassins, Brutus and Cassius, were ex-Pompeians whom Casesar had pardoned. Like Alexander the Great, Caesar was preparing for new wars (against the Parthians and Dacians) when he was cut down; if either man had a wider vision, as has often been suggested, it seems to have taken second place to a compulsive delight in making war.

Caesar's death settled nothing: the republic was too far gone. Despite the

Opposite bottom
Pax Augusta: this inscription, on a coin issued by Vespasian, indicates the propaganda value of the 'Augustan peace' brought by imperial rule after the civil wars of late republican times.

Above left
In the hooded garb of the pontifex maximus – religious head of state – Augustus (centre) takes part in a procession with Agrippa, Tiberius, priests and members of the imperial family. Relief from the Ara Pacis, Rome.

Left
The Altar of Peace (Ara Pacis), dedicated to Augustus by the Roman Senate. First century AD.

version of history made familiar by Shakespeare, the Caesarian party made no immediate attempt to avenge their leader's death; at one point Octavian, Caesar's nephew and heir, was actually at war with Mark Antony (Marcus Antonius), his chief lieutenant. Meanwhile the assassins Brutus and Cassius had become unpopular at Rome, and had been assigned by the Senate to relatively insignificant posts at Crete and Cyrene. Only when they acquired control of the East – with senatorial approval – did Antony and Octavian forget their differences. With Lepidus, who controlled parts of Gaul and Spain, they formed the Second Triumvirate in 43. This, unlike the so-called First Triumvirate, was an official group – a five-year, three-man dictatorship, legally sanctioned by the now-subservient Senate. The Triumvirs proscribed and murdered their enemies, including the sixty-three-year-old Cicero, who had prematurely cheered Caesar's assassination and denounced Antony. In 43 Brutus and Cassius were defeated near Philippi (founded, incidentally, by Philip of Macedon as the focal point of his gold-mining operations); both committed suicide. In the consequent division of the Roman world, Octavian took the West; by 36 he had managed to defeat Pompey's son, Sextus Pompeius, who had been holding out in Sicily, and to take Africa from Lepidus. (Lepidus was a lucky loser in a blood-soaked age: he was allowed to withdraw into private life.)

With the elimination of other contenders, Octavian and Antony were probably doomed to fight for the world. Though Antony had married his rival's sister Octavia, he became more and more closely involved with Cleopatra, Queen of Egypt and Caesar's former mistress. Whatever the strength of their personal relations, this famous union had solid political benefits: Egypt was a rich land, plentifully supplied with the grain so badly needed at Rome; and as a Greek, Cleopatra commanded a good deal of loyalty in the Hellenised East – loyalty that the partners tried to exploit by identifying themselves as Dionysus-Osiris and Aphrodite-Isis in a divine Greco-Egyptian syncretism. On the other hand this highly un-Roman policy – emphasised by territorial

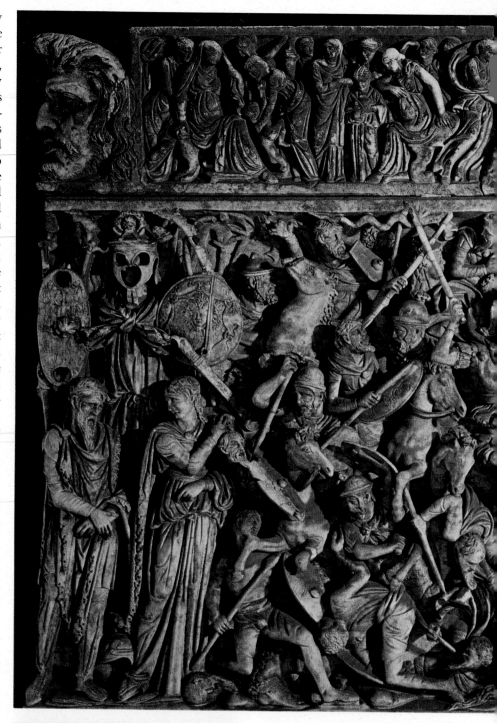

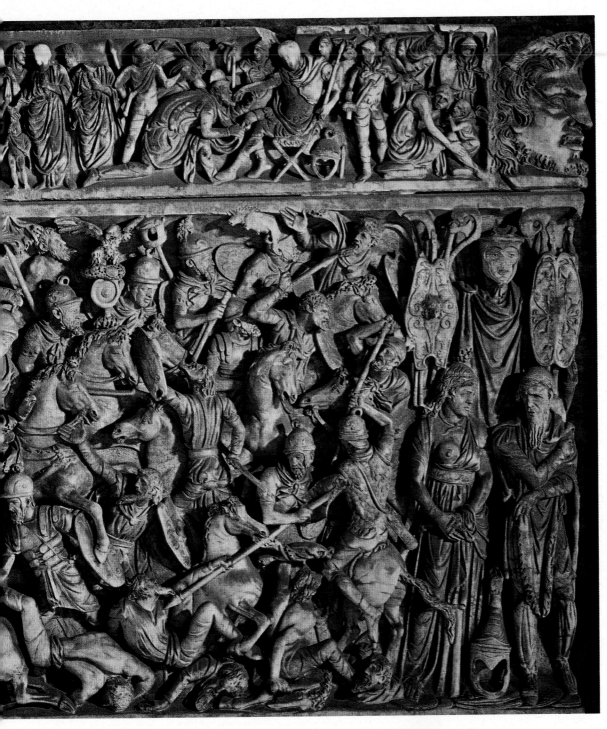

Opposite bottom
Augustan propaganda: coins showing a
barbarian presenting his child to
Augustus, and a kneeling German
surrendering to the Emperor.

Above
Battle between Romans and Germans:
relief from a sarcophagus in the Museo
Nazionale Romano, Rome.

Right
The Roman eagle, symbol of victorious
armies – and, ever since, of imperial
pretensions. Musée du Louvre, Paris.

Opposite
Livia, wife of Augustus. Like her
husband she was eventually deified, and
this figure from Pompeii probably
presided over a domestic cult.

Above
Agrippina, wife of the popular hero
Germanicus (nephew of Tiberius) and
mother of Caligula, who was to become
one of the most infamous of the
emperors. Museo Capitolino, Rome.

ROME: REPUBLIC AND EMPIRE

concessions to Egypt – was bound to alienate Antony's supporters in Italy and the army, and may therefore have cost him his life. When war came at last, in 31, Antony staked everything on a sea battle fought off the promontory of Actium in Greece. Defeated, he fled to Egypt but, deserted by his allies and followers, killed himself on Octavian's approach to Alexandria. Rather than decorate Octavian's triumph, Cleopatra followed Antony's example, allowing a poisonous asp to bite her. Egypt was annexed to the Empire; Octavian's powers were strengthened; some of the legions were disbanded; and the Empire was at last peaceful and united again. The greatest victim of the wars had been the political independence of 'the Roman Senate and People'; and though Romans politely continued to pretend otherwise, the republic was now dead.

AUGUSTUS AND THE EMPIRE

Octavian was probably the wisest and sanest political leader in all Roman history. He had climbed to greatness over the bodies of his opponents, like Sulla and Caesar before him; but once he held power he used it moderately, presenting himself as a traditionalist and capitalising on the universal longing for peace and order after generations of turmoil. He also had a gift often lacking in great leaders – the gift for discovering able and loyal lieutenants. Since he could not be everywhere himself, Octavian employed Gaius Maecenas as his political man-of-all-work and diplomatic troubleshooter; and, no general himself, he found a first-class one in Agrippa, who was mainly responsible for the great naval victories over Sextus Pompeius and Mark Antony.

Having restored order and reformed the state, Octavian formally handed back control to the Senate and People in 27 BC: the Senate would function as before, elected consuls would carry out its wishes, and the people would be represented by their tribunes; Octavian, unofficially *princeps*, 'the chief', was now to be officially distinguished from other citizens as 'Augustus', and given special responsibilities and powers to assist in the ordering of the state. But this restoration of the re-

public was a sham, though perhaps a benificent one that eased an inevitable transition. In reality, Augustus had an overwhelming military force, wealth and prestige that made his word law; and he was becoming the object of religious cults. By accumulating offices he was able with perfect legality to remove recalcitrant senators (the censorship), appoint new members, and prevent trouble-makers from ever reaching the Senate. He was granted a permanent tribunician power (including an absolute veto), so that even the weapons of the popular party were made to serve the new absolutism; and as supreme commander of the armed forces he controlled the provinces in which they were stationed (Spain, Gaul, Syria, Egypt), working through directly appointed legates instead of governors nominated by the Senate. Eventually, he even became pontifex maximus, the religious head of state.

Above
The Emperor Tiberius: early first-century AD statue. Musei Vaticani.

Opposite top left
The Emperor Claudius as the god Jupiter, with laurel wreath and eagle; statue in the Musei Vaticani.

Opposite top right
Head of the Emperor Caligula on a coin. AD 32-38. British Museum, London.

Opposite bottom
Marcus Agrippa, right-hand-man of Octavian (later the Emperor Augustus) and victor over Mark Antony at Actium. Musée du Louvre, Paris.

Augustus' reign was one of harmony between ruler and ruled, in which the question of an appeal to ultimate authority or force scarcely arose; but Augustus is rightly designated not the restorer of the republic but the first Roman emperor.

Augustus brought peace, order and prosperity. A proper civil service was created to run the Empire, giving good government to the provinces as well as Rome. New roads and colonies encouraged industry and commerce. Devolution of authority (albeit mainly in routine matters) breathed fresh life into the cities. And Augustus gradually eliminated the army as a political force by greatly reducing its numbers and distributing it over the frontier provinces; in Italy, the thousand men of the Emperor's own Praetorian Guard constituted the sole military presence. Rome itself was transformed into a worthy capital for universal empire: Augustus boasted that he had found it a city of brick and left it a city of marble. He also left it efficiently supplied with water and food, minimising the risk of political discontent: two hundred thousand people received the free corn dole and were entertained by ever more extravagant public spectacles – the celebrated policy of 'bread and circuses'.

The great foreign conquests under Augustus were of an area roughly corresponding to modern Austria and Hungary, which brought the Roman frontier to the Danube. The Rhine and the Danube were to remain the frontiers in Europe; Augustus' intention to push on to the Elbe was abandoned after AD 9, when three entire legions under the legate Varus were wiped out in the Teutoburg Forest.

Augustus was fortunate even in the literary history of his reign, which produced the poets Virgil and Horace and the historian Livy. All three were generously encouraged by Maecenas (who has become the type of the wealthy patron), possibly with a view to securing politically acceptable sentiments in their works; certainly Virgil's *Aeneid*, the only Latin epic to challenge Homer, is devoted to Aeneas, the 'ancestor' of the Roman people, and culminates in a vision of their imperial

destiny.

Augustus' traditionalist attitude was genuine enough in many respects (though the tradition of liberty was not one of them). He restored religious rites that had been neglected for Greek and Oriental practices, and tried to revive the old Roman virtues. The luxuries of the upper classes were rebuked and legislated against; marriage and paternity were encouraged; and Augustus even exiled his own daughter Julia when he found out about her lurid sex life. Like most such endeavours, this policy showed few positive results. But the most serious of Augustus' family troubles was the succession. He and his wife Livia had no children, though Livia's son by an earlier marriage, Tiberius, became one of the mainstays of the Roman state, both as an administrator and an able and tireless campaigner. The younger men whom Augustus groomed to succeed him died in such abnormal numbers that even in Antiquity there were rumours pointing to Livia as an arch-murderess on Tiberius' behalf; whether they were more than malicious gossip is another matter, despite the ingenuities of Robert Graves's brilliant novel *I, Claudius*. In any event, Augustus was finally compelled to name Tiberius as his successor; when he died in AD 14, there was no serious possibility of a restoration of the republic, though the fifty-six-year-old Tiberius for a time resisted – with real or assumed vigour – the Senate's invitation to carry on the principate. Augustus' apotheosis was a literal one – to be recognised and worshipped as a god, giving his political system the ultimate religious sanction.

Tiberius' reign (AD 14-37) was in most respects a conservative continuation of the Augustan period: the administration of the provinces was, if anything, improved; there was little military activity; and the frontiers remained the same apart from the continuation of a process begun under Augustus, the absorption of the client-kingdoms of Asia Minor and the East. But the disadvantages of an autocracy now began to show themselves. After 23, Tiberius delegated wide powers to Sejanus, the captain of the Praetorian Guard, who perpetrated a large number of judicial murders; and in 26

Above
The consul Romulus gives the signal for the games to begin: ivory carving of a provincial – probably North African – scene.

Opposite top
The Arch of Titus, at the entrance to the Roman Forum.

Opposite bottom
Roman troops sacking Jerusalem (AD 70); they are carrying off the seven-branched candelabrum from the Temple.
Relief from the Arch of Titus in Rome.

Opposite bottom
Roman silver cup of the first
century AD. British Museum, London

Opposite top
The central area of the Roman Forum
seen from the west, with the Colosseum
in the background.

Above
Head of the Emperor Nero, in the
Museo Nazionale Romano, Rome.

Right
Coin with image of the Emperor
Vespasian, characteristically tough and
middle-aged. AD 71. British Museum,
London.

Above
Asphyxiated victims of the eruption of Mount Vesuvius which destroyed Pompeii and Herculaneum at the beginning of Titus' reign: plaster casts of a dog and a man.

Above right
The Emperor Domitian; antique statue in the Musei Vaticani.

Opposite
Domitian greeting his father, the Emperor Vespasian (centre); marble panel. Musei Vaticani.

Tiberius retired permanently to Capri. On Capri he is said to have indulged in infamous orgies; but since the stories, like many accounts of subsequent emperors, emanate from writers of a sentimental-republican outlook, their authenticity is dubious. His residence on Capri, and his feeble reaction to the string of treason trials that disfigured his reign, are just as likely to have been the result of old age (he was sixty-eight in 26). To what extent Sejanus' plotting or Tiberius' fears were responsible for the executions of Agrippina, his deceased brother's wife, and two of her children (his heirs) is now impossible to judge; certainly Tiberius could still act decisively when he felt threatened, as he showed by summarily executing Sejanus in 31.

All these doubts disappear in the case of Tiberius' successor Gaius, nicknamed Caligula ('Little Boot'): he was insane, arbitrary and cruel; and the 'republican' institutions of Rome were helpless to restrain him. The principate was revealed for the despotism it was, with the inescapable weakness of all despotisms – that the benevolence of the despot (let alone his intelligence or sanity) can never be guaranteed.

Caligula was murdered in 41, after a four-year reign of terror. His successor was – ominously – the choice of the Praetorians, though as Caligula's uncle he was also next in line for the succession if the principate could now be regarded as a monarchy. The view that Claudius was simple-minded – current even in Antiquity – hardly fits the facts. He clearly suffered from some kind of impediment or handicap

that made a public career impossible under Augustus and Tiberius; people in Antiquity were even quicker to mock a twitch, a stammer or a limp than they are now. On the other hand, Claudius' physical eccentricity may well have saved his life during the period when Tiberius and Caligula were jealously cutting down their better-endowed relations; and it has been suggested that Claudius was shrewd enough to exaggerate his disabilities in order to be passed over as harmless.

Certainly Claudius' reign was fairly successful, and there seems no reason to deprive him of the credit for its achievements. Though no soldier himself, Claudius was generous in recognising good service, including that of Aulus Plautius, conqueror of Britain;

the invasion of this island at the end of the world took place in 43, and Claudius arrived in time to be present at the storming of Colchester. Eventually the 'lowland zone' of Britain – roughly modern England – was conquered and Romanised, while the highland areas (Scotland and Wales) remained strongholds of the Celtic way of life.

In the Empire, Claudius encouraged the extension of Roman citizenship, mainly through the foundation of colonies and the admission of Gallic nobles to the Roman Senate. The civil service was improved by Claudius' practice of employing freedmen, though other Romans deplored their excessive influence: between them, Claudius' freedmen and his wives ruled him, if ancient authors are to be

believed. The charge has a certain credibility. Even after the spectacular sex crimes of his young wife Messalina were revealed and paid for with her life, Claudius married again when he was almost sixty; his new wife, Agrippina, then persuaded him to adopt her son Nero as his heir; and four years later Claudius died – conveniently, since Nero at seventeen was still young enough to let himself be ruled by his mother. Rumour had it that the uxorious Claudius expired after partaking from a wifely dish of poisoned mushrooms. After his death, Claudius was deified; Nero, in a flash of black humour, is said to have called mushrooms 'the food of the gods'.

Nero, if not quite mad, proved impossible to restrain. After a deceptively

Left
The Emperor Trajan: bust in the Museo Capitolino, Rome.

Far left
The Arch of Trajan at Benevento.

Above
Roman troops besieged by Dacians: scene from Trajan's Column, Rome.

Opposite
Statue of Trajan at Ostia.

quiet start, he did away with his heir (Claudius' teenage son), his overweening mother, and an unwanted wife. Treason trials were revived to raise money from the victims' estates; and when this led to the formation of a genuine conspiracy, its discovery set Nero off on a paranoid round of executions in which any popular soldier or administrator was likely to fall. The disastrous fire which destroyed part of Rome in 64 has been blamed on Nero: possibly unjustly, although instead of replacing the destroyed tenements and temples he erected a vast palace-complex, the Golden House (Domus Aurea), on the spot. That he 'fiddled while Rome burned' (i.e. sang *The Fall of Ilium*, accompanying himself on the lyre) may only be gossip but is absolutely in character: Nero had a mania for art, and went in for extremes of temperament and self-dramatisation. He shocked the Romans by making public appearances on the stage, and preferred to spend his time in Greece, where he carried off a string of prizes as a lyrist and charioteer. The judges were presumably biased – as biased as the historian Suetonius undoubtedly was in the opposite direction: during Nero's performances, says Suetonius, no one was permitted to leave the theatre; women gave birth there, and men dying of boredom shammed dead in earnest so that they would be carried outside.

The performance had to end. Gaul, Spain and Africa rose against Nero, who could think of no remedy except singing them into submission; the Praetorians deserted him; and after an ineffective flight he killed himself in June 68.

COLLAPSE AND RECOVERY

The scandalous doings of the Caesars (which have probably been exaggerated) had little impact on the provinces. The political classes at Rome were sometimes thinned, but the Empire was prosperous, well governed and at peace. The *pax Romana* (Roman peace) was one of the indisputable, widely appreciated benefits of subjugation; an outbreak such as the savage revolt of the Iceni under Boudicca (Boadicea) was unlikely except in a recently conquered province

emperor's, and re-introduced the Empire to the miseries of civil war. First Galba, governor of one of the Spanish provinces, was raised to the purple, only to be murdered and replaced by his colleague Otho. The Rhine army marched on behalf of Vitellius, and the deserted Otho killed himself. Finally the Eastern legions proclaimed Vespasian, a tough commander engaged in suppressing the Jewish rebellion, and his forces overcame and killed Vitellius. This sequence of blood-lettings showed the danger of allowing the army back into politics. It also confirmed that the republic was beyond revival, even when the emperors no long possessed a drop of Julian blood. And outbreaks of local and tribal particularism in Gaul and on the Rhine indicated that the stability of the Empire itself might be at risk as soon as the central power faltered. Fortunately Vespasian was the strong, sane leader the state needed. Being of relatively humble birth, he adopted the pose of a plain, blunt man while taking a conciliatory line with the Senate; but he left them in no doubt that his family, the Flavians, constituted a new dynasty. The army was carefully controlled, Vespasian's son Titus became captain of the Praetorian Guard, civic privileges and membership of the Senate were extended, and the taxes which weaker emperors had remitted to win themselves short-lived popularity were rigorously collected. In 70 Titus ended the Jewish revolt by destroying Jerusalem and the Temple; to this day no Jew is supposed to pass under the Arch of Titus built to celebrate his victory. Vespasian died in 79 and was immediately deified; he evidently foresaw it, since he is said to have made a final deathbed joke: 'Damn it–I can feel myself turning into a god.'

The brief reign of Titus (79-81) was notable for the completion of the Colosseum and the eruption of Vesuvius which smothered the seaside resorts of Pompeii and Herculaneum in the Bay of Naples; layers of ash and pumice choked the citizens and buried the towns, preserving a pitiable but fascinating record of the Roman way of life. Titus was succeeded by his brother Domitian, who governed well

Opposite
Trajan's Column in Rome, with spiralling bronze reliefs commemorating the Emperor's victorious campaigns.

Above
Interior of the Pantheon, Rome.

such as Britain. But the events following the death of Nero affected wide areas of the Empire.

Nero was the last of the Julio-Claudians – the dynasty formed by the combination of the Julian family (Caesar and Augustus) with the Claudians (Tiberius). There was now no obvious heir and the throne was at the disposal of the Praetorian Guard – or of the legions in the provinces, who entered politics for the first time. AD 69 was 'the year of the four

for a few years before he gave way to fears for his own safety (probably not wholly unjustified) and started another epidemic of treason trials. Eventually, when no one could feel safe, even Domitian's wife turned against him and joined a group of conspirators who successfully assassinated him.

THE AGE OF THE ANTONINES

Domitian was the last of the Flavians, but on this occasion the transition from one dynasty to the next was managed without an interval of chaos. The Senate nominated Nerva, an elderly member of the order, and he was shrewd enough to adopt the experienced general Trajan as his son and successor. Nerva's motive was probably to hold the army, and particularly the Praetorian Guard, in check; but the adoption brought such obviously good results that it became a

custom, followed by Trajan and his successors. The Antonines – a dynasty linked by ability, not blood – gave the Empire the most efficient and humane government it had ever had.

Nerva's reign was brief (96-98), but Trajan's was long and energetic (98-117). Despite his Spanish birth, he was a ruler very much to the Roman taste, conquering a large new, mineral-rich province north of the Danube (Dacia), winning splendid victories in the East, and embarking on an ambitious building programme of which Trajan's Column is the most impressive surviving monument. The Senate gave Trajan the official title 'Optimus Princeps' – 'Best of Leaders'.

Hadrian (117-138) may have harboured a different opinion, since his policy makes it obvious that he believed the Empire was dangerously over-extended. He gave up Trajan's

Opposite
The Emperor Hadrian, who travelled all over the empire. This larger-than-life-size bronze head was rescued from the River Thames, where it must have been dumped after being hacked from the body, perhaps during the fifth-century collapse of Roman Britain. Second century AD. British Museum, London.

Above
Hadrian's Wall, spanning Roman Britain from the Solway to the Tyne, was built to contain the fierce Caledonian tribesmen to the north.

conquests beyond the Euphrates and spent most of his reign touring the Empire, supervising provincial administrators, overhauling the armies and tirelessly strengthening fortifications and recruiting on the frontiers. One familiar result of this activity was 'Hadrian's Wall' in northern Britain, a defensive structure which ran for 117 kilometres across the narrow neck of land between the Solway and the Tyne; forts and signalling turrets positioned all along the wall were intended to make impossible a successful surprise attack by the Celts of the far north. As increasingly happened on the frontiers, defence was no longer the business of the legions but of auxiliaries often locally recruited.

Though his policies were essentially defensive, Hadrian was popular with the army and provincials because energetic and omnipresent; the most serious internal disturbance during his reign was the Jewish revolt of 131-135, provoked by his plan to build a new city, with a temple dedicated to Jupiter, on the site of Jerusalem. In Italy his buildings included the Pantheon and his mausoleum (now the Castel Sant' Angelo) at Rome, and a magnificent villa at the popular resort of Tibur (modern Tivoli).

After Hadrian's death, the Senate was slow – perhaps even reluctant – to deify him. Hadrian's nominee for the succession, Antonius, threatened to refuse the purple unless they acted – a 'filial' stance that earned him the name Antoninus Pius. The fact that the Senate gave way is an interesting illustration of the extent to which emperors now seemed indispensable, even in the eyes of the one-time law-givers of the republic. In the heart of the Empire the reign of Antoninus Pius (138-161) was blissfully uneventful, and later generations looked back on it as a golden age. Troublesome outbreaks on the fringes (Africa, the East, the Danube, Britain) were easily contained, and in Britain the frontier was even advanced to the Forth-Clyde line with the building of the Antonine Wall. But Antoninus' successor Marcus Aurelius (161-180) was less fortunate: most of his reign was spent with the armies in the East or in the Danube area. On his accession Marcus chose a co-Emperor, Lucius Verus, who repelled the Par-

thians while Marcus fought the Marcomanni and the Quadi, fierce German tribes who had poured across the Danube and even penetrated northern Italy. This division of imperial functions was the first indication that the Empire might be too big for one man to run successfully in any but the most favourable circumstances; however, Verus died in 169, and for the moment the experiment was discontinued. Meanwhile, his victorious army brought back from the East a plague that swept through the Empire and must have seriously damaged its population, economy and morale. After several years of hard campaigning

Above
Propitiatory sacrifice at a Dalmatian city: scene from Trajan's Column, Rome.

Opposite top
Barbarian ambassadors being received by Trajan: scene from Trajan's Column, Rome.

Opposite bottom
Soldiers unloading a boat: scene from Trajan's Column, Rome.

(interrupted by a revolt in Syria and other worries), Marcus defeated the Germanic tribes, but his death prevented him from adding their territories to the Empire. Marcus' warlike career was unwillingly embraced: paradoxically, he was the only philosopher-emperor — a convinced Stoic whose notebook, published as his *Meditations,* remains a classic account of the mind striving to reconcile itself to the conditions of existence. But his philosophy did not prevent him from violating the Antonine principle of selecting the best man for the job: instead, he chose his son Commodus, who might conceivably have been the worst man. Even less admirable than Nero, Commodus was obsessed with gladitorial displays and himself fought regularly in the arena. Though peace was maintained in the Empire, life at Rome reverted to a pattern of treason trials engendering conspiracies which engendered treason trials – until Commodus was strangled by an athlete hired for the purpose by his own inner circle.

'If a man were called to fix the period in the history of the world, during which the condition of the human race was most happy and prosperous, he would, without hesitation, name that which elapsed from the death of Domitian to the accession of Commodus.' So writes Edward Gibbon, author of the monumental *Decline and Fall of the Roman Empire,*

published between 1776 and 1788. There is still much to be said in favour of his opinion, provided 'the human race' is assumed to exclude slaves and barbarians. Whatever happened on the frontiers, most of the Empire was at peace. Towns flourished and generous civic amenities existed. An efficient system of roads drew the provinces together. Agriculture and industry prospered everywhere. Taxation was light. The number of citizens had been greatly increased throughout the Empire, and the admission of provincials to the Senate had made it far more representative. The civil service was staffed by the senatorial and equestrian classes, whose career opportunities reconciled them to the loss of their old political and judicial functions. And there was even a cultural revival – notably a 'silver age' of literature, not quite comparable with the Augustan golden age but still able to nurture such figures as the poets Juvenal and Martial, the romance-writer Apuleius, the historians Tacitus and Suetonius, the elegant letter-writer Pliny, and Greek authors like the biographer Plutarch and the satirist Lucian of Samosata.

Gibbon names one flaw in the Antonine scheme of things: 'the instability of a happiness which depended on the character of a single man'. But there were others too, less obvious, which came to light as soon as the 'single man' lost his power or his

sanity. Despite state assistance, the Italian smallholders were being driven to the wall by the large slave-operated estates. The flourishing municipalities were losing all power of initiative, compelling the imperial government to take more and more decisions and develop an increasingly large (and potentially rigid and inefficient) bureaucracy. The use of local troops to defend the frontiers risked the development of particularism as soon as the central authority's grip slackened; and the employment of barbarian auxiliaries settled within the frontier — begun by Marcus Aurelius – was potentially even more disastrous.

The political weaknesses rapidly became actual with the madness and death of Commodus. The Age of the Antonines ended, and the Roman Empire plunged into a crisis more serious than any it had known before.

Above
Roman amphitheatre at El Djem in Tunisia, modelled on the Colosseum at Rome.

Opposite top
View of Baalbek, a Roman city in the Lebanon.

Opposite bottom
Roman cavalry attacking Sarmatian warriors: scene from Trajan's Column, Rome.

Life in Ancient Rome

A single chapter is too little for this subject: there is no satisfactory way to encapsulate the life experience of an empire such as Rome's, far-flung over space and time; so what follows is really a series of snap-shots, freezing a restricted number of people in set attitudes at a particular time and place. The generalisations made here are true of Italy rather than the provinces, the town rather than the country, the vocal upper classes rather than the poor; and though some of the most important changes are noted, the descriptions are mainly drawn from the imperial period, which has provided the most abundant records.

City life

Rome, a world capital with a million inhabitants, was different in many ways from Classical Athens and other Greek city-states; she had more in common with the great Hellenistic centres such as Alexandria, which did in fact become the second city of the Empire after the annexation of Egypt. But Rome, like Alexandria, was equipped with the main city-state institutions: her Capitol was an acropolis and her Forum an agora; the Senate and the popular assembly were equivalents to the Council and assembly (though in Greek cities and periods when real power resided in the Council rather than the assembly). Temples, baths, gymnasia and theatres emphasised the similarity in terms of public building, though the Romans added a number of new features – the circus for chariot racing, the amphitheatre for gladiatorial displays and massacres of men and beasts, triumphal arches and columns. Thanks to the might of Rome, this basically Greek pattern was repeated in cities all over the western Mediterranean and northwest Europe from Africa to Britain; the eastern Mediterranean was of course already Greek in its urban culture. Most of these cities, unlike old Rome (or old Athens), benefited from the Hellenistic art of town planning, with its characteristic grid-pattern of straight streets and regular right-angled blocks of buildings.

Roman planning extended even further. The wealth of the empire was employed to provide amenities unknown to the Athenians, whose splendid public buildings rose above squalidly unhygienic streets. The Romans paved their streets, organised convenient water supplies, and constructed efficient sewers, public baths and lavatories. At Rome itself, the sheer size of the population led to the erection of *insulae* ('islands'), great apartment blocks that increasingly outnumbered private houses on the courtyard plan. Most *insulae* seem to have been warren-like tenements, crammed with the dole-fed poor and liable to collapse or catch fire, though some are said to have been designed for 'middle-class' residents. Indoors, appearances in the ordinary house were much the same as among the Greeks. Rooms were larger and details of decoration – metalwork, inlays and the like – richer, but the general effect must still have been one of spaciousness and simplicity, with very little furniture. The Romans too had wall paintings and hangings, and they also made far greater use of mosaics; these patterns and pictures made from small pieces of coloured stone were specially favoured for cool and permanent decorative floors. Just how colourful a Roman room could be is revealed by the interiors excavated at Pompeii, with their bold red-and-black effects, mythological scenes and eye-deceiving paintings of windows with buildings 'outside'. When it was cold, slaves in a wealthy household lit the furnaces under the floors, which caused warm air to circulate through the specially designed spaces between the walls of the house: central heating, one of the most ingenious of Roman inventions, made existence tolerable during the short, sharp Mediterranean winters, and may well have been essential in spreading the Roman way of life to the chillier lands beyond the Alps and the Danube.

Dining customs were much the same as in Classical Greece, the main meal being taken in the cool of the evening, lying on a couch, preferably in the company of friends; following Hellenistic custom, the Romans eventually began to admit women to their more genteel banquets, and with their growing freedom they sometimes misbehaved as badly as the men. By imperial times an astonishing range of food was available, including such delicacies as peacocks' and larks' tongues and stuffed dormice. The general impression that the Romans had less taste and restraint than the Greeks may

Opposite
Slaves working a treadmill to hoist a sepulchral column by a crane. Fragment from a funerary monument, first century BC. Musei Vaticani.

Opposite bottom right
A street of shop-fronts at Ostia, with windows on the first floor and balconies above them.

Opposite bottom left
Shops and apartments in the backstreets of twentieth-century Rome – essentially unchanged since ancient times.

Opposite top
The metropolitan splendour of ancient Rome is still apparent in the ruins of the Forum.

Above
Street in Pompeii with stepping stones, so that pedestrians could remain clean and dry when crossing.

Right
Roman houses: relief showing a village. Museo Torlonia, Avezzano.

CAVE CANEM

be wrong; Hellenistic society had become notably luxury-loving while the Romans were still plain fighting farmers. The most famous description of a banquet is given in a novel, the *Satyricon,* by Petronius Arbiter, who may well be the 'arbiter of taste' employed to supervise the Emperor Nero's diversions (until, inevitably, he fell under suspicion and was compelled to take his own life). The banquet is given by the wealthy ex-slave Trimalchio, and is a wild exhibition of tasteless *nouveau-riche* extravagance, culminating in a maudlin display by Trimalchio himself, who shows off his wealth, vulgarity and ignorance in about equal parts. Perhaps the Neronian period was more gluttonous than some others: for another contemporary, the philosopher Seneca, hits off the most repulsive of Roman gourmandising habits when describing people who 'ate to vomit and vomited to eat'. There is no reason to suppose most Romans were like this, and some of the more high-minded consciously copied the intellectual orientation of the Greek symposium.

Such entertainments were still home-based (though 'home' might be a palace); 'eating out' in the modern sense hardly existed, except at inns used by travellers. Where the standard of home fare was inadequate for a particular entertainment, a man could hire a cook for the night. But as the excavated streets of Pompeii have

Left
Lantern, lamps and weights from Herculaneum.

Far left
An elaborately decorated metal stove from Pompeii. Museo Nazionale, Naples.

Above left
'Beware of the dog' is the inscription on this mosaic, placed in the entrance of a Pompeian house.

Opposite
Buying and selling is energetic in this relief of a shop. Scavi di Ostia.

shown, whole rows of eating-houses and bars existed which catered mainly for a lower-class clientèle.

In wining and dining, as in most things, the Romanised upper class in the provinces copied big-city ways as far as they could, but with local variations; Britons and Gauls, for example, scooped up their delicacies with pieces of bread which they then discarded, in approved Roman fashion, on the mosaic floor; but they were as likely to become tipsy on beer as on wine before they tottered into a litter and let themselves be carried home by their slaves.

For the Roman, as for the Greek, ordinary dress consisted of tunics, mantles and poncho-like cloaks: cut was less important than quality of material, colour and accompanying ornamentation in distinguishing rich from poor and fashionable from frumpish. The most distinctive item of clothing was the toga, a voluminous garment of fine wool worn by male citizens on formal occasions. Draped over one arm, it was evidently tiring and difficult to keep under control, hot, and perhaps scratchy; at any rate, one emperor after another felt compelled to insist that it must be worn at public ceremonies, which implies a degree of public reluctance. There were various types of toga including a grey one for mourning; boys wore the purple-hemmed *toga praetexta* until they could assume the adult's plain *toga virilis;* while various stripes and colours on togas (and, for that matter, shoes) distinguished senators, equites and magistrates. Footwear became more specialised, and cobblers turned out sandals, slippers, fancy town shoes, and boots for heavy work and soldiering. A girl wore an under-tunic, tunic and shawl; when she married she replaced the tunic with the longer and fuller *stola,* decorated only with coloured hems. Though the Roman public style kept up the tradition of sobriety, both men and women dressed more brightly at banquets.

Beauty aids, scents and jewellery were even more abundant by imperial times than they had been earlier in the Greek East; and they were used to a greater or lesser extent by both men and women. Greek craftsmen probably made the finest jewellery, repaid with a characteristically Roman mixture of contempt and envy for their cunning art. One important way in which a Roman woman could appear beautiful and distinctive, while at the same time advertising her wealth, was by adopting an elaborate coiffure: the range of hair styles was such that it left little scope for future invention, and some of the more elaborate must have been triumphs of leisured immobility and the art of the slave-girl-with-curling-tongs. Men too had increasing recourse to the barber in imperial times, though a sterner age had contented itself with a pudding-basin cut and straight combing. Julius Caesar was an early dandy, though forced in middle age to conceal his baldness beneath the victor's laurel wreath. Hair-consciousness was still more intense by the time of Hadrian, who made a mop of curly hair *de rigeur* for the would-be-fashionables of all ages. During the same period beards began to be worn again. Alexander the Great had been clean-shaven, and most Greeks imitated him, though conservatives and back-to-nature philosophers remained obstinately hirsute. Appropriately enough, the Roman most often compared with Alexander – Scipio Africanus, the conqueror of Hannibal – introduced the new fashion to Rome, and by the first century BC it was becoming the norm: Sulla, Cicero, Caesar, Augustus and other men of the late republic – men whose images are perhaps the best-known of Antiquity – were all clean-shaven. Since soap was unknown and iron blades were not very sharp, shaving must have been a painful business even in the hands of experts: nobody shaved himself, and a barber who acquired the reputation of being a smooth worker could make his fortune. The persistence of this fashion suggests that it fulfilled some psychological function, perhaps expressing the sharp-edged nature of ambitious men in a dangerous age. Hadrian is said to have gone against custom by growing a beard to cover a scar; but it is tempting

Above
A luxurious interior with lavish mosaic decoration: the House of Neptune at Herculaneum.

Opposite
Inside the Roman house: a simply furnished but elegant and colourful environment. Villa at Boscoreale in the Bay of Naples.

to believe that the double change he initiated (curly hair and full beard) also corresponded to some change in sensibility, possibly one favouring a more 'romantic' appearance in an otherwise rather staid age.

The family and Roman values

In early Republican times the family, religion and the state were parts of a nexus of feelings and attitudes of peculiar intensity; the values they enshrined can be summarised as *pietas* and *fides,* which translate rather feebly into words such as 'piety' (or 'duty') and 'faith', which have lost much of their old force in English. The household was at the centre of life in a way it never was for the Greeks (or at least the articulate, urban Greeks we know about); and for a farmer-hero such as Cincinnatus it was the small kingdom from which he briefly emerged to rule Rome itself. The oldest male had *patria potestas* – supreme authority over the lives and property of his family. His wife, like all women, was regarded as immutably child-like, and therefore to be kept in lifelong subjection: she passed straight from her father's authority to her husband's, and when he died she could be commanded by her son; her only possible protector was a male relative from her own family, who could be appointed as her legal guardian, empowered to fight the husband for her dowry if he put her away. (In very early times a husband could put his wife away without any shadow of excuse, but this was such an unsatisfactory arrangement that even in the third century BC he was obliged to prove that she had committed some serious offence.) By contrast, a son could hope one day to become a *pater familias* himself, though in the meantime he remained in leading-strings even when he had become the grey-bearded father of a family. A *pater familias* could kill his son, sell him into slavery, or formally expel him from the family. Such actions must always have been rare – and probably unthinkable in most families – but they reinforced the harsh father's authority mightily. The stern rectitude to which Romans aspired is exemplified by the legend of Junius Brutus (not the assassin of Caesar), who is said to have led the revolt that drove the last king from Rome, and to have ordered the execution of his own sons when they were discovered plotting with the Etruscans. In historical times, stern rectitude was exemplified by Cato the Elder, whom we have already met demanding the destruction of a near-helpless Carthage. His puritanism was almost a mania: discipline was rigid in the home, and shows of affection were forbidden; even when holding high office Cato dressed simply, went about on foot and dispensed with retinue and display; he argued for the perpetuation of wartime austerity measures that prevented women from wearing embroidered clothes or driving in carriages within the city; and when, as censor, he was able to purge the Senate, he expelled one member for kissing his wife in public. As censor he also taxed luxury goods and works of art; for above all else he detested the Greek culture and Greco-Eastern refinements of life that were beginning to captivate Roman society. Cato was fighting a losing battle, and his contemporaries' admiration for his unyielding virtue was strongly tinged with hypocrisy – 'the tribute vice pays to virtue'. Both his puritanism and his (to our eyes) more positive qualities – his sense of justice and his incorruptible behaviour in the public service – were increasingly praised rather than copied.

The breakdown of the old Roman

traditions in public life has already been described in the previous chapter. Inside the family a similar change occurred, in this case bringing greater freedom for women and, as far as it is possible to judge, a greater warmth of affection between husband and wife and parents and children. The form of marriage in which the wife had a relative-guardian became universal, while at the same time the guardianship became increasingly perfunctory; so that by the second century AD the wife was a free partner in the marriage, able to keep an eye on her own property and to will it to whomsoever she pleased. Partners were also more or less freely chosen by this period, or at least consented to; among the upper classes 'suitability' and property alliances continued to influence choices, as they have in periods committed to far more romantic conceptions of married love. In both republican and later times, any possibility of female independence must have been restricted by the early age at which girls married – between about twelve and fifteen years old; except in the most sophisticated circles, the majority must have been trained into docility and circumscribed by motherhood before they

became adults. On the other hand, even a very young girl among the better-off became the mistress of a household on marriage, and rapidly learned responsibility or autocratic caprice.

There were certainly plenty of formidable women in Antiquity: in legend, Veturia and Volumnia, mother and wife of the disaffected Roman general Coriolanus, whom they persuaded to give up his planned assault on Rome at the cost of his life; in real-life adversity, Paulina, youthful wife of the philosopher Seneca, who insisted on sharing her husband's (imperially enforced) suicide; in high politics Livia, wife of Augustus, widely believed to be his political partner in governing the Empire; and many others. Not too much need be made of this, since there have been strong-minded and noble women in all sorts of societies, however repressive. More convincing evidence is provided by inscriptions and literary references, which indicate that a loving spouse was increasingly counted as one of life's treasures. Pliny the Younger, a highly successful advocate and imperial administrator of the early Antonine period, appears in his letters as a devoted husband,

Opposite left
The rural simplicity from which Rome sprang: shepherd milking a goat. Relief from a sarcophagus in the Museo Nazionale Romano, Rome.

Opposite right
Elegantly coiffeured lady of the Flavian period: the sculptor has performed a virtuoso feat in rendering the tight curls in marble. Museo Capitolino, Rome.

Above left
Bronze head, perhaps of the goddess Diana or the Jewish princess Berenice; with an appropriately un-Roman hairstyle. Found at Herculaneum.

Above
The Thermopolium, a Pompeian bar that served hot and cold drinks.

221

Left
Wall painting from Nero's palace at Rome, the House of Gold; as so often the painting is an illusionistic 'window' looking out at the exterior of a building.

Above
Ploughing the first furrow. Relief: Museo Archeologico, Aquilea.

Opposite top
Harvesting and treading grapes. Fourth century AD. Vault mosaic from the church of Santa Costanza in Rome.

Opposite bottom
Bride at her toilet. Wall painting from Pompeii. Museo Archeologico Nazionale, Naples.

delighted by his wife Calpurnia's interest in his literary productions and missing her (haunting her bedroom) during her absence. Since Pliny published his own letters, arranged in self-consciously artistic selections, his sincerity can be questioned; but it is evident that he expected his readers to warm to a picture of a marriage based on affection and shared interests. The difference in attitudes between the age of Pliny and the age of Cato is wide and unarguable.

Another aspect of the new freedom was easy divorce. In imperial times, this again became possible for men without the excuse of a serious offence on the wife's part; and under the 'modern' form of marriage, women too could put away their husbands and come away none the worse (though the practical difficulties probably remained greater for them unless they were heiresses). Among the outrageous examples – though hardly unparalleled in our own society – was that of Cicero, who divorced his wife of thirty years to wed a rich young girl. Augustus too, though he later set himself up as a moral reformer, divorced his own wife *and* arranged the divorce of nineteen-year-old Livia (pregnant with her second child by Tiberius Nero) so that he could marry her. This must have been a love match (at least on Augustus' side), but generally speaking the many marriages and divorces of men like Sulla, Caesar and Pompey were politically motivated; and later on, according to Martial and other satirists, high-society people changed partners so often that marriage was no more than legalised adultery. It seems unlikely that divorce was so common among other classes; no doubt it offered much the same pros and cons as it does today.

The sexual availability of slaves must have put a considerable strain on many marriages, though we hear little of the subject. The impression is that female sexuality was not quite respectable, though occasional suggestions that wives should be grateful if their husbands turned their carnal attentions elsewhere smack of wishful thinking (unless we suppose that Roman husbands made their wives frigid by a Victorian combination of brutality and incompetence). As in most societies, sexual attitudes were so contradictory and fluctuating that it is hard to make any meaningful statements about them. This applies equally to homosexuality, which was formally less acceptable than in Greece, yet was often casually referred to in a way that implies complete tolerance. The law prohibited it between citizens (which presumably meant that what was done to slaves was a purely private matter); yet moralists of the second century BC vociferously blamed Greek influence for its prevalence at Rome (between citizens?). Augustus tried to revive the prohibition, yet his poets sang happily of the pleasures offered by boys and girls without insisting on distinctions; whether this was a mere poetic convention – a graceful tribute to the Greek lyric – is unclear. The most famous homosexual relationship in Antiquity was between the Emperor Hadrian and an exceptionally beautiful young man called Antinous, who was the Emperor's favourite for nine years. When he was drowned on a journey up the Nile in Hadrian's company, the Emperor's grief was so intense that his subjects diplomatically joined in: statues of the dead youth were put up all over the Empire, and some cities even deified him; while Hadrian himself founded the Egyptian city of Antinöopolis in his memory.

An even more mysterious fact is the decline in the birth-rate, at least of the upper classes, from the late republican era. Neither Caesar nor Augustus had a male heir, though they married five times between them; and the infertility of the Antonines, though beneficial to

Above
The Aldobrandini Wedding. Detail of a
first-century BC wall painting after a
Greek original. Museii Vaticani.

Right
A Roman married couple. Wall
painting. Museo Nazionale, Naples.

Opposite
Antinous, the Emperor Hadrian's
favourite and, after his death, the object
of a religious cult. Marble statue, second
century AD. Museo Nazionale, Naples.

the state, is not likely to have been deliberate. The old patrician families, having survived for centuries, died out in an astonishingly short time; and the number of freedmen (i.e. ex-slaves) who inherited their former masters' property proves that the phenomenon was a socially significant one. Augustus certainly thought so, since he introduced legislation to combat it, penalising bachelorhood, requiring widows to remarry, and conferring privileges on families with more than three children; but his measures seem to have had little effect. As so often in demographic matters, all the obvious explanations (frivolity, for example, combined with contraception and/or abortion) are impossible or incredible; the mystery remains.

The children who did arrive were better – or more affectionately – looked after. Infanticide by exposure had been practised by the early Romans (as, earlier still, by the Greeks) to dispatch weak, deformed or unwanted children. This extreme example of the *patria potestas* became immoral and finally illegal under the Empire, though the very poor no doubt continued to abandon offspring they could not support; occasional gestures were even made by the emperors towards the upkeep of poor children in Rome. Infant mortality was appallingly high, and in the more humane atmosphere that prevailed from late republican times, monumental and literary laments for dead children multiplied; even Martial, most savage and foul-mouthed of satirists, mourned the little six-year-old slave girl Erotion in verses touchingly reproachful of a criminal Destiny. The declining birth-rate may have encouraged parents to feel that their offspring were precious; at any rate they became far more affectionate and indulgent. Stories about spoiled children began to circulate, though here, as in the case of women, there is no reason to believe that greater freedom and affection led to wide-spread depravity.

EDUCATION AND CULTURE

The earliest Roman education was supplied by the parents themselves, even in the upper classes. As in so many things, Cato the Elder followed the old customs when others were abandoning

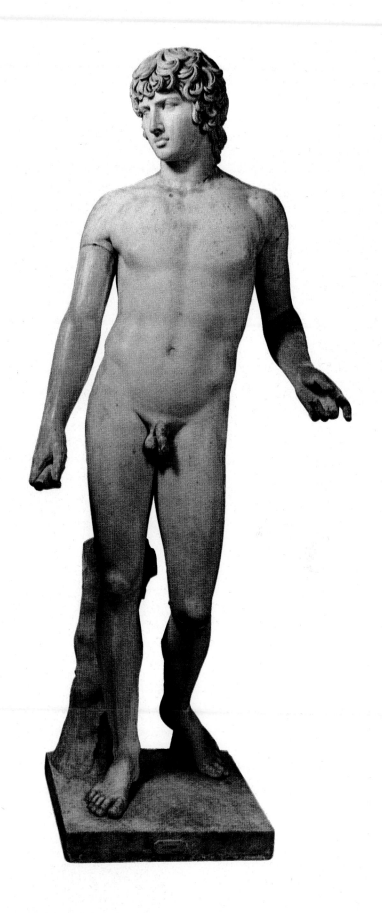

or modifying them: he supervised his son's bath night, taught him to read and write, and personally took the boy through a gruelling course of physical training that seems to have enfeebled him for life. Other parents were already entrusting their children to a *paedogogus,* who taught them the elements or took them to school, just as he did in Greece. All schools were fee-paying, but quite a large number of children seem to have gone through the primary stage and acquired basic literacy; for example, most surviving grafitti are clearly the work of ordinary men. Elementary schoolteachers were low in status and often found it hard to make ends meet; many of them took second jobs. School began at dawn and carried on till noon. Evidently not everybody got up so early: Martial complains that a local teacher wakes the poet and his neighbours, making it impossible to sleep through his bellowings and beatings. An advocate of 'progressive' education appeared in Martial's contemporary and fellow-Spaniard Quintilian, a successful advocate whose book on the training of orators soundly condemns corporal punishment and argues that better results are obtained by making lessons enjoyable and providing incentives for the pupil such as prizes and praises. However, Martial's version is probably closer to the reality of Roman teaching.

Only a small minority of boys went on to secondary education with the *grammaticus,* whose teaching concentrated exclusively on works of literature. In the later centuries of the Republic the literature was mainly Greek, but under the Empire Virgil and Cicero were recognised as Latin 'classics' fit to be studied beside Homer and Menander. The teaching method was uninspiring: the pupil read or recited a prepared passage, then the teacher explained it word by word, concentrating on grammatical and metrical points but also elucidating the mythological, geographical, historical and other allusions as they occurred. In this way a boy could pick up a good deal of incidental information; but that was not the main object. The bi-lingual literary education created a unified ruling-class culture that was inaccessible to outsiders. Criticisms of it on

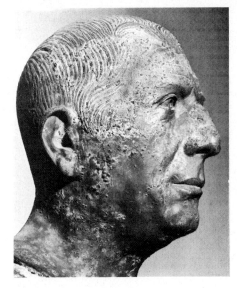

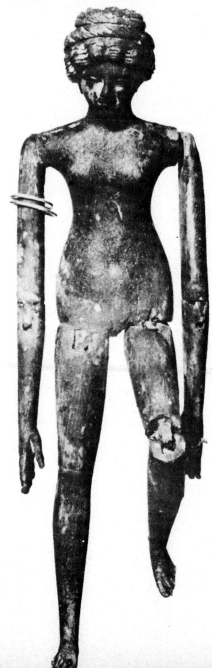

Opposite
The Roman matron: statue in the
Museo Nazionale Romano, Rome.

Top
The great court lady of imperial times:
the Empress Livia, wife of Augustus, as
played by Sian Philipps in the BBC TV
serial *I. Claudius*.

Above
The banker Lucius Caecilius Jucundus;
bronze head found in his house at
Pompeii. Museo Archeologico
Nazionale, Naples.

Right
Jointed wooden doll; she wears gold
bracelets and a gold ring on her finger.
Found in a sarcophagus of the late
second century BC. British Museum,
London.

utilitarian grounds are irrelevant – after
all, a ruling class has no pressing need
for 'useful' knowledge in a relatively
stable, low-technology culture, whereas it does always feel impelled to put
obstacles in the path of would-be
members; the English public school
operated in the same way (and with the
very same languages and literatures) in
the nineteenth and twentieth centuries.

Though physical training with a
military flavour was encouraged, the
Romans had nothing like the Greek
passion for athletics; in fact this was one
pursuit where the associations with
Greek practice – nudity and pederasty
– were a negative influence; even as
spectators the Romans were not enthusiastic about the Greek games
(which Caesar, Augustus, Nero and
other philhellene emperors tried to
popularise), though it is arguable that
Roman taste in this respect was cor-
rupted by addiction to the carnage of
the Colosseum. Music too was not part
of the regular curriculum, though
specialist teachers were available; neither the character nor the fate of the
outstanding amateur practitioner, the
Emperor Nero, can have provided
much inspiration.

At sixteen, when the well-born
youth assumed the toga virilis, he was
attached to some prominent citizen
and served a sort of political
apprenticeship, accompanying his
mentor on civic and ceremonial occasions. He also underwent a period of
army service, at first in the ranks and
later as an officer on a general's staff.
Finally he spent up to three years
studying rhetoric. Here too the cases to
be argued came to have less and less
contact with reality, though 'technique' was constantly refined and
terminology elaborated. This was probably connected with loss of political
freedom under the Empire, which
deprived oratory of its prime subject
matter; even 'practice' political
speeches became dangerous as well as
futile. Declamation remained an admired talent, but decoration and in-
genuity began to loom large when
content became stereotyped and non-
controversial. Stylistic flights, not
relentless arguments, were called for,
and the object was to win applause
(and perhaps advancement) rather
than to influence decisions. That being

Opposite bottom
Master and pupils. Relief of the late second century BC. Trier.

Opposite top left
Proconsul's seat of honour. Museo Archeologico Nazionale, Naples.

Opposite top right
Tools of a trade: Roman surgical instruments. Rheinisches Landesmuseum, Trier.

Above
Shipbuilding: relief showing the building of the *Argo*, vessel of the mythical hero Jason. Villa Albani, Rome.

Above right
Bronze solar clock found at Herculaneum. Museo Archeologico Nazionale, Naples.

Right
A cutler's shop. Relief of the first century AD. Musei Vaticani.

Opposite bottom
A butcher's shop.

Opposite top left
Bronze scales and weights. Museo
Archeologico Nazionale, Naples.

Above centre
Blacksmiths at work: relief showing
Vulcan and Cyclops making the shield
of Achilles. Museo Capitolino, Rome.

Above
Shop sign at Pompeii, advertising oil for
sale.

Left
Cloth being sold. Relief in the Galleria
degli Uffizi, Florence.

Opposite bottom
Fishermen hauling in their catch: a remarkably convincing, action-packed mosaic from Thugga (modern Dougga) in Tunisia. Third century AD.

Opposite top
A banker at his desk. Relief, third century AD. Narodni Muzej, Belgrade.

Above
Shop selling blankets and pillows. Relief. Galleria degli Uffizi, Florence.

Left
Baker's shop. Wall painting from Pompeii. Museo Archeologico Nazionale, Naples.

so, there was something to be said for ingenuity-provoking exercises in historical or legal fantasy (should Agamemnon sacrifice his daughter? is the gold ingot swallowed by a fish part of the pre-sold catch?). So rhetorical teaching was not useless, to those who imbibed it, though its usefulness was not of a kind we see fit to admire.

Given the power of fashion, rhetorical embroidery was probably useful in the law courts, which provided ambitious men with an alternative career to politico-administrative work. In practice the two were often combined; Pliny the Younger, for example, made his name as an advocate in property suits while following a conventional senatorial career, after which he worked in the treasury and finally died while on a troubleshooting mission as Trajan's representative in Bithynia and· Pontus. Special schools existed at Rome for those who wished to study law, offering the detailed knowledge that rhetoric did not concern itself with. This was the most distinctive Roman contribution to education, in line with their devotion to the law, a subject in which they for once outshone the Greeks. Contracts and wills loom large quite early in Roman history, and the sanctity attached to Roman legal agreements was in marked contrast to the more casuistical and often downright unreliable practice of the Greeks. The first coherent body of

Roman law – the Twelve Tables promulgated by the magistrates of the Republic - date from 450 BC. This brief code was expanded over the centuries by 'case law', consisting of rulings and opinions that formed precedents covering more and more possible happenings. Later on, the continuing Roman interest in law must have been further sharpened by the conditions of imperial times, when the courtroom provided the only outlet for qualities once developed in political battles – and when, thanks to the size and wealth of the Empire, litigation flourished as never before. The result was the development of a specialised legal profession – not just advocates but authorities and compilers of textbooks – and of a body of law that increasingly aimed to secure justice rather than merely uphold custom. A code of law as well-made and rational as a Roman road was to be one of the Empire's most durable bequests to mankind.

In most other areas of Roman culture, Greek influence was predominant from the second century BC. Religion, drama, literature, philosophy, art – the subjects of the next two chapters – were all modified by the Greek example or directly copied it, though generally with a typically Roman bias towards the earthy or practical. The Roman genius for conquest and reconciliation spread the Latin tongue all over the western Mediterranean and north-west

Europe, and with it a common Greek-based culture. Some Romans were out-and-out philhellenes (Scipio Africanus, Nero, Hadrian), but most were ambivalent in their attitudes, scorning contemporary 'Greeklings' as degenerate while they imported Greek statuary, studied Greek philosophy and literature, and even employed the living Greekling jewellers and metalworkers who had emigrated to Italy. For their part, many Greeks affected to despise the Romans as uncultured while they rushed to supply them – at a price. Educated Romans were bilingual, and equally familiar with Virgil and Homer, Livy and Thucydides; educated Greeks all too often knew no Latin – to their own loss, since the Greek literary achievement belonged to the distant past, whereas the Latin tradition lived on into the age of the Antonines.

SOCIAL CLASS AND SLAVERY
The chief social distinctions at Rome, in both republican and imperial times, were between the senatorial or noble order, the equites or knights, and the great majority of plebeians, their ranks swollen by ever-increasing numbers of freedmen who took only a generation or so to achieve full citizenship rights. At the bottom of the social hierarchy, vast numbers of slaves laboured in widely varied conditions and with a variety of prospects, from emancipation to death by exhaustion in the

mines.

Under the Republic, the Senate was indirectly elective: a man joined it after holding a number of minor magistracies such as aedile and quaestor, for which he was chosen by the people. However, in practice the magistracies were confined to members of the more or less hereditary class of great land-owners. They had genuine prestige as leaders of a constantly successful state, as well as the resources with which to buy votes if necessary. Most of the equites (roughly speaking the business class) remained outside politics, encouraged by the ruling that no senator could have dealings in shipping or the lucrative state contracts that multiplied with Rome's victories. And for the plebs, unpaid magistracies were of course out of the question. Only a handful of 'new men' (the term used by the Romans themselves) ever reached the Senate from an equestrian background, the outstanding examples being Marius and Cicero.

In reality, then, the republican Senate was an oligarchy. This body of ex-magistrates filled the higher offices including the consulship; the two consuls – the supreme magistrates of the Republic – were chosen annually by the people, but only from the ranks of the Senate. After serving as praetor or consul, a man might continue his political career as propraetor or as a proconsul, taking command of a province: in the late Republic this meant

fleecing it or using it as a base for conquest, depending on the temperament or capacities of the office-holder. The only possible focus for opposition to the senatorial order was the popular assembly (Comitia), which could legislate, though only with a yes or no, on proposals put forward by one of the ten tribunes. However, we have seen that revolutionary tribunes were generally dissident aristocrats such as the Gracchi; and though they may have been genuine reformers, the tribuniciate soon became just another lever in a ruling-class power game which lasted until generals, not politicians, fought over the destiny of the Republic. Under the Empire, the Senate retained its prestige; and, for that matter, it was technically still the Senate and People that held ultimate power in the state, merely delegating it to one emperor after another. But with the real power elsewhere, the actual function of the Senate became the rubber-stamping of imperial policy, and emperors often protested with mock-indignation at the poor attendances. In place of freedom, senators were given privileges and employment. Membership became effectively hereditary; and though wealthy provincials began to be recruited, high property qualifications emphasised the Senate's exclusiveness. Magistracies remained as glamorous as ever, and elections were keenly contested; the consulship, for example, was mainly

decorative but still coveted, both for its glorious name and as a stepping-stone to the governorship of a province. Generally speaking, though vulnerable to the suspicions of the madder emperors, senators could normally expect to hold all the highest responsible offices the Empire could offer.

As their name suggests, the equites originated as a category of citizens enrolled to serve on horseback in wartime; but their membership soon became identical with that of the wealthy business class. Gaius Gracchus gave them judicial functions in the hope of winning their support, but they remained politically apathetic – indeed, equites and people alike disappointed the revolutionaries by their unwillingness to challenge senatorial leadership. Under the Empire the equites flourished, carrying out a broad band of civil and military functions created by the expansion of imperial bureaucracy. More and more offices were opened to them, until only a relatively small number of key posts remained the exclusive preserve of the senatorial order. By the end of the Antonine period it was apparent that the two wealthy classes were beginning to blend into a single ruling class.

The plebeian class can hardly be called a class at all, ranging as it did from well-to-do tradesmen to the 150-200,000 men on the corn dole. Even allowing for this unproductive element, Rome must have been a hive of

industry, with several hundred thousand men (and a much smaller number of women) earning a living at the usual labouring, craft and professional jobs as well as in the booming construction, warehousing, transport and finance businesses stimulated by Rome's unique status. Over 150 occupations have been noted, including carters and other nightworkers whose nocturnal habits were determined by the government decree forbidding wheeled traffic in the city during the daylight hours. (The tired rich man could always get about by litter.) This must have made for restless nights if you lived on a main thoroughfare, or near a big business needing supplies; but it may have been more effective in reducing congestion than the repeated attempts to hold back the shops encroaching on the street – a delightful indication of the Roman trader's commercial enthusiasm.

Romans were bound to one another through various societies such as religious fraternities, mutual-aid clubs and trade guilds. But the most important relationship cutting across classes was that of patron and client. In republican times this was a matter of life-or-death political strategy: Caesar, Pompey and other men of power needed political friends who would return favour for favour, well-settled veteran soldiers who would rally to them at a call, and wealthy provincial cities that would accept their leadership. In the imperial period, patrons and clients abounded. At the lowest level, poor men got up before dawn every morning and went to salute their patron at his house. Each man wore a toga and carefully addressed the patron as 'master' (dominus); failure to do so might forfeit the little gift – probably a few coins – which the client expected on his departure. The most disreputable clients probably expected little more from their patron except this daily hand-out and a more substantial gift of money or food on special occasions; poets and other halfway respectable down-at-heels angled for invitations to dinner; tradesmen hoped for special orders. The patron also extended a degree of protection against legal oppression; all he derived from the relationship was a visible retinue, flattery, verses in his honour, and a train of mourners at his funeral – quite a lot, in fact. As soon as his clients disappeared, he rushed round to *his* patron and went through much the same performance, no doubt with more substantial benefits in view than a few coins. Political support, help in making a career, climbing the social ladder or winning a contract – on this level the process looks familiar. However, one should not underestimate the quasi-ceremonial side of the relationship: the Roman found it

most pleasurable to cut a great public figure surrounded by dependants. The actual extent of patronage is not very clear, though there are some authorities who believe that only the emperor, at the apex of the hierarchy, was not simultaneously somebody's patron and somebody else's client. The whole phenomenon appears less strange when we realise that it has existed at many other times and places under different names. The Democratic political machine in Tammany Hall, New York, 'protected' immigrants and found them jobs in return for votes. The eighteenth-century English nobleman held a *levée* which was crowded with supplicants who hoped his 'influence' would be employed to find them army commissions, pensions, or jobs in the customs and excise; the situation of English writers was so much like those of ancient Rome that one of them, Samuel Johnson, adapted

Opposite
Virgil, greatest of Roman poets, is here shown seated between the muses of tragedy and epic poetry. Mosaic from Susa (modern Sousse) in Tunisia. Musée Bardo, Tunis.

Above
Imperial pleasures: ruins of Hadrian's villa at Tivoli.

Left
Negro slave cleaning a boot; bronze. British Museum, London.

239

Juvenal to lament the scholar's unlucky lot: 'Toil, envy, want, the *patron* and the gaol'.

The criss-crossing of social relationships sometimes concealed economic realities; but the law was quite unambiguously on the side of the rich and respectable. Ignoring other distinctions, it treated men as *honestiores* or *humiliores* – 'honourables' and 'dishonourables'. The categories were not defined: the courts decided in each case where a man belonged; but it seems clear that property and position were the decisive considerations, grouping the better-off plebeians and professional men alongside senators and equites as *honestiores*. The main difference between the two categories lay in the punishments meted out to them. *Honestiores* were most commonly condemned to banishment and confiscation rather than death; whereas *humiliores* were liable to crucifixion, death in the arena, or death by exhaustion and ill-treatment in the mines, working beside slaves.

The *humiliores'* crimes were the more serious because they did not own property; slaves *were* property. Roman slavery was on a quite different scale from that of Greece, and so had a more profound effect on society and the economy. From the second century BC, when Roman arms triumphed in both East and West, enslaved prisoners of war were brought back to Italy in such numbers that they could be allocated to specialised functions, often though not always on a geographical basis: Africans as body slaves; Greeks as nurses, tutors, physicians, craftsmen; Spaniards as herdsmen; and so on. In the following century their ranks were swollen by Gauls who had resisted Caesar, and later by Germans and other barbarians from beyond the Rhine and the Danube; while wars in the Near East brought in a steady flow of more or less Hellenised prisoners.

As a result, the Roman economy became adapted to slave labour, which depressed the wages of free labour and helped to increase the numbers of the Roman unemployed. It also made it difficult for smallholders to compete against capitalist farmers, who could undercut them by large-scale production based on slave-labour. Greek slaves had been relatively dispersed,

Opposite bottom
Perennial pleasures: an old woman, drunk. Roman copy of a Hellenistic original. Museo Capitolino, Rome.

Opposite top
One of the pleasures of the baths: water heater for use in the calidarium. Museo Archeologico Nazionale, Naples.

Above
Women playing knucklebones: wall painting from Pompeii. Museo Archeologico Nazionale, Naples.

except in the very closely controlled Laureum mines; in Italy the numbers were so large that masters could never feel entirely secure. And there were in fact risings in second-century Sicily, followed by the spectacularly near-successful revolt led by Spartacus, which ought to have shaken any belief Romans may have had in their innate superiority. Understandably, then, Roman masters lived under a certain strain: 'so many enemies, so many slaves' was a widely quoted maxim, and in one of his books of advice Cato the Elder warned his readers to watch out for conspiracies when slaves lived together in harmony. In Cato's household, slaves were flogged if the meals they served were not up to standard; they were not allowed to enter any house but their master's; and stable relationships between slaves were discouraged by compelling the females to prostitute themselves within the house according to a tariff fixed by Cato himself. As this implies, even Cato found it prudent to give slaves some incentives to acquiescence by allowing them to earn money; but his general attitude can be summed up in his

celebrated advice to the farmer that he should sell his worn-out oxen and old or sick slaves. Naturally, everybody was not as determinedly unfeeling as Cato, who loved rigour even better than virtue; but many of his attitudes were no harsher than the state of the law. A master could sell, prostitute, castrate or murder his slave; if a slave murdered his master, the whole household was to be executed; and, as in Greece, the evidence of a slave was only regarded as worth having if it was extracted under torture.

In practice, slavery could mean many things, depending on the nature of the slave's employment and the temper of the master. The worst fate was to work in the mines or provide

Opposite
Gladiators fighting beasts. Relief. Museo Teatrale alla Scala, Milan.

Above
Gladiators of various types in action: Astivus and Rodan are dead, as both their prostrate forms and the Greek letter beside them indicate. Mosaic in the Galleria Borghese, Rome.

brief entertainment as animal-fodder in the arena; it seems quite likely that this was the reward of carelessly displayed spirit or intelligence as well as crime, though some safeguards were introduced against sheer vindictiveness on the part of masters. The herdsman was almost certainly better off than field-workers, who could be organised in gangs and locked up together at night; but the household slave had most advantages of all – a relationship with the owning family that became humanised through close contact, plus opportunities to pilfer and benefit from left-overs and discards. Household slaves could also make the most of the Saturnalia on 17 December, a Christmas-like holiday when people exchanged presents and topsy-turvydom prevailed; masters waited on slaves, and slaves were able to indulge in some plain-speaking forbidden all year long – within severe limits, no doubt, since there might otherwise be a reckoning to pay on the morrow. The confusions of town life must have been even more favourable to the household slave, and they also

gave him more opportunities for advancement. If he was a skilled worker he would probably be allowed to take a job on the side, or even to set up on his own and pay his master a percentage of the takings. And eventually, if his master was too mean or too poor to grant him his freedom, he could hope to buy it and join the growing numbers of active, prosperous freedmen.

Under the Empire, the condition of slaves improved remarkably both in law and practice. Claudius laid it down that any master who killed a sick or 'useless' slave was guilty of homicide; castration was forbidden; rights of appeal against injustice were established and could even lead to the enforced sale of a badly-treated slave to a new master; and emperors intervened in a number of legally ill-defined situations to rebuke or punish a cruel owner. Cicero's relationship with his secretary, Tiro, was one of touching friendship, culminating in Tiro's manumission when he was only thirty; Cicero was such a good master that his slaves refused to desert or betray him even when Antony put a price on his head. In the first century AD, Seneca – admittedly the most sympathetically high-minded man in Antiquity – argued that a master should have only so many slaves as he could get to know well, and that slaves should look up to a master rather than fear him. Later still, Pliny the Younger boasted that his slaves' and freedmen's quarters were comfortable enough to be used as guest-rooms; and he affected to be astonished when he heard of some slaves who had attacked their master.

This change in attitudes runs parallel with the milder family situation noted earlier, and probably affected household slaves more than others. The slowing-down of military expansion has been suggested as a contributory reason; with slaves no longer pouring into Italy, slave-holdings stabilised; new generations of slaves were born into households; and a more genial patriarchal relationship inevitably developed. In effect, many slaves were simply domestic servants, perhaps a little less independent than labourers and craftsmen but with greater security; the Roman equivalent to the butler or 'tweeny or maid was arguably a little better off in real terms than his or her Victorian counterpart.

An improvement in the treatment of slaves is easier to account for than the tremendous increase in the numbers who were actually set at liberty. By Augustus' time manumissions had reached a volume so alarming that he imposed age limits (the owner must be

Right
Wrestling and boxing; on the right, the boxer is wearing the *caestus*, a vicious spiked 'glove'. Relief in the Musei Vaticani.

Above right
Athletes and trainers: detail of a mosaic from the Baths of Caracalla. The cropped head and topknot were characteristics of the professional athlete. Musei Vaticani.

Opposite
Fighting between rival groups of supporters at games is nothing new: this wall painting records a brawl between Nucerians and Pompeians, after which gladiatorial shows in the amphitheatre at Pompeii were forbidden for ten years. Museo Archeologico Nazionale, Naples.

eighteen and the slave thirty) and a sliding scale establishing ratios of slaves owned to the number of slaves it was permissible to manumit; Pliny, for example, liberated the maximum number (100) in his will, which indicates that he owned at least 500. Even with these limitations, such numbers had been freed by the Antonine period that a majority of the inhabitants of Rome are believed to have been of servile origin.

This is difficult to explain, and some puzzled historians have been driven back on unconvincing hypotheses such as a – long-term – fashion of generosity. True, a kindlier atmosphere prevailed among the slave-owning classes; but there is no trace of a conviction that slavery as such was wrong: the only people who might have thought so were of a philosophical or religious turn that emphasised inner harmony rather than external liberation. It seems most likely that economics played a large part. An unproductive slave actually consumed his master's resources; and in the unregimented circumstances of town life, slavery was probably even less efficient than elsewhere: no slave in his right mind would work except under supervision. Better, perhaps, for the master to free skilled men to earn their livings, keeping down the number of servants and building up a following of grateful freedmen. For the freedman was not completely free: he owed his ex-master certain services and (perhaps more important) the *obsequium* with which a client treated his patron. In many instances the patron-client relationship survived over the generations, despite the fact that within three generations all the freedman's legal disabilities were removed and he could aspire to any office in the state. (This effective identification of free man and citizen was one of the distinguishing features of Roman practice: in Greece, for example, manumission would have left the slave in a social vacuum, masterless but not a citizen – not even a citizen-at-a-distance, like the resident aliens.) The position of freedmen under Claudius was exceptional, but at a slightly lower level they continued to provide the Empire with many of its best civil servants and businessmen.

Opposite bottom left
Hunting wild animals in North Africa
for use in the amphitheatre. Detail from
a mid-fourth-century AD mosaic. Villa
Imperiale, Piazza Armerina, Sicily.

Opposite top
Theatrical-style scenery and masks were
popular in Roman wall paintings. This
one is from a villa at Boscoreale, about
50 BC. Museo Archeologico Nazionale,
Naples.

Opposite bottom right
The Roman theatre at Arausio (Orange)
in Provençe is splendidly preserved;
unlike Greek theatres it has a massive
stage wall. First century AD.

Above
Mosaic showing actors in the wings of a
theatre. First century BC. Museo
Archeologico Nazionale, Naples.

Naturally they were mocked, liked all newly-arrived men: Trimalchio, the ex-slave and dinner-party host in the *Satyricon,* is the classic new-rich vulgarian. But for all that, freedmen often inherited from their infertile ex-masters, and their role in the later Empire was an important one.

LEISURE AND PLEASURE

Romans, like Greeks, enjoyed their pleasures most intensely in company; as well as gambling, gaming and banqueting together, they preferred communal to private bathing, and congregated in huge numbers to watch spectacles and shows. But there is evidence of a greater inwardness among the educated classes at least, probably connected with the self-scrutiny recommended by Stoicism. Literary composition – almost by definition a solitary activity – was very widely cultivated, though only a fraction of the total output has survived: both Caesar and Augustus, for example, wrote copiously in poetry and prose. Private reading too became common, though many people may have preferred to listen to their slaves reading aloud. Caesar founded the first state library; Augustus established two more; and similar institutions spread through the towns of Italy and the provinces. Booksellers appeared soon afterwards, advertising the latest authors on the colonnade pillars outside their shops. In this way authors might become famous in their lifetimes; Martial, for example, boasts of being read even on the Danube and in Britain. The financial rewards were almost non-existent: there was no copyright, so the author got nothing for his work unless he was so famous that a bookseller would pay him something for the right to copy and publish a new work before his rivals – a temporary advantage only, since there was nothing to prevent such rivals from acquiring a copy, putting scribes to work on it, and publishing their own edition.

Most impecunious authors were therefore dependent on the generosity of one or more patrons. In Augustus' reign, Virgil and Horace were fortunate enough to be taken up by Maecenas; showered with gifts from both Maecenas and the Emperor,

Virgil became virtual poet-laureate, while Horace, perhaps luckier in real terms, was presented with the Sabine farm whose quiet pleasures inspired much of his later verse. Other poets survived by writing grossly flattering verses to their patrons, hoping for a hand-out or a meal.

If he thought his poet-client might do him credit, the patron could arrange a public reading in his house; for the poet this was a chance to win fame and – just as important – to attract new patrons from the audience. Readings had become tremendously popular by the Antonine period, and not merely for the impecunious and ambitious. The Emperor Claudius, who had written several historical works before his accession, gave readings in his palace. Pliny the Younger often performed for an invited audience, and to judge from his letters he felt more nervous on these occasions than when appearing in court. Such is the power of convention that Nero was held to have disgraced himself by performing as a musician, actor and charioteer, while a successful public reading was a social triumph. Many people reserved a special room, the *auditorium,* for readings, and Hadrian built the Athenaeum to hold them. The extent of the Roman reading-mania can be judged from the fact that Pliny went to one every night for weeks at a time, apparently without feeling fatigued – though not everyone felt the same, for Pliny on occasion complains bitterly of audiences' bad manners and inattention.

Less high-minded but still very civilised was the Roman passion for the baths. Even more than in Greece, bathing was a social rather than merely hygienic activity, which is why people favoured public establishments; in the cities, many quite well-off people never bothered to put baths into their houses at all. At Rome there was a multitude of public baths, available on payment of a small entrance fee, even before Augustus' general, Agrippa, built the first imperial baths, which were open to all free of charge. Later emperors outdid one another in building enormous complexes with medium, hot, cold and 'Turkish' baths, gymnasia, massage rooms, lounges, playing grounds for games, walks and enclosures with fountains playing, and

even museums and libraries. The most impressive of the survivors are the Baths of Caracalla and Diocletian dating from the third century AD; but remains on every sort of scale have been found all over the Empire from Hadrian's Wall to the Lebanon. Some kind of bathing establishment was among the earliest constructions in any colony or military settlement, and in cities the baths became as much a part of the civic scheme as the forum. At Rome, mixed bathing became common under the early Empire (though not for really respectable women); but it was banned by Hadrian, who decreed that women should use the baths in the morning and men in the afternoon. The most popular time for men seems to have been just before dinner, although the unemployed poor probably lingered for most of the afternoon, glad to be in a hotel atmosphere after the rigours of tenement nights; those who could not afford the services of bath attendants to scrape them down (steaming and scraping took the place of soap) accomplished it by mutual aid

Excavation at Pompeii in 1895. Archaeological digs at Pompeii and Herculaneum, the cities buried after an eruption of Vesuvius, began in earnest during the eighteenth century and are still in progress.

Above
Manuscript of the *Adelphi*, a play by Terence. Biblioteca Vaticana.

or by rubbing themselves against the marble walls. The central place of the baths in the lives of both rich and poor is summed up in elegiac vein by an anonymous grafitto-artist: 'baths, wine and sex corrupt our bodies, but they make life worth living'.

Infinitely corrupting were the 'games' where untold thousands of men and beasts were slaughtered. As a spectacle 'with a cast of thousands' there has never been anything quite like it – and especially since a high percentage of the 'cast' made only a single appearance. The games were the most unmitigated evil in Antiquity, all the more difficult to comprehend because society was becoming more humane in most other directions. At Rome, the games were the opium of the people: it was policy to entertain 200,000 men on the dole who might otherwise have become dangerously restless; which is why 'bread and circuses' went naturally together. But the games were not just the pastime of the Roman mob; they spread all over the Empire, and even supposedly hyper-civilised peoples such as the Greeks succumbed to their ghoulish allure.

They began as a variation on human sacrifice, suggested by Etruscan funeral games: in 264 BC the sons of Brutus Pera staged three simultaneous gladiatorial combats between pairs of slaves, making a pious blood-offering to the shade of their father. Decade by decade such displays became more elaborate (and their connection with religion more perfunctory) until by the late Republic every ambitious politician borrowed or beggared himself to put on a show that would win the favours of the electors. By this time there were already hundreds of participants; and from the reign of Augustus, when the whole business came under imperial control, both the numbers involved and the calendar days devoted to games began to soar. By the fourth century no less than 175 days were earmarked for games, and these did not include gratuitous shows such as the four-month-long event put on by Trajan to celebrate his victories in Dacia; in this 10,000 animals died and 100,000 gladiators took part. Gruesome entertainment of this sort prompted the invention of the amphitheatre; of which noble ruins survive at Verona, Nîmes, Arles and elsewhere – and at Rome in the Colosseum, built under Vespasian and Titus, which seated at least 50,000 spectators and must still rank as one of man's most awe-inspiring achievements.

In their developed form, the games consisted of two distinct elements: massacres and professional fights. The first involved both animals and humans. Hunts were staged in which the wild animals imported by the thousand were slaughtered – lions and panthers, elephants, bulls, bears, rhinosceroses and hippopotami, crocodiles, snakes, ostriches, seals and similar exotica. At other times men were the victims: criminals and prisoners of war were tied to stakes for ravenous beasts to consume; set to fight one another; alternately armed and forced to kill, and then disarmed and delivered to the next killer-victim (both parties urged on by whips and hot irons); and even primed and lit to create human torches. The dramatic performaces staged in the arena and elsewhere were even more extraordinary, with actors whose tragedies were real: in one, a doomed Icarus might be borne aloft on wires until he was plunged into an enclosure of wild beasts; in another, two parties of prisoners of war might be set to re-enact the battle of Salamis on a lake, fighting each other for survival with all the desperation of the original combatants.

Gladiators proper were a group apart: men trained to fight with skill and style, and more or less evenly matched. Most gladiators were criminals, or prisoners of war, or slaves (though owners were forbidden to dispatch unoffending and unwilling slaves to the arena); but there were always some free men prepared to risk their lives in the hope of recouping shattered fortunes or becoming a star. The gladiator's position was equivocal. In law he was a degraded being and the lowest of slaves, having sworn a terrible oath to endure fire, chains, whips and cold steel at the behest of his master (in imperial Rome a specially appointed praetor). He was a virtual

prisoner, unarmed, in the barracks-like training schools at Rome, Capua, Ravenna and elsewhere. (The military feats of Spartacus were never forgotten by Rome's rulers.) Yet there were rewards too: freedom for the criminal (and probably, though less certainly, for the slave) at the end of a three-year stint in the arena and a period of work around the schools; the palm and prize money for every victory; and, for the star performer, fortune, adulation and women galore. In the training schools gladiators developed a strong *ésprit de corps,* and a pride in their profession such that some expressed their impatience at long spells away from the arena.

The games were surrounded with a ritual and pageantry reminiscent of Spanish bullfighting. The night before their appearance, the gladiators were feasted in their quarters under the eyes of privileged members of the public. Clad in gold-embroidered purple cloaks, they went in procession to the arena, marched round it and greeted the Emperor with the famous words 'Hail, Caesar: we who are about to die, salute you!' In combat too the ritual went on: the defeated man flung away his weapons and held up one finger to appeal for mercy; the Emperor, prompted by the crowds, gave the thumbs-up or down for life or death; and if it was death, the loser was

supposed to prop himself up and offer his throat to the sword without flinching. Then an attendant dressed as Charon, ferryman of the dead, removed the corpse while others raked the sand and sweetened the air with perfume.

The combatants were always unalike in equipment and tactics. 'Thracians', 'Samnites' and 'Gauls' were accoutred in some versions of national arms and armour, whereas *myrmillo, secutor* (follower), *retiarius* (net man) and others were named after their equipment. Labelled pictures and descriptions of the various types are confused and contradictory; but the principle on which they were paired was clearly that of balancing offensive against defensive strengths, and protection against mobility. *Retiarius,* for example, fought almost naked with net and trident against *secutor* or some other armed man with sword and shield; one was mobile and hoped to enmesh and pin his opponent, whereas the other was almost invulnerable, and deadly if he got anywhere near *retiarius.*

Paradoxically, gladiatorial displays – the most notorious part of the games – were rather less repellant than most of the other events. At least they were fair(ish) fights, with something of the atmosphere of a boxing match – audiences shouting excitedly 'Habet!

Above
A street in the thriving Roman resort of
Pompeii, near modern Naples.

Opposite
Treading grapes. Relief. Museo
Archeologico, Venice.

Hoc habet!' ('Yes! He's had it!') – and
chances of victory or mercy. The skill
involved in such displays has probably
been underestimated: gladiators, like
top-class boxers, fought only about
three times a year. And as their training
must have made them valuable investments, it seems possible that bouts were
arranged to give the audience value for
money, so that the eventual loser had
an excellent chance of being spared.
The epitaph of the thirty-year-old
gladiator Flamma suggests that the
mortality rate for gladiators may have
been lower than commonly supposed:
he won 21 victories, fought 9 no-
decision bouts, and was beaten but
spared on 4 occasions.

Despite a few qualifications, however, the games can only be pictured
as a public horror; the brutalities of our
own more recent past, such as would-
be deterrent public hangings and

impalings of traitors' heads, scarcely
make this centuries-long mass sadism
more comprehensible. Even in the
context of ancient warfare and punishment – massacres, burning cities,
chopped-off hands, crucifixion – the
Roman games were unique, since it
was not revenge, hatred, rage or
punishment that motivated them, but
entertainment. The extraordinary
thing is that even Romans who disliked
the games seem to have regarded them
as an unavoidable evil. Tiberius,
Hadrian and Marcus Aurelius gave as
few as possible; Julius Caesar used
them cynically to win popularity,
though he found them so tedious (or
repellant) that he could be seen working during the proceedings. Cicero and
Pliny, otherwise humane men, feebly
recommended the games as a school of
valour; and other intellectuals seem to
have despised the games as the boring

pastime of the boring populace, but to have felt no great impulse to change things. Seneca alone, speaking for the Stoic belief in universal brotherhood, condemned the games unequivocally.

By contrast, chariot-racing seems a genuine sport not so far removed from present-day motor racing. But homicidally dangerous driving was both permitted and indulged in: a driver might try to 'bump' a rival to break his axle, or ram him from behind to smash up the light chariot-car he stood in; and if he cornered too tightly he would be overturned by grazing a track marker. Since drivers raced with the reins wound round them, they needed to react fast in an accident, slashing through the cords before they were dragged along the track behind their horses. The sport was at least as popular as the games, and evoked more permanent loyalties. Though there were star drivers and horses, what mattered was the colour they raced under: red, white, blue and green constituted 'factions' whose successes and failures were followed with the same breathless interest as modern football matches: when his faction won an event, the manager let the city know by releasing a flock of swallows painted with the appropriate colour. Only the big cities could afford a permanent circus or hippodrome, but Rome had no less than five including the famous Circus Maximus, some 600 metres long. As an entertainment the races were more respectable than the games: drivers, though mainly slaves, were unambiguously envied, and Roman intellectuals were not ashamed of being partisans of (usually) the Blues.

A diet of blood and equestrian thrills must have made the drama seem dull fare to a mass audience, and may account for the increasing sensationalism of Roman theatrical performances. Still, the Romans built theatres, each capable of seating thousands, all over their empire, as well as three in the capital itself. These were not built into slopes in Greek fashion, but were free-standing structures. The stage was raised and roofed, with a wall behind it; the actors performed in front of a set designed to look like a row of houses with three doors and 'town' and 'country' street exits at either side. The auditorium was semi-circular (whereas the Greek auditorium was a more-than-semi-circle), and in fact the first amphitheatre is said to have been made from two wooden theatres, placed back to back, so ingeniously constructed that they could be swivelled round after the morning performances and interlocked to accommodate gladiatorial shows in the afternoon. The drama was an integral part of festivals and celebrations, just as the games were; and it is possible that there were rather more theatrical performances and fewer games during any particular period than has generally been supposed.

Despite the magnificence of public provision for the theatre, it was hardly more creative at Rome than it had been in the Hellenistic East. The outstanding comic dramatists, Plautus and Terence, flourished in the late third and early second centuries BC as translators or adapters of Menander and the New Comedy, even retaining Greek settings for their works. Plautus is lively and loquacious, whereas Terence writes in a quieter, more self-consciously finished and aphoristic style; but both dealt in stock characters such as the crafty slave and the professional diner-out, and the plots have a typical fairy-tale love-story quality in which, for example, the slave-heroine proves not to be a slave after all and can marry the well-born hero. Roman tragedy apparently reached its peak in the second century BC, but the works themselves have not survived. After this, drama consisted almost entirely of revivals; 'serious' plays became library productions like the gory tragedies of Seneca, written to be read aloud to a select audience. Pompeii had theatres that catered to both tastes: a large open-air theatre that seated five thousand people, and a smaller covered theatre (by Roman standards a 'little' or intimate one) for an audience of a thousand or so.

As in the East, a 'star system' developed that turned every play into a vehicle for the idol of the day. Ruthless editing of classics, or specially prepared 'scripts' or libretti, focussed attention on the star in spectacularly mounted performances that increasingly resembled opera or ballet, with a chorus singing on stage and instrumental

backing. The supreme star was the *pantomimus* who acted entirely in dumb-show, by all accounts with superb command of gesture, posture and dance-movement. Though such professional performers, like gladiators, were technically *infames* (degraded), they too attracted a devoted following and female attentions; one *pantomimus,* Paris, received the favours of the Empress herself. Comedy seems to have remained closer to conventional drama, though in the debased form of 'mimes', quasi-realistic improvised productions in which women were allowed to appear and masks were not worn. They seem to have mixed sentimentality, sex and violence in soap-opera style, but with the occasional distinctively grim Roman note, as when a real criminal was substituted for the fictive villian and tortured and excuted on stage.

The provinces

Until the end of the second century AD, there was a steady growth of urban culture in the provinces of the Empire, based directly on Greco-Roman models; the rich also followed the Roman example in developing a passion for rural leisure based on well-equipped and often self-sufficient villas. The East was urbanised before the arrival of the Romans, but large areas of the West were transformed by Roman initiatives, whether in the form of military colonies or of army camps around which native settlements grew up. Conquered Gaul became thoroughly Romanised, and even chilly Britain supported a widely distributed villa culture; Tacitus, torn between imperial pride and a tendency to romanticise a freedom he had never known, describes the Romanisation of Britain in terms that might have been used of many other peoples:

Those who once refused to learn the Roman tongue now aspired to become eloquent in it. Our national dress was honoured, and togas became a common sight. Gradually the Britons succumbed to the lure of Roman vices: lounging under arches, at the baths, and at elegant entertainments. The naive referred to all this as 'gracious living' when it was simply an aspect of their servitude.

This cultural homogeneity was an urban upper-class phenomenon, and the Romans not only promoted cities but also favoured oligarchies within them; otherwise they hardly interfered in municipal affairs. Each city had its own senate and magistrates, who expressed their local pride through public works duly recorded by a marble inscription. Such endowments turned into a competitive frenzy, became expected of each and every magistrate, and ended by making men reluctant to assume the burden of office. By the late Antonine period the imperial government was being compelled to take over responsibility in many places – a development that encouraged the growth of an over-extended bureaucracy and actually weakened the real cohesion of the Empire. This was an early symptom of Roman weakness: the Empire was simply too large to control effectively except during the inevitably brief period of internal balance and lack of critical challenge from outside.

However, the overwhelming impression given by the Empire at its height in the second century is of cosmopolitan splendour. Rome tolerated most religions and was remarkably free from national or racial prejudice. A Spaniard like Trajan could become emperor; an African like Terence, who was a slave too, could become the favoured playwright of a sophisticated élite. If Italy was no longer supreme over the provinces, Rome herself was still the first city of the Empire; and both city and empire now appeared to be Eternal.

Opposite
A less pleasant side of Roman rule –
paying taxes. Relief found in the
cemetery of Noviomagus (modern
Lisieux), Rheinisches Landesmuseum,
Trier.

Above
Roman life in Tunisia: this villa at Utica
is the only example to survive on
African soil.

Religion and Ideas

GODS AND SPIRITS OF OLD ROME

The primitive religion of Rome was a religion of hard-working farmers, concerned to ensure the goodwill of the spirits (numina) felt to be all around them. Each stream, glade, copse or other natural feature had its numen, to which it was wise to make offerings. The household itself had its lares and penates, spirits of whom carved figures would often be brought to the table so that they could share the family meal; the goddess Vesta guarded the blazing hearth; and the pater familias had his own guardian spirit or genius (a word with a long and interesting history). The household spirits were benevolent unless offended, whereas others needed to be carefully handled and propitiated – amongst them the manes or spirits of the dead.

On this level Roman beliefs are not far removed from those of Pacific islanders in the recent past. But at an early date some numina must have been given the wider powers and significance of gods, and we find Jupiter, Quirinus and Mars on the Capitol. This triad apparently represented a Roman-Sabine coalition, later replaced by Jupiter, Juno and Minerva as Rome fell under Etruscan influence; these three – the sky god, his wife and their daughter the goddess of wisdom – remained the three chief deities even when revamped as Olympians. At this stage the Romans do not seem to have thought of their gods as super-humans with tempers and appetites; unlike the Greeks, they had a powerful capacity for abstraction, inventing a god for every conceivable function (Janus, two-faced god of gates; Terminus, god

of boundaries) and even for qualities such as Virtue and Fortune; yet they abstained from giving their creations personalities or mythical adventures. The legalism so characteristic of the Romans appeared in the scrupulous care with which ceremonies were conducted and the curious lack of warmth in the relations between men and gods; instead of the hot-blooded deities of Greece, Jupiter and his family were thought of as exacting their rights with lawyer-like precision; and men behaved with equivalent nicety to win their favour. This was emphatically a state religion, with a supreme pontiff - the pontifex maximus – who was a layman; Julius Caesar held the office, and it became in effect hereditary among the emperors. (The arrangement is not particularly unusual; the British monarch is the head of a church, just as the Caliph of Bagdad once was.) However, the gods were not entirely reasonable beings or it would not have been necessary to ponder every unusual event in case it proved to be an omen or portent; further information was acquired by the augurs, who studied the flights of birds and scrutinised the entrails of slaughtered animals for clues to the future. The conclusions drawn from such exercises might forward or delay the actions of Senate and consuls, already enmeshed in ritual. However, though the formalism of Roman religion sometimes hindered effective action in an emergency, it also gave Roman society a cohesion and reliability that the more volatile Greeks lacked. Its connection with morality (except for the imperative morality of contracts, derived from religious oaths) was curiously oblique; the *pietas* and *fides* of the family – and by extension the state – formed almost a separate value-system from the elaborate propitiatory mechanism of the state religion.

THE IMPACT OF GREECE

The intensity of Roman Hellenising from the second century BC has already been indicated. But some Greek influence was felt on religion even earlier, either through the Etruscans or from the Greek cities to the south of Rome. The famous Sibylline books – oracular pronouncements which the Romans consulted during great crises – were written in Greek verse and according to legend had been brought to Rome from the Greek city of Cumae; the last Roman king, Tarquinius Superbus, was said to have been the purchaser. The prestige of the Sibylline books may well have encouraged the identification of Roman with Greek gods that now took place: Jupiter was equated with Zeus, Juno with Hera, and Minerva with Athene. Eventually a Roman pantheon emerged that matched the Olympian line-up (Mars/Ares, Venus/Aphrodite, Diana/Artemis, Neptune/Poseidon, Vulcan/Hephaestus, Ceres/Demeter, Mercury/Hermes, Eros/Cupid, and so on); gaps were filled by directly bringing in a few Greek deities, notably Heracles (re-named Hercules), Apollo and Asclepius (Aesculapius). The gods were anthropomorphised, and Greek myth became a common Greco-Roman possession – to the enrichment of the Roman literary sensibility, if less obviously to the benefit of religious and moral convictions. The final triumph of Greek ways occurred when the Romans, shaken to the core by Hannibal's victories, sent a special embassy to Delphi for the oracle's advice. However, most Romans continued to honour the lares and penates, and to seek the help of Fortune and other abstract deities.

In the last centuries of the Republic, Rome conquered the Mediterranean and made peace with the gods of its peoples. As is well known, the Romans were remarkably tolerant; they suppressed some British cults that involved human sacrifice, but otherwise left local customs undisturbed, if possible absorbing their deities into an increasingly flexible system of religious ideas. Under the Empire, Augustus and Livia even had offerings made in their names at the Temple in Jerusalem, despite the Jews' belief that theirs was the only true god, and that therefore all the Romans' gods were false.

By this time, many educated Romans had come to believe that all temple gods embodied aspects of the divine; clearly Augustus and Livia believed something of the sort, or were polite enough to pretend they did. Such an attitude was a natural development from Roman syncretism, which was bound to weaken faith in specific deities and myths. In effect, it encouraged the most reflective men to turn from religion to philosophy.

The philosophy too was a Greek import, and one of the many that were

Opposite
Ancestral spirits (lares) worshipped in the home; these are made of bronze. Musée du Louvre, Paris.

Left
The master of the house with his guardian spirits (genii). Wall painting at the House of the Vetii, Pompeii.

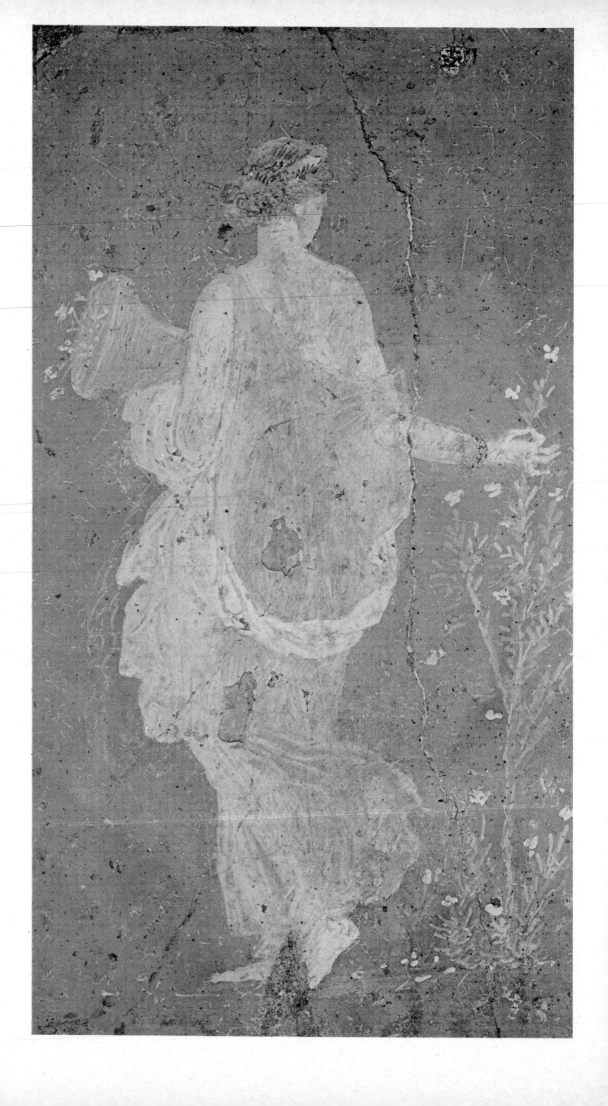

Opposite
Flora, goddess of flowering plants; wall painting from Stabia.

Above
Mosaic from Hadrian's Villa at Tivoli; the figure is one of the ancient spirits of the earth (*pales*), who were responsible for the wellbeing of crops and flocks.

Left
Augur (*haruspex*) reading the omens by examining the entrails of a bull. From a relief in the Musée du Louvre, Paris.

regarded at Rome with a mixture of admiration and suspicion; from time to time philosophers were banished from the city but, like other Greek luxuries, they were always readmitted in the end. The Romans themselves gave noble expression to Epicurean and Stoic attitudes, but added little to their substance. In a long philosophical poem, *On the Nature of Things,* Lucretius gave the most detailed and lucid exposition of Epicurean doctrine that has survived; but though Epicurus had followers, the prevailing philosophy among serious men in imperial times was Stoicism. One of its most influential exponents was a lecturer at Rome from the Greek East, the ex-slave Epictetus from Phrygia in Asia Minor; after his death around AD 135, his lectures were published and read by Marcus Aurelius, whose own Stoic *Meditations* were jotted down in Greek in the midst of his campaigns on the Danube and in the East. Epictetus taught the Stoic doctrines of fortitude and self-sufficiency, placing particular emphasis on his conviction that a man might be 'happy on the rack' if he chose to be so. Though Epictetus also argued for a divine scheme of things and the brotherhood of man, these are even more strongly present in the writings of Seneca, whom we have already encountered as an enemy of the games. The brotherhood of man was a reasonable deduction from the belief that men represented sparks from the divine flame, that inner control was the supreme achievement, and that a man's position in the world was an external accident to be dutifully ('stoically') endured, not praised or blamed: only the Sage was worthy of admiration, and there was no reason why an emperor, or a slave, or even a barbarian, should not become a Sage. This emphasis, in itself new to the more aristocratic form of Roman Stoicism, acquired a surprising emotional, even religious, force in Seneca's works. All men need the help of God, he says; but prayer is pointless: the divine spirit is 'near you, with you, within you'. In this life, the soul is in prison: a man resembles a soldier who has signed on for a term of years and must make the best of it, with the prospect of finer things to come – for Seneca sometimes appears to believe in a future life, if

Right
The entrance to the shrine at Cumae; here dwelt the Sibyl, whose prophetic books were consulted by the Romans whenever a crisis occurred in the state.

Above
Marcus Aurelius sacrificing as pontifex maximus. Relief. Museo Capitolino, Rome.

Opposite
The Emperor Augustus garbed as pontifex maximus (religious head of state). Statue in the Museo Nazionale Romano, Rome.

only as part of the world-soul. Like other Stoics he preaches 'happiness in adversity', but in his case the austere Stoic ideal is modified by belief in the importance of human sympathy and mutual help. Understandably, he was later considered a proto-Christian, and for centuries a fake correspondence between Seneca and St Paul was in wide circulation. In life, Seneca may have been less admirable. A Spaniard, he made a successful political career at Rome, tutored the young Nero, and in collaboration with the praetorian pre-fect Burrus ran the imperial govern-ment during the early (i.e. good) years of Nero's reign; on the other hand he is accused of having amassed an en-ormous fortune in government, and of lending money at such extortionate rates that the British under Boudicca were provoked to revolt. When Nero began to take a hand in government, Seneca prudently retired, and even presented the Emperor with his for-tune to blunt his jealousy. However, when a conspiracy against Nero was discovered, Seneca was implicated (justly or otherwise) and ordered to kill himself; which he did by opening the veins of his wrists and ankles.

INVASION FROM THE EAST

Seneca was unusual in his own time, but a century later the emotional-religious note was being sounded even more strongly. In Marcus Aurelius' *Meditations,* the Emperor's world-weariness is much more apparent than any vestigial Stoic's pride in self-sufficiency; duty is joyless, the world has become the soul's prison indeed, and it longs to be away. Some of this reflects Aurelius' personal situation – that of a sensitive man tied by a sense of duty to camp life and the slaughter of fellow creatures; but it also expresses a more general mood. In the second century AD – Gibbon's happiest age for mankind – a sense of futility had begun to gain ground; there was a vague mood of dissatisfaction with life and its rewards, and a yearning towards some otherworldly state. It was not nec-essarily the mood of the majority, who probably continued to worship the old gods, whether from full-hearted belief or just because it was good form to do so – part of what it meant to be a Roman and a kind of civic duty.

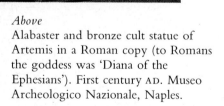

Above
Alabaster and bronze cult statue of
Artemis in a Roman copy (to Romans
the goddess was 'Diana of the
Ephesians'). First century AD. Museo
Archeologico Nazionale, Naples.

Above right
Greek myth as taken over by the
Romans: wall painting from
Herculaneum showing the centaur
Chiron teaching the young Achilles.
Transferred to panel and now in the
Museo Archeologico Nazionale, Naples.

Opposite bottom
Carving from the temple of Sulis
Minerva at Bath in England; the linking
of British Sul with the Roman goddess
of wisdom was typical of the Empire's
conciliatory religious policy. Roman
Baths Museum, Bath.

Above
Bronze group of Cybele enthroned on a
cart drawn by lions; the orgiastic cult of
this goddess from Asia Minor was only
allowed into Rome as a measure of
desperation, at a critical moment in the
war against Carthage. Metropolitan
Museum of Art, New York. Gift of
Henry G. Marquand, 1887.

Right
Dionysus on an ass: Greek coin. The
god was also worshipped – as Bacchus –
by the Romans.

Besides, given the un-exclusive religious outlook of the Romans, there was no reason why the doubtful should not hedge their bets by honouring the lares and penates, worshipping the Capitoline triad, and also taking part in one or more cults that promised exciting mystical experiences and a more fulfilling after-life. The early third-century emperor Alexander Severus took this policy to an extreme, filling his private chapel with cult figures of Jesus, Orpheus and other assorted sages and deities (which did not, however, prevent him from coming to a sticky end).

In response to the new mood, cults and religions poured into Italy – almost exclusively from the East, whose sophisticated creations had an appeal for the Romans that the tribal rites of Celts and Germans were unlikely to match. Cybele, the non-Greek Great Mother, had been imported from Asia Minor as early as 205 BC; but her state recognition had been exceptional, reflecting the Romans' desperate casting-around for any forces that might help them in the struggle against Hannibal. A few years later Bacchus (the Roman version of Dionysus) also became established, though the orgies associated with his worship were for a time regarded as dangerously subversive; the ritual of initiation, culminating in flagellation, is portrayed in the superb painting on the walls of a room in the Villa of the Mysteries at Pompeii. But it was in the imperial period that a bewildering variety of non-state cults emerged and achieved respectability. Temples of Isis, for example were built at Rome itself and at Pompeii, where its steps still lead up to an altar-area now exposed to the sky and surrounded by broken walls and columns. Isis became a popular deity all round the Mediterranean, claiming a more exclusive allegiance than most, yet remaining thoroughly Egyptian in the priests she employed and the Nile water prescribed for her ceremonies. Though associated with her husband Osiris and their son Horus in a 'trinity' concerned with death and rebirth, outside Egypt Isis seems often to have achieved a superior or independent status. She was also linked with the Greco-Egyptian god Serapis; and both frequently presided over what were in

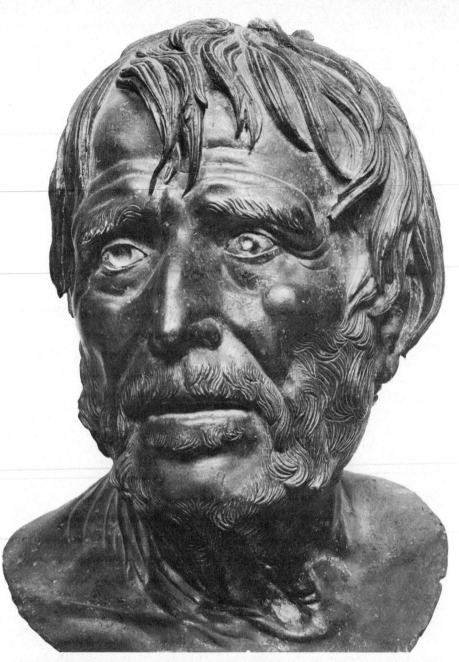

was Plotinus, an Egyptian-Greek who posited union with God as the aim of existence and rearranged the Platonic 'Ideas' into a hierarchy supposedly accessible to intellectual contemplation.

Neither mystery religions nor mysterious philosophies was likely to provide the basis for a new world religion, which would need to be more accessible, easily understood and ethically definite. A more likely candidate was the cult of the Unconquered Sun (Sol Invictus), with its immediate appeal as the ever-renewed source of light and life, and its easy identification with an emperor who was himself increasingly a cult in his own lifetime. In the third century the main rival of Sol was Mithras, originally an import from Persia. He too was a god of light, and was represented as leading the struggle of good/light against evil/darkness. The bull was the potent symbolic animal of Mithraism, its sacrifice signifying the renewal of all things and the rebirth of the participants. The whole tone of the religion was more sober and disciplined than that of most Oriental cults, and this presumably accounts for its popularity among soldiers, who took it to the ends of the Empire; British evidence of Mithraism includes a temple uncovered in the City of London not many years ago.

With its notion of a struggle between good and evil, its shepherds worshipping the new-born Mithras child, and its communion service of bread and wine, Mithraism had important points in common with Christianity. In fact, the ultimate victory of Christianity is easier to understand in the light of the myths and beliefs prevalent in late Antiquity: virgin births; divine trinities; deaths and renewals; the divinity within; mutual love; immortality; and so on. Some doctrine permutating such beliefs was likely to unite the Roman world if it was to be religiously united at all. Christianity had a hard fight·of it, and was more liable to persecution than most of its rivals; so it almost certainly possessed compensatory advantages in terms of its appeal and capacity to inspire loyalty.

The difficulty here is that we do not know precisely what form Christianity

Opposite bottom
Sarcophagus with funereal relief. Museo d'Arte Nazionale d'Abruzzo, L'Aquila.

Opposite top
Bust of the Stoic philosopher Seneca. Museo Archeologico Nazionale, Naples.

Above
The god Serapis. The Romans, with their all-embracing religious outlook, took over this god, who was himself a Greco-Egyptian composite. Statue in the Musei Vaticani.

effect mystery religions. Rival versions of these – the Eleusinian mysteries, Orphic cults - also had a great appeal, satisfying the growing craving for magic, secrets, miracles, salvation and immortality. One of the more touching indications of a craving for immortality is the great increase in the number of sarcophagi made in the second century AD: whatever their precise religious allegiance, people who believed in the resurrection of the body abandoned cremation, presumably lest it over-taxed the powers of their deity.

Belief in magic and mystery drove out belief in reason; the process, visible in the stable world of the Antonines, accelerated in the disordered third century. Even philosophy took on a mystical hue: the outstanding figure

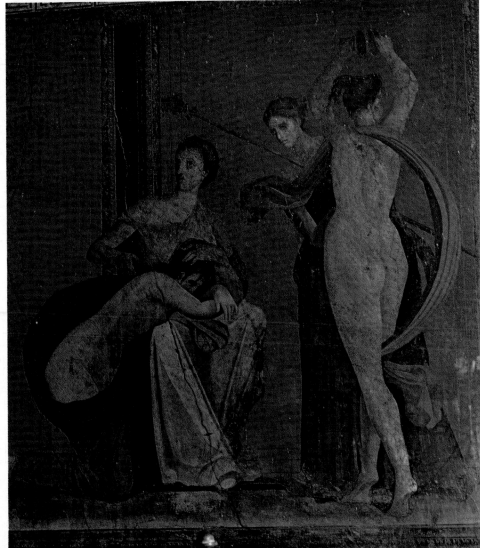

Opposite
Apollo as sun god. Mosaic.

Above
Bacchanalian dance. Wall painting from Galleria Doria Pamphilj, Rome.

Left
Flagellation as part of the initiation ceremony at the Villa of Mysteries, Pompeii.

267

Above
Sacrifice of a bull to Mithras. Musée du Louvre, Paris.

Opposite top
Mosaic designed to avert the evil eye. Museo Capitolino, Rome.

Opposite bottom
Chronos, lord of infinite time, a traditional figure reinterpreted in Mithraic terms. The serpent represents the ecliptic, the course of the sun through the heavens as it appears to an observer on earth. Marble statue from the late second century AD. Museo Arqueológico, Mérida.

took in the early centuries, let alone how people reacted to it: it is hardly mentioned by surviving Roman writers before its victory, and those who notice it tend to dismiss it as a criminal conspiracy. Tacitus, for example, says (possibly wrongly) that Nero put the blame for the great fire of Rome on the Christians though it was his own doing – not that one need be sorry for the Christians, who are 'the enemies of mankind'. The reasons for the intermittent persecutions are clearer, and may provide clues to the eventual success: Christianity was both fiercely

exclusive and accessible to all. Like the Jews, Christians insisted that theirs was the only god; unlike the Jews, they opened their ranks to all without making tiresome stipulations. The Jewish refusal to worship the emperor was allowable – so great was the Romans' tolerance – because they were a distinct people who could be excused on the grounds of respect for national custom; but the Christian refusal had the aspect of an international conspiracy of indefinable dimensions. Worshipping the emperor did not necessarily entail religious sentiments (which is not to say that such sentiments never existed); it was above all a civic act, pledging loyalty to the state. In refusing his pinch of incense the Christian was guilty of treason as well as lèse-majesté; and given his vehemently expressed contempt for all other gods, respectable and religious people cannot have felt much sympathy when he was punished for it.

In the long run, however, refusal to compromise was probably one of Christianity's strengths: in ages of uncertainty, dogmatic conviction attracts as many people as it repels, and the mutual tolerance of other cults was ultimately a source of weakness. By proclaiming that it alone held the truth, Christianity called men to make a complete break with their old lives and gave them certainties that seemed worth dying for (which they would hardly have done if other cults had been seen as having some share in the truth – a civilised Stoic point of view, but not one likely to win over the world). Poor men, slaves and women were promised a glorious future life that would compensate them for their miseries in this one, but the rich were not excluded and the social order was not threatened – not, at any rate, after a very early stage when Christain groups may have practised some form of communism. In time, other 'antisocial' features disappeared, notably belief in an imminent Second Coming (which made effort seem futile) and pacifistic tendencies (which were, so to speak, more appropriate to a loyal opposition than to a government). With this achieved, it needed only the conversion of an able and ambitious general to give Christianity a chance to re-fashion the world of Antiquity.

Roman Art and Architecture

THE ENGINEERS' ART

The Romans were far less artistically creative than the Greeks, who influenced them deeply in this as in other aspects of culture. The Romans' greatest contributions were the results of their practicality and realism. In the engineering works of their empire they created a functional art using all the technological resources of Antiquity - roads, bridges, aqueducts, sewers, great public buildings, arcades, and a range of monuments including triumphal arches and commemorative columns. The roads, measured off with regular milestones from the Golden Milestone in the Forum, linked the cities of the Empire from the Euphrates to Hadrian's Wall, promoting trade and travel as well as military and political control. The aqueducts are among the most impressive of all Roman remains, their greatest arches and piers space-stepping majestically over land and water; the finest surviving example is the 'Pont du Gard' at Nîmes, one of the great cities of Roman Gaul. The principle of the arch was known to the Greeks, but the Romans were the first people to use it on a large scale. This was the true arch spanning two pillars in a curve by means of wedges—not the ancient overlapping-stone corbel arch, used for example in Mycenaean fortresses. The vault and dome are extensions of the same principle, and in combination with the Roman invention of concrete they could be used to span areas previously impossible to cover without employing a forest of columns for support. Strong walls and skilful distribution of stress turned the

Above
Head of the Empress Livia. Musée du Louvre, Paris.

Opposite
Roman bridge over the Tagus at Alcántara. AD 105-106.

column into a primarily decorative feature which could be partly sunk into the wall ('engaged') or even flattened against it to achieve a more rectilinear effect. As Roman confidence grew, Doric, Ionic and Corinthian orders were varied or permutated according to a taste that grew more florid (though not more certain) during imperial times. Roman public buildings, like Roman houses, tended to be unspectacular outside; they were not decorated with paint and lavish sculptures, so that their present appearance is less misleading than that of Greek temples, which now look equally austere. Roman architecture is seen at its best from inside, where the Roman mastery of handling space is shown to best advantage.

ROMAN REALISM

Much Roman sculpture was either influenced by the Greeks or actually created by Greek craftsmen for Roman customers. The earliest Greek impact was indirect, through the Etruscans who dominated the early history of Rome. Many Etruscan bronzes and terracotta figures, such as the famous life-size *Apollo of Veii*, are clearly derived from Greek Archaic art, their faces wearing the wide give-away 'Archaic smile'. Later, the Romans came into contact with the Greeks in Southern Italy, and later still they conquered Greece itself, looted or bought Greek works of art (contemporary and 'classic') and were such enthusiastic purchasers that copying became a skilled industry; as we have seen, most of the great individual masterpieces of Greek sculpture survive only in these Roman copies.

The Greek achievement may well have had an inhibiting effect on the Romans; certainly they never challenged the Greeks' mastery of the gods and god-like men as subjects. On the other hand, they were more down-to-earth – curious about real people and the real world, and impelled to document at least some aspects of them. They were probably encouraged by the realistic element present in Etruscan art, and by the contemporary realistic tendencies of the Hellenistic world. But Roman realism has a sober, literal look that refuses emotion or exaggeration, and this makes it quite distinct from the slightly eerie Etruscan tomb art or the sensationalism never far away in Hellenistic work. Roman taste was expressed – and influenced – by the portrait busts of ancestors that were customarily displayed in the house. These were intended as records of people as known and remembered, not of mythologised heroes; and there is evidence that many of them were made directly after the death-masks cast from the faces of the deceased. With such a precedent – and a temperament to match – the Romans went on to reproduce plain and truthful portraits of emperors, commanders, farmers, freedmen and slaves, on busts, statues, coins, sarcophagi and memorials. Except for a few periods of glamorising 'official' art, even emperors and victorious generals allowed their jug-ears, stubbled or doubled chins, warts and other defects to be included in portraits of suitably Roman *gravitas*. Realistic observation of animals, plants and everyday life also occurs, especially on reliefs of the imperial period.

MONUMENTS AND MEN
Relatively little survives from the republican period; at Rome in particular, most buildings were swept away

during the imperial city-development boom. One of the most interesting survivals is a provincial temple, the Maison Carrée at Nîmes. This first-century BC building is a stolid Roman adaptation of the Greek temple-style, raised on a podium and undecorated outside; but instead of a peristyle of columns surrounding the body of the temple, the walls are placed wider apart and the columns are decoratively engaged to them except at the porch – as if the Roman builder was insisting on the supremacy of the load–bearing wall. The *Orator,* a bronze in the Florence Archaeological Museum, is the best-known example of Roman realism in sculpture from the same period.

Rebuilding at Rome actually began with Julius Caesar, though Augustus built on a larger scale and left the city marble – or rather marble-faced, since Romans were more sparing of the material than Greeks. Caesar, Augustus and the Flavians and Antonines built great public squares (fora) to beautify the city and relieve traffic congestion, as well as rebuilding *the* Forum (the Forum Romanum). A distinctive Augustan style of official sculpture was developed which gave a noble or idealised turn to realistic portrayals, no doubt for conscious propagandist reasons: the famous statue of Augustus from Livia's villa, his arm extended in an oratorical gesture resembling a benediction, is evidently the portrait of a real man, but very much the real man seen in the most

Left
Roman cistern for supplying a city with water – in this case Pergamum in Asia Minor.

Above
Bronze head of the Jewish queen Berenice. Museo Nazionale Archaeologico, Naples.

Opposite top
Roman realism: portrait bust of the Emperor Decius. About AD 250. Museo Capitolino, Rome.

Opposite bottom
Vines and other naturalistic decoration; relief of the Flavian period. Musei Vaticani.

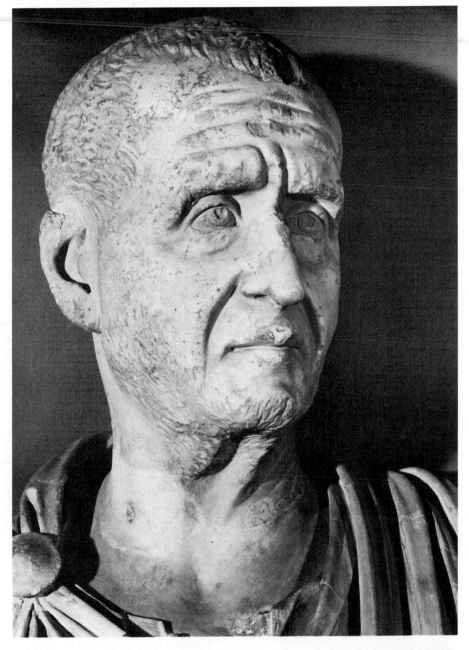

favourable light, as universal peace-bringer. The reliefs on the almost exactly contemporary Altar of Peace (Ara Pacis) are Roman in subject matter but consciously 'classical' in style, featuring a great procession that echoes the Panathenaic procession on the Parthenon frieze. Though the carving is technically assured and animals and plants are more closely observed than in Greek art, the overall effect is rather insipid – a sort of chocolate-box classicism. Augustus himself is ever-youthful in his portraits, as befits the saviour if not the man. Flavian portraits go back to the realistic tradition, modified under the Antonines by a certain soft romantic tendency, sometimes with retrospectively disconcerting effects (the odius Commodus, strangely benign-looking, with glamorous curly locks and beard, and the lion's skin and club of Hercules). Sometimes the same emperor was treated in different ways – like Marcus Aurelius, whose images can be seen in the Capitoline Museum at Rome, first impossibly youthful-smooth and beautiful and then nobly middle-aged; and then, on his column in Rome, trouble-scarred and disillusioned at the end of his life. An outstanding feature of Antonine portrait sculpture was the treatment of hair; by carving and drilling the sculptors managed virtuoso effects suggestive of the wild-and-wavy fashions of the time.

The most famous surviving Roman monuments date from the Flavian and Antonine periods. The Arch of Titus in the Forum celebrates the victories of Vespasian and his son over the Jews; one relief shows Roman soldiers carrying off the seven-branched candelabrum. A triumphal arch of this sort took time to build, and was put up some years after the triumph it records. (The triumph was an official honour granted to a victorious general; he rode laurel-wreathed through the city in the midst of a great procession of captives, soldiers, senators and magistrates.)

By contrast with the reliefs on the Arch of Titus, tucked away inside the arch, Trajan's column is florid and boastful: the reliefs wind round and round the column from bottom to top in a continuous scroll. The style too is less restrained: instead of action shown

Right
The Pont du Gard at Nîmes, most
splendid of surviving Roman aqueducts.
First century AD.

Above
The Colosseum at Rome, scene of
gladiatorial shows and other cruel
spectacles.

Opposite
Bronze equestrian statue of Marcus
Aurelius in the Piazza del Campidoglio
at Rome.

274

realistically in 'profile', Trajan's soldiers and their enemies are arranged in registers, one above the other, as if on a slope, filling up the available space vertically as well as laterally. This is not a matter of clumsiness: at the expense of photographic realism, the column provides a continuous, crowded, thrilling narrative. In its details the relief is highly realistic, giving a particularly clear picture of throwing a pontoon across a river, setting up a camp, and other operations involving the Romans' military engineering skills. The column of Marcus Aurelius, erected under Commodus, obviously derives from Trajan's and has the same subject: imperial victory over Northern barbarians. But its spirit is different: the figures, deeply cut, are more emotionally expressive: instead of a smooth narrative of victories, their horrors blunted by a kind of imperial calm that emanates from emperor and army, the Aurelian column is discontinuous and violent, as if designed to turn men against war. Even in triumph, the later Antonines manifest a certain discontent with the world. This is evident even in the famous equestrian statue of Marcus Aurelius – a bronze that survived the Middle Ages only because it was wrongly believed to represent Constantine, the first Christian emperor. Even on horseback – the traditional emblem of man in full pride of life – the Emperor is thought-oppressed, and his raised hand gives him a prophetic rather than military air. But perhaps it once drew a more physical splendour from the gilding of which a few traces still remain.

The Flavians' greatest building, and certainly the most famous of all Roman buildings, was the Colosseum, the overawed medieval name for what the Romans knew as the Flavian Amphitheatre. Finished in Titus' reign only nine years after it was begun, the

Opposite bottom
The Maison Carrée at Nîmes.

Opposite top
The Pantheon, Rome.

Left
The *Orator*: bronze sculpture of the first century BC. Museo Archeologico, Florence.

Opposite
Steam baths in a second-century AD
Roman villa at Ephesus; the walls are
decorated with mosaics.

Above
Wall painting from the Villa of Livia;
the whole room, all four walls
decorated with a continuous landscape,
is in the Museo Nazionale Romano, Rome.

Left
Girl with tablet and pen; she has been
nicknamed 'Sappho'. Wall painting
from Pompeii.

279

other emperors present them as perplexed men for whom the weight of the world is too heavy. By contrast, the developing Christian style rarely touched on the individual psychology; it presented religious truths or events with an emotional force derived from its increasingly hieratic treatment, frontal and schematised after the Eastern fashion; truth and meaning were the subjects of this art, for which realistic details from the visible world could only serve as distractions. Mosaic lent itself superbly to this treatment, most notably of all in the great wall-scenes of Justinian, Theodora and their courtiers in the church of San Vitale at Ravenna, which had replaced Rome as the imperial capital in Italy.

The city, the multi-domed church in Eastern style, and the mosaics themselves already belong to a new age in which even Constantine seems remote

and Roman. Elsewhere, men were turning away from the old world in a different sense by entering monasteries to escape the brutalities of life and find salvation outside the fray. In the new age, even the Latin language ceased to be universal, disappearing altogether in outlying parts such as Britain, and developing provincially into independent languages such as Italian, French, Spanish and Romanian; the Western Church alone maintained the universality of Latin, just as it maintained the Roman claim to universal dominion. A heaven-directed art, monasteries, church-Latin, unlettered local lords and peasants – here Antiquity has been left behind and we are in the turbulent world of the early Middle Ages. In 529, Justinian performed an action rich in symbolism when he ordered the closure of the great schools of Greek pilosophy.

Opposite
Keen observation of nature – soon to disappear – is evident in this sixth-century AD ceiling mosaic in Santa Costanza, Rome.

Above
The hieratic and frontal style derived from the East is already forming in this early sixth-century AD mosaic of Justinian and his courtiers from San Vitale, Ravenna.

The Legacy
of Greece and Rome

THE BYZANTINE EMPIRE

Catastrophes aside, there are few clean-cut endings in history. In the East, the Roman Empire went on without Rome; the emperor continued to reign at Constantinople; and when Edward Gibbon wrote his *Decline and Fall of the Roman Empire,* he took the story right down to the fall of Constantinople in 1453 – a true catastrophe which put a clean-cut ending to the state.

Still, there is no denying that these Eastern Romans who spoke Greek are not the people we normally mean when we talk of the ancient Greeks and Romans; and historians have generally agreed to regard the reign of Justinian as the watershed between the East Roman Empire and what is now known as the Byzantine Empire, which properly belongs to the history of the Middle Ages. The distinction is also geographically justified: hardly more than a century after Justinian's death, some scraps of territory in the south of Italy were all that remained of the Empire in the West, and the Arabs, inspired by the doctrines of Islam, had flooded out of the Arabian peninsula, destroyed the old enemy Persia, and incorporated Syria and North Africa in a huge new empire that stretched from Spain to India.

The heartland of the Byzantine Empire was now Asia Minor, with more or less precarious extensions in the Balkans and Italy; she was beset from west and east by Slavic and Islamic enemies, and much of her subsequent history represents a struggle for survival. Nevertheless Byzantine wealth, luxury and culture

Above
The Dark Ages ape the Roman achievement: the ninth-century cathedral at Aachen was built by Charlemagne in direct imitation of Justinian's San Vitale at Ravenna.

Opposite
Constantinople besieged: illuminated manuscript of 1455, two years after the greatest city in Christendom had fallen to the Turks. Bibliothèque Nationale, Paris.

were the astonishment of barbarians, both west-European and Slav: the wonders of Constantinople, the size and splendour of her palaces and churches, and her mechanical and military marvels (including the famous Greek fire, a sort of Molotov cocktail) had a great deal to do with the conversion of the Slavs to Christianity. Unwilling to defer to a 'barbarian' Rome, Byzantine Christianity asserted its independence, ultimately breaking with Rome and emerging as the Eastern Orthodox Church which still commands the allegiance of most Slav and Greek Christians. Byzantium produced a flourishing Greek literature, a Greek version of Roman legal codes, and a splendid and opulent art which found expression in illuminated manuscripts, wall paintings, mosaics, ivories, metalwork and enamelling.

From the ninth to the eleventh century the Empire was at its height, culturally, economically and even politically: under the vigorous Macedonian dynasty the Balkans were reconquered and the Arabs pushed back in Asia Minor. Then disaster struck. The Normans expelled the Byzantines from Southern Italy; and in 1071 the Byzantine army – prudently nurtured and conserved for centuries by a limited-risk strategy – was shattered at the battle of Manzikert by a new people, the Seljuk Turks, who had accepted Islam and proceeded to conquer its eastern realms. Manzikert, and the loss of Anatolia with its supplies of manpower, were blows from which the Byzantine Empire never properly recovered. When help came from the

West in the shape of the Fourth Crusade (1204), the predatory 'Latin knights' were subverted by their Venetian creditors to turn on their Byzantine hosts. Constantinople was stormed for the first time in its history, and the Empire was carved up into a group of Latin kingdoms. Within half a century most of the Latins had been driven out, but the Empire was now visibly on the decline. A new Turkish people, the Ottomans, surged into Asia Minor and on to the Balkans, bypassing Constantinople. Reduced to the confines of the beleaguered capital, Byzantium was little more than an Ottoman vassal state during its last years; the storming of Constantine's New Rome in 1453 – nominally the end of one of the great epochs of world history – was almost an anticlimax. However, as events in the West were already demonstrating, ancient Greece and Rome had disappeared but continued to live on.

THE CLASSICAL LEGACY

The extraordinary afterlife of the Greco-Roman world has no parallel in history. The barbarians had wandered into the Roman Empire like bulls (or children) into a china shop: they broke its enfeebled culture and institutions, and then naively tried to put them together again. In 800, when the Frankish king Charlemagne had made himself ruler of western and central Europe, he crossed the Alps into Italy and allowed the pope to crown him emperor - a sanctified, a Holy Roman Emperor. So began an institution that lasted throughout the Middle Ages and finally disappeared only in 1806, when the new Caesar-Charlemagne, Napoleon Bonaparte, swept it away. Though its claim to universal secular supremacy was never taken entirely seriously, the relationships between emperor and pope were for centuries one of the key issues of European politics. The pope himself was a successor to the Roman emperors, deriving his authority from his position in the old world capital as well as from St Peter and the (fake) Donation of Constantine; and, of course, as pontifex maximus, the pope inherited his title from a long line of Caesars, and, back beyond great Julius, from the notables of the Roman Republic.

Above
Renaissance Platonism found pictorial expression in *Primavera* (Spring) and other paintings by Botticelli. Galleria degli Uffizi, Florence.

Opposite bottom
Byzantine ship using the dreaded 'Greek fire' against an enemy. Twelfth- or thirteenth-century Byzantine manuscript. Biblioteca Nacional, Madrid.

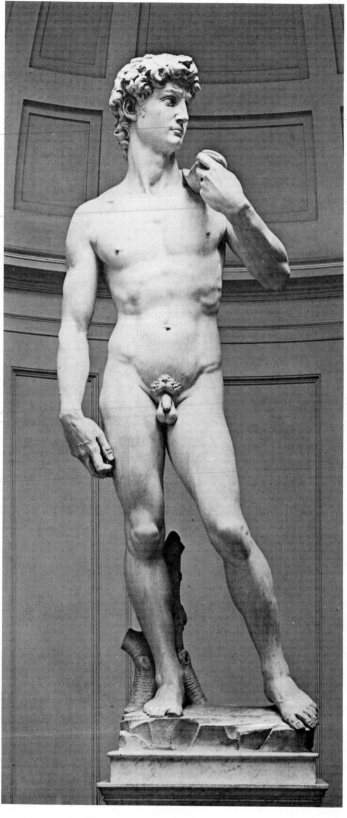

Above
The ideal of heroic manhood, enshrined in the *Apollo Belvedere* (Musei Vaticani), inspired later sculptors; its affinities with Michaelangelo's *David* (Accademia, Florence) are clear, although the latter's colossal size and troubled expression are distinctly un-classical.

Opposite
Cool in style but ardently accumulated: the Pantheon-like interior and statuary speak volumes for British attachment to the Classical. Ince Blundell Hall, Lancashire.

Struggling to recreate civilisation, men like Charlemagne could think of nothing better than to imitate Antiquity – sometimes in a literal reproduction like Aachen Cathedral, which is San Vitale, Ravenna, with some refinements absent. The rulers of the Dark Ages continued to use the Roman solidus, and copied it when they became confident enough to mint their own coins. The culture of the Ancient World, as is well known, was largely preserved through the efforts of monks, despite their suspicion of the morals and messages of pagan authors. And the earliest attempt to create a Christian drama was undertaken by a Saxon nun who cleaned up Terence for convent use.

The first great European style of architecture also betrays its affinities in its name – Romanesque. In the twelfth century, builders at last broke out of the classical or quasi-classical mould: Gothic is the supreme achievement of an independent sensibility and a quite new understanding of architectural dynamics. But intellectually western Europe was still dependent on the authority of Aristotle in logic and science, just as it remained dependent on the authority of Galen in medicine. And everywhere in the West, Latin

was the language of learning, law, theology, diplomacy and debate, though long since 'dead' as the vernacular of a people.

When a reaction occurred against the failing scholasticism and gloom of the late Middle Ages, it expressed itself as a renewed cult of Antiquity – the Renaissance. Petrarch, like the Roman poets, was laurel-crowned on the Capitol. The Dutchman Erasmus polished his Latin style through the study of Cicero and wrote pointed witty satires when he was not editing the original Greek text of the New Testament, thus implicitly criticising the infallibility of the Latin Vulgate. Architects studied the Roman author Vitruvius and built domed churches and country villas. Sculptors were inspired by Roman copies and occasional originals that appeared; Michaelangelo's attitude to the *Laocoön,* mentioned earlier, is a case in point. Even painters were classically inspired – not by Roman painting, which was then unknown, but by history, literature and even (like Botticelli in the *Primavera* and *Birth of Venus*) by the Platonism that was replacing Aristotelian philosophy among the sophisticated. Beginning in Italy, the Renaissance spread out over

Above
The Palladian villa, a sixteenth-century interpretation of the ancient Roman villa: this one, the Villa Rotonda, was begun by Palladio (1518–80) himself. The Italian 'Palladian' style was taken up in eighteenth-century England and widely used for country houses by Lord Burlington and others.

Opposite top left
Women dressed in the 'Empire' style as worn in London, 1804. As so often, the imitation is all the more interesting for being wildly inaccurate.

Opposite top right
The ancient myth in modern art: *Minotaur leaning over a sleeping girl*, by Picasso.

Opposite bottom
Deliberate resurrection of the Roman spirit by a new Caesar: Napoleon giving eagles to the army. Engraving after a painting by Jacques-Louis David.

Europe in various guises. Of course it was far more than a movement of revival – among other things it was closely connected with the Reformation, which split the Church and plunged Europe into a century and a half of intermittent wars. But it remains astonishing that, then and later, a change in sensibility and general outlook could only express itself through the medium of a 'classical' revival.

In the sixteenth and seventeenth centuries, the vocabulary of art remained classical, but the Mannerist and Baroque movements put it to uses that would have outraged the Greeks and Romans. In the eighteenth century came the first extensive discoveries at Pompeii and Herculaneum, and with them a renewed interest in Antiquity; in this cool, aristocratic age, Neo-Classicism reflected the prevailing temper, bringing a superb gilt-and-icing look to interior decoration and placing a little temple in the grounds of the English milord's country house or Palladian – that is, Roman-style – villa.

At the end of the eighteenth century the hold of Antiquity seemed as strong as ever. Rousseau's *Contrat Social,* often regarded as the textbook of the French revolutionaries, begins 'Man is born free; yet everywhere he is in chains' – and then discusses the political problem wholly in terms of Greek and Roman practice. The revolutionaries themselves, partly inspired by Neo-Classical painting, aped Brutus and Cato while their ladies (once things had relaxed a little) dressed in sexy dampened 'classical' shifts. Napoleon was even more history-conscious – First Consul, then Emperor, with his legion of honour and eagles; the pose was only interrupted when he substituted Charlemagne as his model, imitating an imitation by having himself crowned by the pope.

And so Greece and Rome remained powerful as images even as their connection with contemporary reality was becoming remote, thanks to the replacement of Latin by vernacular languages, the rise of science and the advent of the gigantic, fearful and utterly alien Industrial Revolution. In the nineteenth century Greek and Latin remained central to upper-class education, though increasingly criticised as irrelevant – which in a sense they were, though it is worth remembering that a man like Gladstone could combine profound Homeric scholarship with a deep involvement in the political life and culture of his time. In architecture, Neo-Classicism (like Neo-Gothic, Neo-Renaissance *et al.*) too often became a cover for stylistic bankruptcy; and in art the 'classical' came to mean lifeless marble nudes and insipid, technically admirable paintings of rose-leaved Roman 'decadence', interesting only for the erotic impulses to which it allowed covert expression.

This identification of Greece and Rome with the most out-of-touch and repressed aspects of Victorian culture gave Antiquity a bad name for several decades of the twentieth century; some people still think of it as dull, though the 'blockbuster' epic film has done a great deal to cure that. The images have remained inescapable even down to yesterday, when an Apollo landed on the Moon. But now that only images are left – when, after the longest apprenticeship in history, we have finally become independent of the Greeks and Romans – we are in a position to appreciate their gigantic achievements and enduring influence all the more clearly.

Opposite above
Ben Hur (Charlton Heston) drives his
chariot furiously in a race at the Circus
Maximus; scene from the 1959 MGM
film. 'Epic' productions of this sort –
visually if not always psychologically
accurate – have helped to stimulate
interest in the ancient world.

Above
Classicism adapted to charm: the
Temple of Love in the gardens of the
Petit Trianon at Versailles, built 1778.

Index

Page numbers in italic refer to illustrations

THE GREEKS

THE ROMANS

Acknowledgements

PHOTOGRAPHS

Alinari, Florence 29 bottom, 81 bottom, 98, 102 left, 113, 116 bottom, 122 centre, 124 bottom, 132, 167, 169 bottom, 183, 187, 188-189, 189, 192-193, 197 top, 200 bottom left, 202 bottom left, 214 top, 231 top left, 232-233, 241, 264 bottom, 265, 272 top, 277, 301 bottom, 304, 305, 312; P. Almasy, Neuilly-sur-Seine 125; Anderson, Florence 42, 184, 194, 202 bottom right, 216 top, 244 top, 260 top, 276 top; Antikenmuseum, Berlin 25, 54 bottom; Archives Photographiques, Paris 106, 146, 156-157; Ashmolean Museum, Oxford 40 left; BBC, London 229 top; Biblioteca Vaticana 249; Bibliothèque Nationale, Paris 307; Gad Borel-Boissonnas, Geneva 97 top right; 102 right, Federico Borromeo, Milan 149 right; Jean Bottin, Paris 17, *173*, 210; E. Boudot-Lamotte, Paris 36, 109 Bottom, 290; British Library, London 152-153; British Museum, London 11 bottom, 28, 33 bottom, 50 bottom, 56 bottom, 61 bottom, 64, 68 top, 82 bottom, 84 bottom, 85 top, 89 top, 93 top, 97 centre left, 99, 100 top, 103 bottom, 107 bottom, 109 top right, 116 top, 117, 121 left, 129 top, 138, 138-139, 151 bottom, 152 bottom, 158 left, 158 right, 206, 229 bottom right, 284, 285, 313 bottom; J. E. Bulloz, Paris 172; Committee for Excavation of Antioch and its Vicinity, Princeton University 280 top right; *Country Life*, London 311; W. F. Davidson, Penrith 207; Deutsches Archäologisches Institut, Athens 40 right; Walter Drayer, Zurich 169 top right; Werner Forman Archive, London 31 left, 31 right, 35 bottom, 38, 94 bottom, 103 top, 126 top, 126 bottom, 130-131, 150 top, 174, 186 top right, 190 left, 190 right, 215 top, 219, 222 bottom, 229 bottom left, 237, 255, 267 top, 267 bottom, 279 bottom; Fototeca Unione, Rome 251, 257, 260 bottom, 289; Gabinetto Fotografico Nazionale, Rome 168, 239 top, 292; Photographie Giraudon, Paris 21, 62, 70 centre left, 70 bottom left, 127 left, 135, 191, 195 bottom, 256 top, 256 bottom, 258, 259 top, 270, 274 bottom, 280 bottom, 288 top, 288 bottom, 297 right; Government of Pakistan Department of Archaeology, Karachi 144; Sonia Halliday, Weston Turville 110 top, 234 bottom; Hamlyn Group Picture Library 14, 19 top, 27, 32 centre, 32 bottom, 34, 43 top, 43 bottom, 51, 55, 60, 66 top, 79 bottom left, 79 bottom right, 80 bottom, 89 bottom left, 91, 93 bottom left, 94 top, 104 top, 108, 110 bottom, 118, 119, 122 left, 122 bottom right, 123 left, 123 right, 124 top, 127 right, 130, 131 left, 131 right, 141, 143 top right, 143 bottom, 149 left, 151 top, 154, 155 top, 163, 169 top left, 176, 182, 186 bottom, 188, 192, 195 top right. 198 top, 198 bottom, 199 bottom, 200 top left. 205, 214 bottom left, 214 bottom right, 216 bottom right, 221 left, 221 right, 223 top, 233 right, 238, 252, 262 left, 268, 269 bottom, 271, 272 bottom, 273 top, 275, 279 top, 280 top left, 283 top, 283 bottom, 286, 287, 291 top, 293 294 top, 295 top left, 295 top right, 300, 301 top, 303, 313 top left, 313 top right, 315; André Held, Ecublens 266; Hans Hinz, Allschwil 15, 111, 246 top; Hirmer Verlag, Munich 8, 13 top, 16 top, 16 bottom, 18, 20

bottom left, 20 bottom right, 23, 29 top, 30, 32-33, 37, 50 top, 53, 59, 63, 67, 69, 70 top, 70 bottom right, 76, 77, 78, 79 top, 83, 84 top right, 85 bottom, 88 bottom, 88-89, 93 bottom right, 95 top, 95 bottom left, 95 bottom right, 96 top, 97 bottom, 100 bottom, 104 bottom, 112, 122 right, 128, 129 bottom, 136, 137 left, 142 bottom, 161, 211 top, 263 bottom, 294 bottom, 297 left; Michael Holford Library, Loughton 45 left; Istanbul Arkeoloji Müzeleri 143 top left, 162; A. F. Kersting, London 35 top, 274 top; Koninglijk Penningkabinet, The Hague 147 bottom left, 147 bottom right; Kunsthistorisches Museum, Vienna 71 left; Mansell Collection, London 22 left, 22 right, 33 top, 33 centre, 44, 47 top, 54 top, 56-57, 57 bottom, 61 top, 65, 66 bottom, 68 bottom, 72, 73 top, 73 bottom, 74 right, 75, 80 top, 89 bottom right, 90 left, 101 top, 103 centre left, 109 top left, 121 right, 156, 185, 196, 230 top right; 231 bottom, 232 bottom, 239 bottom, 248-249, 253; Mansell-Alinari 45 right, 49, 84 top left, 90 right, 101 bottom, 164, 177, 178-179, 197 bottom, 200 right, 202 top, 208, 209 top, 209 bottom, 211 bottom, 213, 215 bottom, 216 bottom left, 220 left, 220 right, 224 top, 225, 230 top left, 230 bottom, 232 left, 233 bottom, 236, 240 top, 240 bottom, 245, 254, 259 bottom, 269 top; Mansell-Anderson 74 left, 87, 165, 204, 224 bottom, 228, 261, 264 bottom, 308-309; Mansell-Brogi 180, 231 top right; Mansell-Giraudon 281 top; Bildarchiv Foto Marburg 12, 47 bottom, 58, 81 top, 134 bottom, 276 bottom, 306; E. Mariani, Como 134 top; Mas, Barcelona 309; Metro-Goldwyn-Meyer 314; Metropolitan Museum of Art, New York 152 top, 263 top; Musée d'Archéologie Borély, Marseilles 186 top left; Musée Guimet, Paris 147 top; Musées Nationaux, Paris 160; Musei Vaticani 137 right, 157, 195 top left, 201, 244 bottom, 273 bottom, 310 right; Museo Archeologico Nazionale, Naples 133, 148, 262 top right; Museo Nazionale, Reggio Calabria 97 top left; Museum of Fine Arts, Boston, Massachusetts 71 right, 103 bottom left, 120; Ny Carlsberg Glyptotek, Copenhagen 145; Photoresources 10; Pontificale Commissione di Architettura Sacra, Vatican 302 bottom; Paul Popper, London 246 bottom right; J. Powell, Rome 10-11, 13 bottom, 140, 150 bottom, 155 bottom, 291 bottom; Crown Copyright, Royal Commission on Historic Monuments 302 top; Scala, Antella 82 top, 107 top, 115, 166, 171, 175 top left; 175 top right, 190-191, 199 top, 203, 222 top, 223 bottom, 226 top, 226 bottom, 227, 234 top, 235 top, 235 bottom, 242, 242-243, 246 bottom left, 247, 250, 282 top, 282 bottom, 295 bottom, 298-299, 310 left; Schweizisches Landesmuseum, Zurich 296; Editions d'Art Albert Skira, Geneva 142 top; Soprintendenza alle Antichità Roma III (Scavi di Ostia) 217; Nick Stournaras, Athens 96 bottom; H. Roger-Viollet, Paris 9, 11 top, 20 top left, 20 top right, 24, 41, 105, 159, 174 bottom, 175 bottom, 252-253, 296-297; Warburg Institute, London 262 bottom right, 281 bottom; ZEFA (UK), London 218, 278; ZEFA–Konrad Helbig 19 bottom, 39.